INFINITE
MONSTER

INFINITE MONSTER

COURAGE, HOPE, AND RESURRECTION
IN THE FACE OF ONE OF AMERICA'S LARGEST HURRICANES

LEIGH JONES AND
RHIANNON MEYERS

PenlandScott Publishers
Dallas, Texas

Published by PenlandScott Publishers.

PenlandScott and colophon are trademarks of Red Honor Ventures, Ltd.

Copyright © 2010 by Leigh Jones and Rhiannon Meyers

PenlandScott publications are available at special discounted rates for volume and bulk purchases, corporate and institutional premiums, promotions, fund-raising, and educational uses. For further information, contact:

PenlandScott Publishers
P.O. Box 166677
Irving, Texas 75016
specialsales@penlandscott.com

Front cover design by Publications Development Company.
Back cover photo credit: Jennifer Reynolds/The Galveston County Daily News
Front cover photos credit: Andrejs Pidjass/Dreamstime.com
and Alexandr Tkachuk/Dreamstime.com
Book layout and design by Publications Development Company.

Printed and bound in the United States of America.

ISBN-13: 978-0-9823-1524-8
ISBN-10: 0-9823-1524-4

Get informed & inspired at
www.penlandscott.com

10 9 8 7 6 5 4 3 2 1

It was a sort of infinite monster, tossing its million heads and frothing at its million mouths as it hungered to devour the city. I stood there and heard the monster's growl—his cry for blood—and looked into the black terror of his murderous frown.

—Pastor William Mercer Harris
Galveston Island, September 9, 1900

This book is dedicated to the people of Galveston, who refused to accept defeat. You are the personification of perseverance. Your example is an inspiration to anyone whose possessions, stability, and security have been swept away.

CONTENTS

FOREWORD

WE HAVE A tendency to compare disasters, to measure death tolls and dollar amounts, to weigh images of this submerged town against that shaken village half a world away. Even when disasters invite these comparisons, the sum usually amounts to little more than a heap of superlatives: the worst, the deadliest, the largest, the costliest.

Hurricane Ike, as it pushed the Gulf of Mexico into the streets of Galveston, killing people, and destroying thousands of homes and businesses, never invited much of this kind of contemplation because it arrived in September 2008, just as the nation began to topple into another superlative—the worst economic meltdown since the Great Depression.

Even if the storm had arrived at a time more convenient for the national news cycle, it could never have measured up, in breadth, damage, death, and destruction, to Hurricane Katrina—or even to the nameless storm that killed 6,000 Galvestonians in 1900 and still holds the dubious record for death tolls among U.S. natural disasters.

The terrible truth is that the scope of one disaster means nothing to the victim of another. For every person who mucked out a home, or simply fled and never returned, leaving a home to rot, there is no worse disaster than Hurricane Ike.

The stories collected here are stories of everyday people performing extraordinary acts in the face of annihilation, stories of government working and failing to work, of people relenting or refusing to relent, and of a rebuilding that will continue to reshape and redefine a great Texan city indefinitely. The themes seldom stray from those that have emerged amid other calamities. Some got more press, but the lessons from Ike can be no less important.

An island is many things to many people. Galveston has been the Wall Street of the South; it was also a pirate's last resort. It was home to prohibition-era speakeasies and gambling parlors. Today it hosts a crown jewel of modern medicine. For thirty miles—from the West End beach houses and condominiums, east to the port, the housing projects, and the University of Texas Medical Branch—nothing on the island was spared from the lasting uncertainty that came with the hurricane.

Can we learn from our mistakes? Will our families return? For those who stayed, how will we help ourselves and each other?

Nearly two years have passed since the city lay submerged and in ruin, and the questions remain. But with this account of one of the island's darkest chapters, it can no longer be said that the nation was never told the story of Galveston, and how against terrible odds, this weird little star-crossed sliver by the sea manages yet again to adapt and survive.

—CRAIG EILAND, *Texas State Representative*

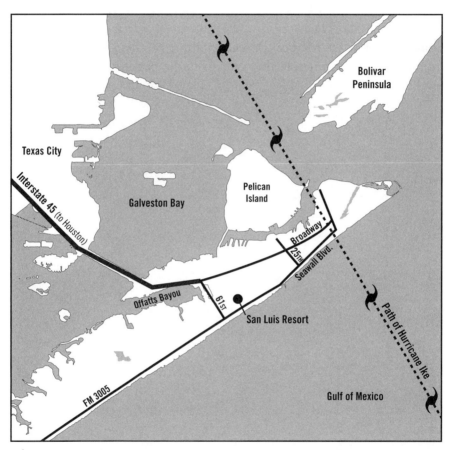

This map shows the major streets in Galveston and the path of Hurricane Ike as it tore across the island. While the seawall protected the southern edge of the island, the storm surge rose from Galveston Bay, covering everything in the city except for a narrow strip along the seawall, in water.

CHAPTER

ONE

HURRICANE IKE SPUN into life just off the west coast of Africa on August 28, 2008. Ten days later, it ripped into the Turks and Caicos Islands as a Category 4 storm. Ike's 127 mile per hour winds shredded the tiny islands, damaging 80 percent of the houses on Great Inagua Island.

But in Galveston, residents were too busy watching Hurricane Gustav to worry about a storm in the eastern Caribbean Sea.

By September 8, Ike had vented its wrath on Cuba, where an estimated 50-foot storm surge tore apart the coastline near Cabo Lucrecia and killed seven people. In Haiti, heavy rain fueled mudslides that killed 74 people. Although the storm lost most of its fury as it rolled over Cuba's western tip, storm watchers nervously noted that the warm waters of the Gulf of Mexico were the perfect incubator to nurture Ike into a Hurricane Katrina-like monster. But forecasters with the National Weather Service confidently predicted the storm was headed up the Atlantic coast.

Galvestonians heaved a sigh of relief and felt a passing pang of sympathy for the Carolinas.

But when they awoke the next morning, they learned that Ike had missed its northerly turn and was headed for the Gulf of Mexico. It was the fourth named storm to threaten the Texas coast in 2008. Galvestonians reluctantly began their storm preparations—checking updates from the National Hurricane Center every two hours, thinking about buying bottled water, and praying Ike would ruin someone else's weekend.

Galveston had a long history of dodging storms. Every 25 years or so, one would hit close enough to leave a mark. But after surviving the Great Storm of 1900, still the deadliest natural disaster in United States history, the defiant island and its resilient residents believed they could withstand anything. Most people thought the 17-foot-tall seawall, built in the early 1900s after the Great Storm, could restrain nature's worst. Many residents had lived through Hurricane Carla in 1961 and Hurricane Alicia in 1983. The city bounced back from both.

But on September 13, 2008, Galvestonians learned that some storms demand respect. Ike left more than just a mark.

■ STEVEN RUSHING NEVER evacuated for a hurricane. It was a family tradition and a source of pride. So when he heard that Hurricane Ike had entered the Gulf of Mexico, he was more excited than scared. With shining green eyes, a confident grin, and a year-round tan earned by spending almost every day trawling for shrimp in Chocolate Bayou, the Galveston native exuded the easygoing attitude that most islanders maintained through every hurricane season.

On Monday, September 8, four days before the storm was expected to make landfall, most shrimpers took their boats inland to Moses Lake. Protected by tidal floodgates, the sheltered inlet is on the western shore of Galveston Bay. But Steven had never left his boat, the *Tiffany Leann,* behind. He had ridden out every storm on board, making sure his boat stayed afloat.

Lupe Rushing, Steven's wife, never stayed for hurricanes. She and the rest of the family always evacuated early. But she wasn't ready to sit in another 20-hour traffic jam, like she had during the Hurricane Rita evacuation almost three years before. Her son, 13-year-old Tyler; her stepson, 19-year-old Stevie; and her stepdaughter, 17-year-old Tiffany, all wanted to stay. Like their dad, they were excited about watching the storm come in.

Outvoted, Lupe reluctantly agreed to stay.

The Rushings both grew up listening to stories of Hurricane Carla, the storm that most islanders remember as the worst since the Great Storm of

1900. Carla's 10-foot storm surge washed over the West End but mostly stayed out of the city's core behind the seawall, where tornadoes kicked up most of the damage. They were old enough to remember Hurricane Alicia, which devastated the island's unprotected West End but left the rest of the city mostly unscathed. Their elderly neighbors in the Gulf Village neighborhood, many of whom rode out both storms in the houses where they still lived, told the Rushings that floodwater never reached their front doors. Sure, the streets would probably be underwater, but that could happen in any heavy rain.

Confident of their safety, the couple kept an eye on the weather reports and prepared for what Steven and the kids hoped would be an exciting but safe weekend.

◾ FROM HIS SUBURBAN Dallas home, Dave Harris watched Hurricane Ike take a sudden jaunt toward Galveston. He phoned his father more out of a sense of duty than anything else. He knew how the conversation would go with the stubborn old man even before the phone stopped ringing. Dave made his usual pitch to evacuate his 83-year-old father Fletcher Harris. But this time, he also gave an ultimatum. Fletcher had to decide now to leave—before the state opened the inbound lanes of the Gulf Freeway to outbound traffic—because Dave would be unwilling, and probably unable, to come get Fletcher if he changed his mind later.

As predicted, Fletcher declined his son's ride out of town with less-than-convincing assurances of his stockpiles of hurricane supplies. As Dave would learn months later, Fletcher's friends spent days trying to convince him to leave.

It's a wonder anyone even tried. The old man would be damned before he fled from a storm. He stayed through Hurricane Carla in 1961 and through Alicia in 1983.

He stayed during Rita in 2005, which veered toward Galveston only two weeks after Hurricane Katrina changed history in New Orleans. The television news was then splitting coverage between the devastation in New Orleans and the new monster in the Gulf aiming for a direct hit over Galveston. Typically apathetic to storms, islanders who had spent the past two weeks watching the people in New Orleans being plucked from roofs panicked. They boarded up windows. They picked grocery shelves clean. They loaded their cars with pets, clothes, and children and headed north on the Gulf Freeway. They didn't look back.

During Rita, Fletcher Harris, in his ground-floor townhouse near the seawall, chatted on the phone with Fox News' Greta Van Susteren. He was a big hit on the show. E-mails flooded Van Susteren's inbox.

"Serious news programs such as yours are enhanced on the rare occasion when 'stupid humans get on TV,' " wrote Elliot Bressloer of Ft. Lauderdale, Florida. "I only regret that Fletcher was not on camera. Please, I beg of you to get Fletch that we may see him and get even more of a laugh than when you spoke with him via telephone. Milk and frozen dinners with no power. A bathtub full of drinking water will be used to flush the toilet. I can only imagine your thoughts at that moment. Just how far above stupid is this guy? No matter. I look forward to you having him on tomorrow."

Enthralled with Fletcher, Van Susteren's producers booked him for Rita coverage the next night, too. "Fletcher Lives!" proclaimed the headline on the conservative anchor's blog.

As the nation poked gentle fun at crotchety old Fletcher Harris, the World War II veteran once again comfortably rode out what had quickly become a non-event for Galveston.

In a rare moment, before it became clear that Rita was not the threat to Galveston that the forecasters had predicted—the neighboring communities of Beaumont, Orange, and Port Bolivar would not be so lucky—Fletcher admitted to local newspaper reporters that he was getting too old to run from storms. He simply didn't feel like messing with an evacuation.

But that was only partly true. In reality, staying through a storm was a source of pride for the man whose father and grandfather survived the 1900 Storm. Fletcher was raised on a diet of storm survival tales. He grew up hearing the saga of how the Harris family climbed to the roof during the raging hurricane and clung to life as a storm surge rushed over the barrier island and swallowed thousands of friends and neighbors.

■ IN 2001, EMORY and Merlinda Brockway bought a house on Bayou Homes Drive, just a few hundred yards from Offatts Bayou. Like other neighborhoods near the shore, Bayou Homes is a mixture of expensive waterfront mini mansions backed by more modest homes on the streets that stretch inland. The Brockway's house, built in 1965, was a typical example of most of the island's middle-class housing—well-worn but livable. Its proximity to the water had nothing to do with its appeal. It was in the Brockway's price range, and the neighborhood was quiet, just what they wanted.

Neither Emory nor Merlinda had experienced a hurricane in Galveston. But after watching three other storms pass by the island that summer, they weren't alarmed when Hurricane Ike entered the Gulf. On Monday, Emory was at his usual spot behind the counter of the convenience store in the Shell gas station at the corner of 75th Street and Stewart Avenue. His customers talked about the storm; some of them even started to buy provisions. Business also continued as usual in Jamaica Beach, where Merlinda worked at the Subway sandwich shop. But by Wednesday, most of the people stopping in for lunch were just taking a quick break from boarding up their beach houses before heading out of town.

■ FORTY MILES INLAND, in the Webster office of the National Weather Service, Meteorologist Gene Hafele and his team of 24 forecasters tried to figure out where Ike was headed. On Tuesday, computer models showed the storm going south, toward Corpus Christi and Brownsville. During his morning conference call with state and local officials, Hafele could almost hear a collective sigh of relief from Galveston.

On Tuesday, Galveston was still in Ike's cone of error, the wiggle room forecasters give themselves on either side of a storm's projected landfall. But Hafele realized the island's leaders thought they were going to escape a Gulf hurricane for the fourth time that summer. Officials, tired of warning residents to prepare evacuation plans and gas up their cars, were relieved at the thought of putting Ike in the "near miss" category.

The state's emergency management coordinators ordered all of the evacuation buses and fuel tanker trucks to head south down the coast.

But Hafele was afraid officials were letting their guard down too quickly.

"Even though it looked like it would go south, we were still putting remarks in our forecasts saying that we were four days out and a lot could change."

■ WHILE STEVEN RUSHING continued to take the *Tiffany Leann* out into the still placid waters of the Gulf, Lupe, who worked in the city secretary's office, prepared for Thursday's city council meeting. The mayor, the city manager, and the city's emergency management coordinator continued to have regular conference calls with state officials, but other than the occasional e-mail update sent to all city employees, business went on as usual at city hall.

It wasn't until Wednesday that anyone really started getting worried. By then, the storm was projected to make landfall 100 miles south of Galveston. With predictions of moderate flooding in low-lying areas, Mayor Lyda Ann Thomas called for a mandatory evacuation of the West End, the long and skinny half of the island unprotected by the seawall. Charlie Kelly, the emergency management coordinator, begged Lupe to start getting ready to evacuate.

But Steven assured her they would be fine.

By Thursday, Ike had turned north again, putting Galveston uncomfortably close to the projected landfall. At 9 AM, Mayor Thomas ordered a mandatory evacuation for the entire island. Although Steven always stayed with his boat during storms, Lupe told her husband of five years that if the whole family was going to stay, he was going to have to be at home with them. So Steven had the *Tiffany Leann* hauled ashore at Payco Marina, at the base of the Galveston Causeway, the bridge that spans the Gulf Intracoastal Waterway and connects the island to the rest of the state. If he couldn't be aboard to loosen her ties as the water rose and the waves pitched and rolled, Steven thought the boat would be safer on land.

Once the boat was secure, Steven prepared for a hurricane-watching party at home. He gassed up the generator and filled two big coolers with $220 in food, more than enough to get them through the few days he expected them to be without power.

Lupe went to work that morning at city hall but almost immediately left for the Island Community Center to help with the evacuation of poor, elderly, and disabled residents. As she assigned each one to a bus, making sure everyone who wanted to leave got a seat, Lupe reminded herself of what Steven had been saying for the last four days: We'll be fine.

■ **Fletcher Harris still** owned the family copy of a history book simply titled: *Galveston in 1900,* an account published just months after the devastating storm in an effort to raise money for hurricane recovery.

The old, fragile leather-bound book was covered in pencil markings where Harris' grandfather edited the writer's mistakes.

The book was in the apartment with Fletcher as his neighbors fled from Rita and into a horrifying gridlock that became a textbook example of a bungled evacuation.

Harris had once again outsmarted those who had no faith in the island's resiliency against devastating storms.

Those who panicked because of what had happened to New Orleans, he quipped to a local reporter, well, they were just stupid, as were the people who lived in New Orleans.

"That was a case of people dumb enough to live 10 feet below sea level and having a faulty levee system," Fletcher told *The Galveston County Daily News.* "They made their bed, and they better lie in it."

Unlike the Louisianans, Fletcher lived above sea level in a first-floor condo within walking distance of the 17-foot seawall that had been built after the 1900 Storm to protect the island from future hurricanes.

It was no matter that Fletcher was 83 years old, missing one hand from a World War II injury, and showing some disturbing, but infrequent, signs of dementia. He had boxes of government-issued meals-ready-to-eat (MREs), bottles of water, a generator, a cooler full of ice, a mini armory of pistols and shotguns, 30 years of experience with the Red Cross and, most importantly, a track record of surviving hurricanes that were predicted to do untold damage to Galveston, but then inevitably veered west or east at the last minute. The storms always spared the island that had come face-to-face with the Big One and survived.

There was no way he would run from a hurricane, and no way in hell would he run from one named after a World War II army general.

■ BY TUESDAY AND Wednesday, most of the Brockway's neighbors had boarded up their houses and headed out of town. But the fiercely independent and stubbornly self-sufficient couple never considered joining them. Emory collected what was left of the candles, batteries, and canned goods from the convenience store before boarding it up and heading home on Thursday afternoon. He didn't bother boarding up the windows at the house or doing anything else to prepare for the storm. The eerie quiet on his street didn't bother him.

"People said we were crazy to stay, but I wasn't afraid of no hurricane," he said.

■ LUPE RUSHING WORKED late Thursday night. The last bus of evacuees didn't leave until about 6:30 PM. When she got home, she, Steven, and the kids headed over to The Spot, one of the only island restaurants still open. With television newscasts predicting death and destruction in the background, restaurant owner Dennis Byrd served beer and margaritas at the bar. Ike had given islanders a three-day weekend. What better reason to party?

The Rushings saw many of their friends at the bar that night. Some were planning to leave the next morning, but most were staying. No one seemed worried.

"We were ready to bunker down," Steven said.

■ T<small>WENTY-FOUR HOURS LATER,</small> water spewed from the electrical outlets in the Rushing's bunker as Steven scrambled to find a way to keep his wife and children from drowning.

The Brockways retreated up a ladder into their attic and, for the first time, realized some hurricanes should be feared.

And Fletcher Harris awoke where he had fallen asleep, on a mattress that had floated off its frame. He had made his bed and damned if he wasn't lying in it.

CHAPTER

TWO

THE MARBLE HALLWAYS outside of the city council workshop room echoed with the click-clack of TV reporters' high heels as they paced back and forth, fielding anxious phone calls from producers and editors irritated that the 5 PM press conference was delayed.

It was Wednesday. Hurricane Ike was less than three days away.

The lead news story that afternoon was evacuation, or, more accurately, the lack of an evacuation. Everyone wanted to know why—as a monster hurricane swirled in the Gulf of Mexico—Mayor Lyda Ann Thomas hesitated to order people to leave the island.

The 6 PM news broadcasts on every television in Houston would lead with Thomas' announcement to evacuate. Or so producers thought. At 5:15 PM, Thomas, holed up behind closed doors with her advisors, did order the city's legal department to draw up the necessary paperwork for her to call the evacuation in the morning, but only if the storm's track changed and shifted closer to Galveston.

With cameras rolling 30 minutes later, Thomas coolly assured reporters she had no intention of ordering a mandatory evacuation for the whole island. Hurricane Ike was too close to landfall for everyone to leave safely, she said. The mayor encouraged residents to leave, if they wanted to. But she emphasized that they should consider sheltering in their homes. Thomas ordered a mandatory evacuation only for those few people living on the West End—the 20-mile strip of land unprotected by the 17-foot seawall.

"Asking people to leave the island is the very last thing I want to do," Thomas said. "I feel that sheltering in place is the best option now . . . Go to the store and go home."

Reporters were shocked, and television news anchors looked grave when they reported Thomas' shelter-in-place order on the evening newscast. But few islanders questioned the mayor's decision. Ike was a weak storm. Galveston had certainly withstood worse. No one wanted to evacuate unless they could be absolutely sure the threat of staying outweighed the frustration and inconvenience of leaving. Memories of the botched evacuation ahead of Hurricane Rita, when more people died on the road than in the storm, were still fresh.

No one wanted to go through that again, especially not for a Category 2 storm.

■ THE SUMMER OF 2008 was sunny and dry—ideal weather for lounging on Galveston's beaches, watching the Gulf of Mexico's chocolate-brown waves roll ashore. But what Galveston's long, dry summer lacked in rainfall, it made up in hurricane threats. Three times during the first three months of the storm season, beginning June 1, islanders had listened to forecasters issue warnings for the upper Texas coast. And three times, the hurricanes veered away from the 64-square-mile barrier island 50 miles southeast of Houston.

In late July, Hurricane Dolly came ashore at South Padre Island. Hurricane Edouard, which for a few days seemed certain to give Galveston a wild ride, ended up making landfall northeast of High Island, at the base of Bolivar Peninsula, on August 4. And Gustav came ashore near the unincorporated fishing village of Cocodrie, Louisiana, on September 1.

Hurricane Ike followed Gustav almost immediately, but City Manager Steve LeBlanc didn't let it ruin his weekend. He barely noticed as the storm ravaged Cuba late Sunday, and when he walked into his office at city hall on Monday morning, he was more worried about the upcoming vote on the city's 2008–2009 budget than about the storm. Four new council members had taken office in May, bringing with them a slate of campaign promises they wanted to fund.

But Ike had state officials worried enough that they started holding their twice-daily conference calls with officials from the National Weather Service, coastal cities, and counties. On Friday, the storm was expected to turn north during the weekend, spinning past Florida and heading for the Carolinas. Instead, Ike stubbornly maintained its slow march toward the Gulf of Mexico. Cuba's northern mountain ranges ravaged Ike just as Ike had ravaged the mountains. The storm landed in Cuba as a Category 4 hurricane, but left as a Category 1.

Charlie Kelly, Galveston's emergency management coordinator, sent an e-mail early Monday morning warning staffers to keep an eye on Ike. Although it was expected to enter the Gulf on Tuesday, the storm looked like it might head away from Texas. But Gene Hafele, the chief meteorologist for the National Weather Service in Houston, also cautioned officials that things could change quickly. He continued to warn them not to get too complacent with Ike still five days out.

On Tuesday, forecasts had Ike landing in far South Texas, near Brownsville. Kelly's morning e-mail told city staff the news had improved for Galveston. But he urged them not to let their guard down. Hafele and his staff still said Ike would likely strengthen into a Category 4 or 5 storm, fueled by the Gulf's warm waters. But the state directed its attention south, and evacuation buses that had cautiously moved toward the island changed direction and headed for Corpus Christi.

Before leaving city hall on Tuesday, LeBlanc held a late afternoon press conference with Mayor Thomas. Both urged residents, especially those on the West End, to stay watchful. Tides on the island were predicted to be about 6 feet higher than normal and some low-lying areas were likely to flood, he told a small group of reporters. The reporters wanted to know whether the city was considering an evacuation. Emphatically, Thomas said no. After the city's last disastrous evacuation, the mayor wouldn't call for another one unless she absolutely had to.

■ THREE YEARS EARLIER, almost to the day, LeBlanc and his staff scrambled to get out of the way of another storm, Hurricane Rita. Less than a month behind Hurricane Katrina, which killed 1,836 people and filled New Orleans with floodwater for a week, Rita was expected to make a direct hit on Galveston. State officials warned of annihilation. With images of New Orleans families stranded on rooftops and bodies floating for days in flooded streets, Thomas ordered a mandatory evacuation for the entire island. Residents hit the road within hours. The University of Texas Medical Branch, the state's oldest medical school and the region's only major medical facility, evacuated its patients and left the hospital staffed with only a skeleton crew for the first time in history. Thomas and LeBlanc commandeered Galveston Independent School District buses and evacuated 3,000 people who couldn't drive.

Millions of panicked Houston residents also hit the road. More than two million Texans left home in a matter of hours. People in suburban towns 100 miles from the coast—far away from any potential storm surge—fled and ended up ensnarled in traffic for up to 24 hours. Every major route inland was gridlocked. Cars overheated. People relieved themselves alongside pets on highway shoulders and medians. A bus evacuating nursing home residents from Houston burst into flames on Interstate 45 near Dallas after a wheel caught fire and medical oxygen tanks exploded. Twenty-three people died.

While almost all island residents fled, national media crews arrived in Galveston in droves, convinced they would soon be covering another national disaster. Thomas made appearances on all the major networks. After weighing the possibility of evacuating themselves, city officials decided to ride out the storm at The San Luis Resort, on the seawall. Although the 20-year-old upscale, beachfront hotel sits only about 200 yards from the Gulf, it rests atop Fort Crockett, a former military installation. The old fort's 8-foot-thick walls make the hotel's bottom floors the safest place on the island during a storm. The night before Rita was expected to make landfall, nervous city staffers gathered in one of the hotel's underground ballrooms. Standing at the front of the room, LeBlanc told them he felt like praying. They eagerly bowed their heads.

Watching Rita's march toward the island was like staring down the barrel of a gun and getting a reprieve at the last minute, Deputy City Manager Brandon Wade recalled. As Hurricane Rita neared land, it veered east and came ashore over southwest Louisiana, west of Johnson's Bayou but east of Sabine Pass, punching Beaumont square in the face. The island did have some strong winds and heavy rain, and several of its historic houses burned to the ground while the fire department watched helplessly from the hotel's top floor. But for the most part, Galveston escaped disaster. The near miss and the traffic snarls reminded many residents why they usually chose to ride out storms at home.

■ LIKE GALVESTON CITY officials, County Judge Jim Yarbrough was little concerned about Hurricane Ike, even as the storm wrecked Cuba and aimed for the Gulf. But unlike other Galveston natives—who call themselves BOIs, short for "born on the island"—Yarbrough was not one to take storms lightly.

When he took office in January 1995, Galveston County treated emergency management as an afterthought. One full-time employee and one part-time secretary coordinated all of the emergency operations in a county struck by nine major hurricanes since the United States started keeping records in 1851. The county had no formalized hurricane plan. The emergency operations center was set up in the basement of a dilapidated county court building.

The mayors and city mangers of Galveston County cities were notorious for their mutual silence on hurricane planning. Island leaders didn't cross the Galveston Causeway to share hurricane plans with the leaders of nearby Texas City, an oil refinery town protected by a 17-mile levee. Texas City officials worried more about industrial disasters than hurricanes. And no one talked to the leaders of Bolivar Peninsula, a narrow strip of land a ferry ride away from the rest of the county.

As county judge, Yarbrough authorized the construction of a new emergency bunker in League City, a growing bedroom community 24 miles inland. He hired John Simsen—who had a degree in emergency management from the University of North Texas—to head the county's emergency operations full time. And he organized a meeting between top county officials and the leaders of Galveston County's dozen or so municipalities. For the first time, county leaders sat around a table and scrawled on a white board the things they'd need in the event of the next Big One.

They talked about emergency equipment and reentry procedures. They talked about signing contracts ahead of time with companies to clear the tons of debris chewed up and left behind by massive storms. While the state continued to treat emergency management as a local issue, Galveston County built a regional plan so unconventional that the state sent a delegation to the county to learn from it.

In many ways, hurricanes are the easiest disasters to manage. They announce themselves slowly and spin for days over pockets of warm water, gradually building strength, all the while giving emergency management officials time to plan, stockpile, coordinate, and prepare. But hurricanes are also notorious for playing hopscotch, skipping around for days while forecasters endlessly write and rewrite landfall projections.

Yarbrough was not thinking about evacuation in the week Ike entered the Gulf. Like Galveston's city manager, Yarbrough had business on his mind. The judge was busy strategizing a $135 million bond election in November to pay for new streets, better drainage, and an upgraded health clinic for the poor. Hurricane Ike was just another storm in the Gulf, a minor threat overshadowed by the upcoming election.

■ AT 7 PM Tuesday, the forecast track had Ike maintaining course for Corpus Christi. But at 10 PM, forecasters shifted the track north, predicting the storm would land near Matagorda Bay, just 120 miles southwest of Galveston.

Mayor Thomas decided late Tuesday to call for a voluntary evacuation of the island's low-lying West End. Ike was wide enough that even a landfall at Matagorda would be felt on the island. Forecasters continued to predict the storm would come ashore early Saturday morning, right at high tide. Without the protection of a seawall, the low-lying West End was likely to flood. But its houses, built on pilings, were designed for water to wash under them and back out to sea without causing much damage.

By Wednesday, the forecasting models shifted the hurricane further north. Yarbrough summoned his good friend Bill Read on the phone. In September 2007, Read had left his post as head of the National Weather Service in League City to take the National Hurricane Center's top job.

"Give me the off-the-record," Yarbrough told Read.

"This storm is pretty big and it's pushing a lot of water," Read said.

Yarbrough didn't hesitate. At noon Wednesday, he joined Thomas for a press conference broadcast live on almost all of Houston's television stations. He ordered a mandatory evacuation of the county's most vulnerable areas, the unprotected Bolivar Peninsula and the low-lying bayside communities of Bacliff and San Leon. Mayor Thomas urged West End residents and visitors to consider leaving but stopped short of ordering a mandatory evacuation. Flanked by Jamaica Beach Mayor Vic Pierson, Thomas urged West End property owners to prepare for high winds and flooding.

Many didn't need Thomas' encouragement to start boarding up windows and tying down deck furniture. About 80 percent of West End houses were vacation or rental homes. Property management companies asked visitors to leave and sent crews to roll down storm shutters. Homeowners from Houston left work in the middle of the afternoon to drive to the island and move furniture away from windows. Trucks drove north towing boats to safety.

By 1 PM, Ike had strengthened to a Category 2 storm, but the forecast track held steady through the afternoon. Cautious residents who lived behind the seawall started to board windows. Some, with memories of hurricanes Katrina and Rita fueling their panic, loaded up prized possessions and headed inland. At 4 PM, the National Weather Service issued a hurricane watch for the entire Texas coast, indicating hurricane conditions were possible within 48 hours.

After the conference call with state emergency management officials, Thomas and LeBlanc gathered the city's department heads and legal staff to discuss their options. People had already started to question why the city hadn't called for a mandatory evacuation of the whole island, but Thomas was adamantly opposed to asking people to leave, with the storm's track and intensity still so unlikely to cause much of a problem for the island.

Ordering an evacuation ahead of Hurricane Rita was an easy call, LeBlanc said. But this was different. Despite forecasters' initial fears that Ike would strengthen as it spun over the Gulf, the storm remained what many considered a weak hurricane. The city's emergency plan called for evacuation only for storms that were a Category 3 or higher. The Saffir-Simpson scale was designed to reflect the damage hurricane-force winds could inflict, but Deputy City Manager Brandon Wade worried more about the storm's surge than its winds. Wade and other city officials had traveled to Gulfport and Biloxi, Mississippi, after Katrina and saw firsthand what kind of damage the rushing water left behind. If Galveston suffered the kind of surge those coastal cities had endured three years earlier, the island wouldn't survive, he thought. Still, he knew asking people to leave ahead of such a minor threat during one of the summer's last weekends would be difficult.

"You always have to worry about hurting the tourist season," he said.

Outside the city council workshop room, where Thomas was holed up with her advisors, reporters and television cameramen waited impatiently. The 5 PM press conference didn't start on time, and every station wanted to lead its 6 PM broadcast with news of the evacuation. But all they got was the shelter-in-place order. Thomas told only West End residents they had to evacuate.

Contrary to the city's emergency plan, which mandates no shelters in a high-risk zone, which includes the entire island, Thomas told residents shelters would open on Friday for anyone who wanted to stay on the island but was afraid to ride out the storm at home. Pets would be welcome at the shelters, and medical personnel from the University of Texas Medical Branch would be on hand to take care of any emergencies, she said. Both Thomas and LeBlanc bristled when asked by reporters whether they had waited too long to make the call to get residents to safety. LeBlanc pointed to the storm's constant changes and said officials made decisions they thought were best based on the information they had. But looking back on those decisions months later, LeBlanc admitted he and Thomas had a difficult time making the call for evacuation. Based on the problems people had during the Rita evacuation, everyone at city hall knew it would be difficult to make people leave, he said.

■ THE SITUATION DETERIORATED rapidly overnight. By 10 PM Wednesday, the National Weather Service moved the storm's projected landfall to San Luis Pass, on the western tip of the island. The residents of Bolivar Peninsula and Galveston's West End who didn't heed the mandatory evacuation order on Wednesday night found themselves trapped by rising water early Thursday morning, a full 72 hours before Ike was set to come ashore.

Judge Yarbrough was amazed as he looked at the early morning reports of rising water and widespread flooding. From his bedroom, he placed a private call to Jack Colley, the state's top emergency management director.

Galveston Island needed to evacuate now, Colley said.

The call was the mayor's to make, but Yarbrough was determined to try to force her hand. At 7:15 AM Thursday, September 11, Yarbrough headed to city hall to make his pitch to Thomas and LeBlanc. If they bucked, Yarbrough would point out that this storm was no Rita. The outbound roads weren't snarled with traffic yet. If Thomas called the evacuation that Thursday morning, islanders could flee, safely and quickly. There would be no evacuation by zone, either, as there had been for Rita. The zones—divided into A, B, and C, depending on how close the resident lived to the water—were too confusing and no one knew which zone they were in anyway. Instead, the evacuation would be ordered by zip code—those closest to the Gulf and Galveston Bay would be allowed out first.

The Galveston County delegation had a quick talk with Harris County Judge Ed Emmett, too, to make sure the coastal residents got out first.

"You got to help us make sure people in Katy and The Woodlands and Sugar Land don't get on the roads," Yarbrough told Emmett. "They're not near the water. Tell them to stay put."

At a press conference that morning, Emmett told Houstonians to "hunker down." The plea worked so well that he rode the catchphrase all the way to reelection in November.

But Yarbrough didn't need a sales pitch after all. When the judge arrived at city hall early Thursday morning, Thomas and LeBlanc had already decided to call for the mandatory evacuation. At 7:50 AM, not long after he had talked to Yarbrough, Colley shot LeBlanc an e-mail. Attached to the message was a map of the island, swallowed by 12 feet of blue waves.

The body of the e-mail contained only two words: Call me.

"Based on that e-mail, I got on the phone with Lyda Ann and told her we needed to call the evacuation immediately," LeBlanc said.

■ **AT 9:30 AM** on Thursday, Thomas, Yarbrough, and LeBlanc again stood before the television cameras. This time, they all looked tense, and they didn't waste time getting to the point.

"This has been a hard call to make," said Thomas, who then stepped aside from the podium to let Yarbrough announce the evacuation.

Yarbrough said Ike's swing northward had prompted their decision.

"When we saw that last movement, we thought, if it's going to make an error, it's going to come toward us," he said.

Critics questioned whether Thomas was trying to separate herself from the decision, hoping to deflect any angry backlash by having Yarbrough make the announcement. But letting the judge take the lead was just part of the emergency team's command structure, she said later. Yarbrough was helping to coordinate evacuations in all Galveston County cities, to make sure the people living closest to the coast got a chance to leave first, she said. His role in the press conference was a symbol of the group's unity, she said.

The late evacuation order confused islanders. Why would Thomas wait until two days before the hurricane was supposed to arrive to tell people to leave? And why leave for a Category 2 storm?

After telling those who could leave on their own to get off the island as soon as possible, Thomas and LeBlanc urged the island's neediest residents—the old, the sick, and the poor—to head to the Island Community Center, at 47th Street and Broadway, where state-chartered buses would soon be waiting to evacuate them.

Within an hour of Thomas' press conference, buses descended on the island. Hundreds made their way to the community center carrying suitcases, duffle bags, and trash bags filled with medicines, a few days' worth of clothing, and some personal hygiene items. Families gathered in little groups in the parking lot, waiting their turn to register. With no overhead shelter, the sun was brutal. At least three people fainted. Pallets of bottled water evaporated into the hands of thirsty, sweaty evacuees.

While buses headed for shelters in Austin began filling up and rolling away by late morning, some evacuees ended up waiting for hours just to register. At 3 PM, city staffers were still taking down names and handing out seat assignments. Rumors that there wouldn't be enough buses for everyone started to ripple through the parking lot. But dozens of buses were lined up in the Target parking lot, just a few miles away, waiting their turn to load up and move out.

While the city scrambled to evacuate its residents, the University of Texas Medical Branch decided to get its patients out of harm's way as well. As it was three years before, the hospital remained staffed with just a skeleton crew. The medical branch used chartered medical jets and helicopters to fly those patients too sick to go by bus or ambulance. Doctors discharged or evacuated more than 400 patients in less than 24 hours. On Thursday morning, an empty terminal at Scholes International Airport greeted medical personnel and the patients they pushed in wheelchairs and on stretchers. The usual flurry of activity from helicopters serving Gulf oil rigs had already stopped.

Traffic stayed light all day on the roads out of town. The fuel trucks state officials had pre-positioned along the highways to help stranded motorists were hardly used.

■ **AFTER THE EVACUATION** announcement, city staffers began clearing out their offices and getting ready to head home to board up their own windows. At first, the city's IT department told staff to put their computers on their desks, but two hours later employees were told to move all of the electronic equipment to the second floor. Ike's storm surge was expected to be much higher than previously thought, IT Director Ryan Young told his coworkers.

David Smith, the city's garage manager, ordered all city vehicles to head to the Galveston Island Convention Center at 57th Street and Seawall Boulevard. Following the plan developed on the fly for Hurricane Rita, city staffers drove as many of the city's vehicles as could fit, bumper to bumper, into the center's ballrooms and parking garage.

The Galveston Park Board of Trustees spent Thursday morning securing the island's five beachfront pavilions and moving its ATVs and other beach equipment to the agency's maintenance facility on 29th Street. The agency, which oversees all the island's beaches and operates its convention and visitors bureau, had already plucked the red and yellow lifeguard towers from the beach and moved them to a parking lot at 24th and Church streets. During Hurricane Rita, the park board moved almost all of its equipment off the island to save it from flooding. But this time, Executive Director Lou Muller decided to leave everything just a few blocks from downtown. Muller and his department heads had heard the surge predictions, but no one really thought a Category 2 storm could produce that much flooding, Muller said.

"We probably didn't pay as much attention as we should have," he said.

■ OFFICIAL PREPARATIONS AND evacuations were complete by late afternoon, just in time for the storm to shift again. In its 4 PM advisory, the National Weather Service announced Ike was likely to move directly over the urban core of Galveston when it made landfall early Saturday morning. Although the weather advisories talked about the storm's increasing threat, officials and area residents still didn't seem to grasp the storm's real danger, Chief Meteorologist Gene Hafele said.

"I don't think we did an adequate job of trying to communicate that to the officials, even though, if you look at our products, the numbers are in there," he said. "We kept saying it was a Category 2 and expect it to remain that way. That's what people were hearing. Then we would talk about the storm surge. Maybe they weren't understanding what a 10- to 12-foot storm surge would do."

LeBlanc later acknowledged he didn't fully understand Ike's destructive potential. As an island native, he was numb to the hype that precedes every storm. When Hurricane Alicia made landfall in 1983, LeBlanc and his wife Jolene, then newly married, sat on the seawall at 25th Street and watched the wind rip off chunks of wall from the Flagship Hotel, which sits on a long pier stretched out over the Gulf. Storms just weren't that big a deal, he said. The hype only seemed justified when Hurricane Rita, a Category 5 storm, was headed toward them.

But Ike wasn't even a major hurricane.

Although city officials set up their base camp at The San Luis Resort for Hurricane Rita, LeBlanc decided to keep the 200 city staffers on duty at city hall. The building, built in 1916, was 6 feet above street level. At just one block off Broadway on 25th Street, it was far enough away from both the port and the seawall to be safe, LeBlanc thought. Despite seeing Colley's surge map and listening to the weather predictions, LeBlanc was still focused on the storm's Saffir-Simpson scale rating.

"We thought, heck, it's just a Category 2," he said.

About one-third of the island's 56,000 residents shared LeBlanc's nonchalance. Although Thomas and LeBlanc cancelled plans for a shelter when they ordered the evacuation, an estimated 20,000 decided to brave Ike on their own. Only 1,500 residents took the city up on its offer of a ride to Austin. Almost twice that many had boarded buses ahead of Rita.

Many people later said it was too late to leave by the time Thomas called the evacuation. Less than 48 hours later, they would blame the mayor for the horrifying night they spent fleeing Ike's storm surge. Had she called the evacuation sooner, they would have heeded her warning, they complained.

Months later, Yarbrough defended Thomas. Sitting in an overstuffed brown leather recliner, chomping on a thick, unlit cigar, Yarbrough said it's tough making calls in advance: "Nobody likes to cry wolf."

CHAPTER

THREE

DONALD DAVIS AND Louis Gross sat on a bench in front of the Island Community Center, where evacuees had filled the parking lot waiting to board buses just 12 hours earlier. Both men had duffel bags and plastic grocery sacks packed with the few things they would need during the evacuation. Although they missed Thursday's buses, they heard rumors that more would be coming this morning. Davis kept looking down the road. Gross said his whole family left without him because he wanted to wait on his paycheck.

The dawn revealed an island that was slowly drowning. Davis walked all the way from his apartment complex at 81st Street and Seawall Boulevard–50 blocks–hoping he wasn't too late. He frowned as he continued to look down the street, occasionally leaning forward when he thought he caught a glimpse of a bus. But no buses were coming this day.

Davis and Gross, both without transportation, were stuck. Others, who woke up frightened by the early flooding but lucky enough to own cars, tossed bags of clothes into sedans and SUVs and fled. Vehicles crawled through flooded streets, leaving wakes that ebbed and flowed across front yards.

Those unafraid of the rising water went sightseeing along the seawall, capturing photographs and videos of the churning ocean. Waves crested over the road, regurgitating shells, driftwood, and seaweed that piled along a sidewalk usually reserved for cyclists and roller skaters. Cars and trucks making their way slowly down the seafront boulevard drove over trash and tiny crabs trying to scuttle to safety. People stared out of car windows, gawking at the foamy, coffee-colored waves shooting over the seawall like dancing fountains in Las Vegas.

They watched the waves batter a popular fishing pier on 61st Street, a 100-year-old gift shop, a restaurant, and the historic Balinese Room nightclub, once the hub of the island's midcentury gambling industry. All four of the buildings, built on piers that extended into the Gulf, gave way piece by piece to the pounding surf, washing onto the seawall in incongruous bits: a heap of wooden shards, one side of a staircase, a cash register, a souvenir conch shell left mysteriously intact.

Those who left had no idea what, if anything, they would have to come home to. Those who stayed had no idea what desperation nightfall would bring.

■ "I JUST CAME from our West End. It is starting to go under." Galveston County's IT Director Chris Gonzales, crisscrossing the island like a storm chaser in the predawn hours Friday, fired off an e-mail to the county judge, recording with chilling precision the storm's early arrival.

The hurricane—still more than a day away according to the National Weather Service forecast—funneled a storm surge into the streets, transforming the roads in the tiny village of Jamaica Beach into miniature canals. As the waves crept closer to sherbet-colored beach houses, the surge chewed up the sandy beach, the dunes, and the sand socks—thick tubes designed to prevent beach erosion. Along the seawall, waves splashed 15 feet high even though the storm was "still 20 hours out," Gonzales wrote to County Judge Jim Yarbrough in his 2:39 AM message. The surf was already crashing over the lower deck of the Flagship, a once-glorious hotel that stretched out over the Gulf of Mexico.

"We have about 8 feet to give before the water is over the seawall," Gonzales predicted.

In downtown Galveston, the rising tide backed up through the drains and flooded the streets. The Strand, the city's historic, tourist-attracting downtown shopping district, was slowly being swallowed by Galveston Bay.

■ BILL AND KATHY Moll spent Thursday night packing up everything they didn't want to risk losing—her best jewelry, his mother's silver, their clothes, wills, passports, family pictures, and a carefully built wine collection. Moll packed it all away in the bed and cab of his Ford F150 truck. By the time he was done early Friday morning, the water in the canal behind their bayfront West End home had risen to the top of the bulkhead that protected their yard from erosion. The couple, who had lived in Galveston since 2001, didn't decide to evacuate until Thursday morning, even though Mayor Lyda Ann Thomas had asked West End residents to leave Wednesday evening. Ike just didn't seem that threatening, Moll recalled.

But as Thomas ordered the islandwide evacuation, Moll decided it was better to be safe than sorry. He hoped to have both their canal home in Spanish Grant and a beach house rental property in Karankawa Beach boarded up by the end of the day so that they could drive to Houston that night. But the handyman he usually called on for help with the heavy plywood had already evacuated to Dallas. Moll gratefully accepted his neighbor's offer to help, and together the two men boarded up the house. It took them all day. By the time he made it back to Spanish Grant at 6:30 PM, he was ready for a breather. Moll was just sitting down to enjoy his first glass of wine when his son called and begged him to leave immediately. Ike was now predicted to be a direct hit on the island, and the Houston television stations predicted certain death for anyone who stayed.

Moll couldn't see any water in the streets or drainage ditches. They still needed to pack the truck. The couple decided to leave in the morning.

When the last box was stowed away, Moll opted for a quick nap before hitting the road. He was exhausted, and the tide wasn't that high yet. He had lived in Galveston long enough to know that FM 3005 and Stewart Road, the only two routes off the West End, flood quickly during a storm. But Ike was still 18 hours away. The situation didn't seem desperate yet.

■ THURSDAY EVENING, DEPUTY City Manager Brandon Wade and his wife Belinda, also a city employee, met at Kroger to stock up on a few things they would need during the next few days. The store was starting to close as Wade ordered the couple's dinner from the deli. Because Ike's storm surge was not expected to get bad until Friday morning, they decided to stay at their home on the West End, just past 12 Mile Road. After dinner, they packed up the things Belinda would take while evacuating in the morning, including their two dogs and one cat.

At 5:30 AM Friday morning, Wade woke up and walked out onto the second-story deck. The water was already at the foot of the driveway. His plan had been to have Streets Superintendent Mike Dricks pick him up so that Belinda could drive off the island without stopping to drop him off at the San Luis. But watching the water start to creep up the driveway, Wade knew if they waited that long to leave, they'd be stuck. While Belinda frantically packed the last of her things, Wade called Dricks and told him they needed to leave immediately.

Dricks headed down Seawall Boulevard in the bucket truck his crews used to fix traffic signals. It was taller than most trucks, but the water was already dangerously high when he got to 7 Mile Road. Dricks called Wade and told him they'd better be in the car, waiting to go when he got there. The three set off as soon as Dricks got his truck turned around. Wade, at the wheel of his personal truck, followed the larger vehicle as closely as he could to take advantage of the lower water levels flowing in its wake.

When they got to the end of the seawall, the road was already littered with logs, trash and seaweed coughed up by waves. As the churning Gulf waters crashed into the base of the 17-foot-tall protective barrier, the spray splashed up and on to the groups of people who had gathered to witness Ike's fury. Most were snapping pictures. Some panned video cameras up and down the street. Wade was shocked by the carnival-like atmosphere. After escorting Belinda over the causeway to make sure she made it safely, Wade and Dricks headed back into town. Instead of going directly to city hall, the men drove down 57th Street, through neighborhoods that backed up to English Bayou.

"It just looked like a sunshiny Sunday morning," Wade said. "Everybody was just out, kind of walking around. There didn't appear to be any real level of urgency. People were walking around just visiting with one another. That struck me as very concerning because I knew at that point we had a lot of people on the island that really didn't plan to leave. And I knew it was going to get pretty tough after that."

■ **LESS THAN TWO** miles away, Mayor Thomas was on her way to check on one of the houses she owned on Offatts Bayou. Once a fishing camp on the outskirts of town, the house had become part of the Hollywood Heights neighborhood when the city started to spread west. To accommodate the growth and the additional traffic, the Texas Department of Transportation rebuilt 61st Street, raising it to make it less vulnerable to flooding. But the road improvements had turned the adjacent neighborhood into a big bowl. Thomas expected the streets to flood during the storm. She was surprised when she got there to see the water already too high for her to drive through it. Determined to get to the camp, she went back to her house on 37th Street, grabbed her boots and the keys to her son's truck and headed back toward the bayou. She made it through the second time, but only just.

"I knew then that we were in real trouble," she said. "The water was already too high in that part of town."

■ **WHEN COUNTY JUDGE** Yarbrough left his New Orleans-style mansion around 8 AM Friday morning–carrying with him the necessities he'd need for his stay with county officials and dozens of reporters in the emergency operations center in League City–the water in the manmade "lake" behind his home already lapped at the top of the bulkhead in his backyard. That was unusual, even for a high tide in Lake Madeline, which was connected to Offatts Bayou by a long, thin canal. He gave the encroaching water little more than a passing glance, locked the house and left. As he headed toward the causeway, it dawned on him that he'd forgotten the cigars sitting in the desk drawer in his downtown office. He changed course and headed east along the seawall, where the water already sprayed high into the air, eerily similar to his boyhood memories of Hurricane Carla.

Yarbrough was five years old when Carla came ashore over Port Lavaca in 1961–the last Big One in the recent memory of most islanders.

Carla flooded the island and spawned 26 tornadoes that tore apart 120 buildings and killed six people in Galveston.

As Carla came ashore, Yarbrough, a round-faced, chubby boy, walked with his family to the seawall to watch the spectacle of waves shooting upward over the protective wall. Yarbrough remembers the waves and the seal—or was it a sea otter?—that floated into a neighbor's pool. Yarbrough watched the frightened mammal swim in frantic laps around and around the edge as the storm inched closer to Galveston. When the deadly storm passed, Yarbrough and his father, then the president of the local school board, canvassed the town, assessing the damage and tallying the loss.

For the young Yarbrough, Carla was an adventure, not a threat. And Ike—well Ike was a *Category 2,* for God's sake.

Yarbrough picked his way downtown, dodging debris and pooling water that in some streets measured several feet deep. At the county courthouse, just a few blocks off Broadway in the island's historic East End, Yarbrough plucked the cigars from his desk, poured a cup of coffee, and pondered checking on his house one last time before heading north. He bid farewell to the staff planning to ride out the storm in the courthouse and headed home for one last look.

On his way back west, Yarbrough noticed with growing alarm that in the hour or so he'd spent at the courthouse, the water in the streets had deepened. At home in his bedroom, the ex-Longhorn linebacker pulled from a safe his coveted football season tickets. Instinctively, he moved a pair of custom-made University of Texas cowboy boots from the floor to the shelf, but he left everything else in its place, including the dozens of potted hibiscus plants encircling his backyard pool. He didn't bother to let his two cats—Magic and Spice—inside.

Before he left, he set the burglar alarm and locked the doors. By that time—around midmorning—the storm surge was so high in the streets that Yarbrough was forced to pick his route carefully to stay out of the flood. As he drove over the Interstate 45 bridge crossing 61st Street—the island's main north-south thoroughfare—he noticed everything below him was underwater.

"This is going to be bad," he thought. It had taken five days, but the dreaded storm finally arrived.

■ **WHEN BILL MOLL** woke from his nap, the water in the canal had risen almost three feet. But the street was still clear when he, Kathy and their orange tabby Goldie left the house and headed into town. By the time they got to the entrance of their subdivision at Stewart Road, they were driving through shallow water—nothing their high-clearance truck couldn't handle. But as they reached 8 Mile Road, two miles from home, the water was almost to the top of their tires. Bill was starting to get nervous. When he turned onto FM 3005 at 7½ Mile Road, the current was so strong the truck started to float. Fearing it might stall, Bill rolled down the windows, in case he couldn't get the doors open if they needed to escape.

"We were slinging water like a Mississippi paddle boat," he said.

When the engine died a few minutes later, they were "too scared to be scared," Bill said. The pressure against the door was so strong he had to push with both feet to get it open. Water poured in, filling the cab to Kathy's waist as she sat in the passenger's seat. Bill first lifted Goldie's carrier onto his shoulder and then helped his wife out into the slow but steady current. Kathy was still clinging to her purse, but they didn't have time to grab anything else they'd so carefully stowed in the truck. The water was up to their chests as they started to walk down the highway.

Clutching the cat carrier with one hand and Kathy with the other, Bill tried not to show how worried he was. Waves occasionally splashed them in the face as the water flowed past them. They could tell it was gradually getting shallower as the road rose toward the seawall, probably the only thing that kept them going, Bill recalled. He turned around only once to look at the truck. All he could see was its roof.

When they were close enough to the seawall that the water was just below their knees, Bill saw an old farm truck headed toward them. It was only slightly taller than the couple's newer Ford, but it was high enough to get through the flood. The driver stopped and offered to take them to a shelter, if they could find one. Like everyone else who had driven past the same sights just a few hours before, Bill was shocked by the waves pounding the seawall. At 90th Street, the punishing surf began to shred a fishing pier.

■ BY MIDMORNING, IT was clear to city officials driving through neighborhoods that about one-third of the islanders had ignored the mandatory evacuation order. Mayor Thomas and City Manager Steve LeBlanc had planned earlier in the week to open shelters of last resort for the stragglers who refused to leave. Thomas and Galveston Independent School District Superintendent Lynne Cleveland agreed on Wednesday that the district would open three schools as shelters, if needed. Cleveland offered to give the city Ball High School, Central Middle School, and Alamo Elementary School. In total, the district could house almost 4,000 hurricane refugees.

Cleveland agreed to throw in six buses, three of which were equipped with lifts for people with disabilities, some food and snacks for people who arrived unprepared, a few rolls of toilet paper and paper towels, some hand soap, a team of 10 police officers, a few bus drivers and other district officials to help manage the shelter. As Cleveland understood the agreement, the city would provide water, bedding, and extra manpower. But early Thursday morning, Thomas and LeBlanc reversed the decision and pulled the plug on the shelters. Seeing no need to keep a team on standby, Cleveland sent the police officers and bus drivers home to evacuate.

On Friday morning, LeBlanc phoned Cleveland to say the city needed the shelters after all. But Central Middle School was not an option any more, he told her. The historic campus—the heart of the African-American community on the island's north side—was already flooded. It was Cleveland's first inkling that Hurricane Ike was damaging the island's bay side. LeBlanc gave her no time to ponder the school's fate, however. The city needed a shelter in two hours, and LeBlanc wanted it set up in Ball High School. Cleveland phoned the members of her cabinet—the district's police chief, the budget officer, and the transportation director.

"Find me whoever you can," she told them.

Many of the district's shelter team had evacuated, but a few were close enough to return.

Several cafeteria workers showed up at the school to help. One bus driver brought her teenage son to work. Officer Dwight Gaines, heeding the call from his boss, gathered enough extra uniforms to last a few days and left his wife behind in their Houston home. Heading south, Gaines cruised along the empty interstate while everyone else fled north in a panic. Gaines knew the storm would be much worse than he expected when he drove over the causeway and saw his hometown underwater. It would be a long night, he told himself.

Cleveland swears the city promised to send extra employees–those who weren't already pulling people from their flooded homes and cars–to help the district operate the makeshift shelter. But no one ever came. She understood LeBlanc was busy, but where were the pallets of water, the pillows, and the bedding he had promised? Cleveland called LeBlanc's cell phone over and over. She got no response.

Frustrated, Cleveland ordered district police, cafeteria workers, and bus drivers to scavenge whatever supplies they could get their hands on in the school to give to the hundreds of victims showing up at the school's doors.

"Bust into whatever you have to bust into," she told them. "The juice, the water, we'll take care of that later. We gotta take care of the people first."

■ LEBLANC, THOMAS, AND the other city staff members who were riding out the storm on the island met at city hall at 8 AM. But they didn't stay there long. From his corner office on the second floor, LeBlanc could see almost all the way down 25th Street to the port. The bay had crept up to Postoffice Street, and it was obvious the water was over the curb on The Strand. The island's downtown streets flood even in a heavy rain, so it was not unusual to see so much water between the buildings. But this time it was flowing.

"It was just like a river coming toward us," Thomas said.

Realizing the water would be at their doorstep soon, LeBlanc decided to retreat to The San Luis Resort. By the time everyone was loaded into trucks and the convoy was ready to roll out of the parking lot, the water was a foot deep in front of city hall.

As city officials were evacuating the rapidly filling downtown, John Augelli and Mike Christiansen were frantically trying to get there before it was cut off completely. Augelli, executive director of the Rosenberg Library, hadn't planned to retreat to the library until the afternoon, but one of the two employees who planned to stay with him during the storm in the 104-year-old building called early that morning to say he needed to get down there soon. The rest of the library's 40 staff members evacuated on Thursday, but Augelli wanted someone to be on hand to keep an eye on the building and be ready to start any necessary cleanup work as soon as the storm passed.

The library, three stories set with wide windows trimmed in classical scrollwork, had never suffered any major structural damage during a storm, and 18 inches was the most water it had ever taken on during a flood. The first floor, which contained the entire children's collection, sat several feet below street level. Before they left on Thursday, employees had picked up computers and moved them to the second floor. They didn't attempt to move the rest of the first floor's books, furniture, and equipment. It was just too much, Augelli said. But because the storm wasn't very strong, he was confident the books would be fine.

As soon as he hung up the phone, Augelli finished closing up his house in the Denver Court neighborhood, between 52nd and 43rd streets just a few blocks from the seawall. His wife Gloria had left town on Thursday, headed not only away from the storm but also to her father's funeral. Augelli planned to join her as soon as Ike passed through. Calling his German Shepherd mix, Enzo, Augelli climbed into his Toyota Corolla and headed for the Frost Bank parking garage at Market and 22nd streets. During storms, the bank opened the garage to people who wanted to protect their cars from street flooding and flying debris. When Augelli arrived at 8:15 AM, it was already so full of other cars that he had to squeeze the compact car into a walkway next to the elevator. Augelli and Enzo waded through knee-deep water for part of their six-block walk to the library, but the building was still dry.

Christiansen, the executive vice president and chief accounting officer of Moody National Bank, planned to ride out the storm in the bank's seven-story headquarters at 23rd and Postoffice streets. Like Augelli, Christiansen didn't intend to start his vigil until late Friday afternoon, but a friend who worked for the Galveston Police Department called before 8 AM to tell him he needed to go immediately if he wanted to be dry when he got there. Curious to see what the Gulf looked like, Christiansen and his wife Julie detoured down the seawall on their way downtown. Both of the eastbound lanes were so covered in debris they had to drive on the wrong side of the road.

"It was the most horrifying sight of my life," he said. "I couldn't believe it."

The couple; their 98-pound Labrador, Kelsey; and their cat, Mr. Palmer; got to the bank at about 9 AM. Christiansen parked their truck on the building's wide porch, about five feet above the street. They would stay on the windowless second floor, but Christiansen first went through the rest of the building to make sure all of the windows and doors were closed tight. From the top floor he could see the water streaming past Market Street, just one block away.

■ BY NOON, EMORY Brockway watched the water in his street rise over the wheel well of his truck. He and his wife Merlinda had decided early in the week they wouldn't leave. Now they had no choice. Although the couple liked to keep to themselves and didn't really know their neighbors, they did have some friends on the island. But Emory, determined he could take care of himself and too stubborn to ask for help, didn't try to call anyone. He just stood at his front door, chain-smoking cigarettes, and watched the water get closer.

Emory came to Galveston in 1990 to visit a friend after losing his job as an airport cargo manager in St. Thomas, in the U.S. Virgin Islands. He had nowhere else to go, and he liked Galveston well enough, so he stayed. Several years later, he took a trip to the Philippines to attend his friend's wedding. In Manila, he met Merlinda, a friend of his friend's bride. One wedding turned into two before Emory returned to the United States. After wading through the tedious immigration process, Merlinda finally joined him in Galveston a year later.

They were determined not to let Hurricane Ike chase them out of the home they had shared for the last seven years, and Emory had declared he wasn't afraid of a hurricane. But watching the water get closer to his front door, he started to worry. He wasn't in the best of health, his slender five-foot-five frame was weakened by breathing problems that left him short of breath after even a little exertion, and Merlinda couldn't swim. But they never thought about calling 911 and asking dispatchers to send a rescue team their way. They just watched the water creep toward them. By about 4 PM, it seeped under the door and started to soak through the carpet.

"I'm thinking, that's the worst it's going to be, and we'll just have some soggy carpet," Emory recalled. "But that damn stuff just kept coming."

■ THE RESCUE OPERATION was in full swing when Judge Jim Yarbrough finally arrived at the emergency operations center. The U.S. Coast Guard spent the morning plucking Bolivar Peninsula residents from their rooftops—a scene eerily similar to the post-Katrina visuals that captivated the nation's attention after the levees broke in New Orleans. The rescues and the waves crashing over the seawall dominated the news coverage. Yarbrough's Blackberry buzzed unceasingly with phone calls, e-mails, and requests from reporters to get inside the bunker with the county's top officials.

As Ike slowly swallowed Galveston and Bolivar Peninsula, a thin spit of land north of the island that didn't have the benefit of a protective seawall, the mayors of the relatively hurricane-proof mainland started to worry. Would the Texas City levees hold? Or was the small bayfront refinery community, anchored by its four chemical plants, doomed to the same fate it suffered during Hurricane Carla, which drowned the older parts of the city in as much as 11 feet of water?

With the eye of the hurricane just hours away, Texas City Mayor Matt Doyle contemplated a mandatory evacuation—a drastic and dangerous move this late in the game. The Department of Homeland Security— the parent agency of the oft-maligned Federal Emergency Management Agency—by then was predicting a Category 3 storm with maximum winds of 127 miles per hour and landfall over Quintana, Texas—a small town southeast of Freeport. The surge would cover land where half a million people lived, the federal predictions warned.

This was a worst-case scenario, the homeland security advisors warned. Yarbrough summoned the county's engineer, Mike Fitzgerald.

"Will that levee hold?" Yarbrough asked.

"It was built to handle this storm," Fitzgerald said.

End of discussion. Mainlanders behind the levee wall would stay put.

Days later—after the worst of the storm—Fitzgerald made his way to the levee and found debris near the top of the 21-foot wall. Had the storm been any wider, any stronger, any farther west, it would have topped the levees.

■ **AFTER EACH CONFERENCE** call with state officials, Yarbrough's optimism about escaping Ike unscathed waned. The storm stopped moving east, dashing Yarbrough's hopes that it would eventually curve around to hit Louisiana. Gene Hafele, chief of the local National Weather Service office, painted a bleak picture in a noon press conference for those planning to ride out the storm. Hurricane Ike would inundate the island with a storm surge as deep as 15 feet in some places. Bolivar Peninsula would get it worse—people there could expect to see water as deep as 20 feet. Once Hafele was done, Yarbrough addressed the reporters about the ongoing rescues on Bolivar Peninsula.

"The state is working to get out helicopters to evacuate people, but at some point that will be impossible from the winds," he said. "At that point, I wish them Godspeed and to get to the highest shelter. We'll be there as quickly as we can."

Throughout the afternoon, the Coast Guard shuttled peninsula residents from their rooftops to the massive empty parking lot at a La Marque dog-racing track, Gulf Greyhound Park. But 27 people holed up at Fort Travis—a concrete bunker that in World War I housed American troops defending Galveston—refused a ride on a Coast Guard helicopter, preferring instead to take their chances in the 110-year-old fort.

"The weather is allowing us to extend this mission," David Popoff, the liaison officer for the governor's division of emergency management, reported in a 2 PM e-mail blast to public officials. "On scene report indicates that several of the victims are highly intoxicated."

"Unbelievable!" County Commissioner Pat Doyle, who represents the peninsula, shot back in an e-mail to Yarbrough. "Those sons of bitches are crazy!!!"

■ IN GALVESTON, FRIGHTENED residents arrived by the dozens at Ball High School. Firefighters started depositing people at the building's front doors around 1 PM. Bill and Kathy Moll were among the first to arrive. Sitting in the school's cafeteria with Goldie wide-eyed but silent on the table between them, the couple took stock of what they had left. Moll pulled his cell phone from his soaked pocket and pressed the power button. Nothing. He pressed harder. Still nothing. Kathy fished hers from the innards of her purse. It was dry. Worried it might lose service at any minute, Moll dialed his son's number and closed his eyes as he waited for him to pick up.

Bill Jr. was at his own son's Little League baseball game in Houston but agreed to leave immediately and head for the island. About an hour later he called to say he was in Dickinson, about 20 miles from the island. He wanted to know if it was safe to keep coming. Moll asked a policeman walking through the shelter if the causeway was still open. It was, but only just. Bill Jr., almost the only driver on the road, sped 90 miles per hour past a state trooper who did nothing more than wave at him to slow down.

Bill and Kathy were waiting outside when Bill Jr. pulled up in the street out front. He stopped just long enough for them to jump into his Suburban before he sped off again. As they drove back down Broadway and onto Interstate 45, the water had started to pool on the outermost lanes of both sides of the freeway. Only the main lanes of the freeway remained above water.

The Molls were the only ones who left the shelter that afternoon. Everyone else who arrived in the school's lobby was there to stay. Most, like the Molls, didn't have much with them when they checked in at the front desk. Some brought trash bags full of clothing and kennels full of dogs and cats. One man brought a ferret.

It was clear to Cleveland that many of the district's temporary guests lacked the ability to care for themselves. There were old people, sick people, tiny children, alcoholics, drug addicts, and people with disabilities, mental and physical. Some of the little kids—the babies—had bare feet.

"I really felt bad for most of them," Cleveland said.

She remembered how, in the aftermath of Hurricane Katrina, 30,000 people had holed up in the Superdome, New Orleans' shelter of last resort. As they waited days for rescue, conditions in the football stadium became horrendous. There was no air conditioning and not enough food or water for everyone. Toilets backed up and the stench forced people outside to sit on the sidewalk in the sweltering heat. Six people died there.

Cleveland fretted that Galveston public school district didn't have enough food and supplies to care for the dozens of people now under her charge, especially if the damage left by Ike forced people to spend days in the school. She sent school district officials to retrieve whatever food and toiletries they could from other schools. They doled out whatever food they could find; refugees munched on crackers and frozen cheese sandwiches only partially defrosted.

■ THE RUSHINGS SPENT most of Friday morning sitting in their driveway watching the water fill up the street gutters. It came from the west at first, but they soon could see it flowing steadily at both ends of the street. The boys, 19-year-old Stevie, 13-year-old Tyler, and their cousin, 19-year-old RJ, splashed around with the two family dogs while Steven, Lupe, Tiffany, and Jason, another cousin, watched. Before Steven decided to ride out the storm at home, he talked to some of his elderly neighbors. They told him no water ever came into the houses in the Gulf Village neighborhood, just south of Moody Gardens, during Hurricane Carla. He figured Ike couldn't be worse than Carla because all he had ever heard was how bad the 1961 storm had been. So when the water started to flow like a stream down the street, Steven couldn't believe it.

At about 3 PM, he took the kids and walked about a mile to the seawall. When he saw how high the waves were, he knew the storm was going to be worse than he had expected. He had never seen the water that high. As they watched the surf pound the top of the wall, he told the kids maybe they should leave. But raised to crave the excitement of watching a storm come ashore and oblivious to Ike's destructive potential, the kids begged him not to make them go. When they got back home, Steven told Lupe he was going to get his truck out of the parking garage at Moody Gardens, just a few miles from their house. He grabbed his bicycle from the garage and pedaled north, splashing through the water that had already collected in the streets.

He thought he would make it, until he rode to the top of the small bridge that spans the canal entrance to Lake Madeline. From there he could see the entrance to Moody Gardens and the southern edge of the airport. It was like an ocean; every bit of it under water. Cut off from the truck and his only hope of getting his family off the island, Steven rode home and told them it was time to hunker down.

Gathered around the television in the living room, they talked about what would happen the rest of the night. Lupe suggested climbing into the attic if the water got too high. But Tiffany, who was three months pregnant, was scared they might end up sharing their refuge with rats. Steven had forgotten to bring home his chainsaw and didn't want to get trapped under the roof without a way to cut through to the outside. His initial plan was to swim outside and tie his family to the top of a tree. He even got the ski ropes out of his fishing boat in the garage and started to try to figure out how he could lash everyone together.

"We just thought of all these different scenarios, what we were going to do," Lupe said.

■ WHILE THE RUSHINGS watched the waves on the seawall, Steve LeBlanc grew restless holed up in The San Luis Resort. Anxious to see what was happening around the rest of the city, he asked Brandon Wade to find someone who could drive them around in a dump truck. Their first stop was LeBlanc's house, not far from where Steven Rushing looked over the airport ocean. LeBlanc's house was still dry, but Lake Madeline lapped at the back door. He knew the house would take on water. But he still hadn't grasped what was in store.

"I thought we would get about a foot," he said. "I was still being a little apathetic about having gone through this before."

LeBlanc, Wade, and Municipal Utilities Director Eric Wilson, their driver, continued down Stewart Road to 69th Street, where three or four helicopters hovered over Parker Elementary School. When they got closer, they realized police and firefighters had started pulling people out of houses in Hollywood Heights and Gulf Shores, neighborhoods between Offatts Bayou and Stewart Road. It was truly an American flag-waving moment, Wade said. They had stopped to talk to one of the firefighters when they noticed a small white Hyundai driving toward them through the surging tide. The car, with the words "U.S. Army, Retired" written in block letters under the driver's window, rolled right into the middle of the emergency response scene before it stopped and they could finally make out Fletcher Harris at the wheel.

Harris shook his finger at them, chastising Wade and LeBlanc for riding in the same vehicle together. The city manager and the deputy city manager had a duty to preserve the city's chain of command, Harris shouted at them.

"He really couldn't understand why it was that Steve and I were in the same truck," Wade said. "He kept shouting that at us, and we kept shouting to him, 'Fletcher, go home!'"

Wade and LeBlanc eventually persuaded the old man to head home, where they hoped he'd be safe. After he drove off through the rising water, Wade, LeBlanc, and Wilson headed for Broadway. It was still dry, but the tide had already swallowed the poor neighborhoods to the north. As they drove east, they could see a column of thick black smoke rising from somewhere in the East End.

As the water rose, it crept into circuit breakers, power outlets and refrigerators, stoves and toasters no one thought to turn off. When water met live electricity, wires shorted. Sparks flew and fires grew into blazes that consumed entire rows of houses. Firefighters stood helplessly by watching the ever-growing infernos fanned by the hurricane's winds that grew stronger by the minute.

Fire Chief Mike Varela had to stop his men from hurting themselves, and the department's pricey equipment, to fight fires he knew they couldn't reach.

"Firemen not only think they're invincible, but so are the trucks," he said.

The expensive electronics on the bulky red fire engines wouldn't last long if firefighters submerged them in water. And if firefighters ruined the equipment before the storm, what use would they be to fight fires and save people after Hurricane Ike passed?

"Sometimes you have to lose the battle if you want to win the war," Varela said.

When boats started to catch fire in the dry dock area of the Galveston Yacht Basin on Friday afternoon, firefighters couldn't get within a two-block radius of the blaze. Firefighters racing to the waterfront found the streets too flooded to navigate. Water swamped the trucks up to the wheel wells. They tried different routes, but no luck. Every street was like a river. At one frustrating point, men carrying 100-pound packs of gear waded in the chest-deep water to get to the blaze. They couldn't see the end of the pier under several feet of water, and realizing that they risked drowning, the men turned back. It was a cruel irony: An abundance of water prevented them from extinguishing the blaze.

As they stood by helplessly, the fire grew, feeding on fuel from the hundreds of boats islanders had docked there to save them from the hurricane. Black smoke drifted from the boat basin to the University of Texas Medical Branch across the street and over downtown Galveston, where scores of frightened islanders were holed up in their condos and lofts. The holdouts in downtown had spent the afternoon watching the city's green trash bins bob down flooded streets, and they wondered with growing anxiety how high the water would get. Now they worried about the black smoke that seemed to be coming from all around.

Varela consulted the captains on Galveston's fire squad. They elected to allow the blazes to continue to burn rather than risk equipment, and more importantly, firefighters' lives. Varela couldn't live with himself if a firefighter died needlessly fighting a blaze that couldn't be stopped.

Conditions worsened and Varela called for the firefighters to return to the hotel, where they would ride out the storm. They stowed away the trucks in the Galveston Convention Center parking garage and returned to their rooms to catch some sleep before daybreak. They would be needed for rescues and to comb through collapsed structures until the state's special rescue team—Texas Task Force One—could arrive. They needed to be fresh for what was sure to be a long, grueling day ahead. But no one could rest. Firefighters gathered outside their hotel rooms in the carpeted hallways facing wide windows overlooking the island. Some sat on the floor. Others leaned against the thick panes of glass. They watched in silence from their birds-eye vantage the dark plumes of smoke and the bright flames engulfing the houses below.

CHAPTER

FOUR

I T WAS EARLY in the day and slightly windy when Pastor William Mercer Harris stood on the beach, watching in awe the foamy, churned-up waves of the Gulf of Mexico.

"It was a sort of infinite monster, tossing its million heads and frothing at its million mouths as it hungered to devour the city," he wrote. "I stood there and heard the monster's growl—his cry for blood—and looked into the black terror of his murderous frown."

By nightfall, the "enraged sea" had swallowed Galveston Island. Tied to the back porch of the First Baptist Church parsonage, the Harris family dairy cow, Betsy, treaded water, desperately trying to stay afloat. Thelma Longfellow Harris, Pastor Harris' wife, eventually dragged the terrified animal inside the kitchen, where the Harris family had sought shelter from the storm. At 6:30 PM, a tornado hit the church at the corner of 23rd and Sealy streets, felling all seven steeples and damaging the upstairs bedroom of the parsonage.

"I saw our chapel blown into a thousand fragments; I heard the crash when our beautiful church fell," Harris wrote. "One portion of it struck the corner of the parsonage and drove myself and family out into the storm when the water was five feet deep in front of our gate. The wind was blowing a hundred miles an hour."

In a desperate attempt to get to safety, Pastor Harris laid a board from the parsonage windowsill to the stone wall of a nearby house, and he, his wife and their children "walked the plank to safety," church historian Diane Zimmerman wrote.

There they waited for the hurricane's fury to subside. When dawn broke over the island and the skies cleared, Harris watched wagons pass by carrying loads of dead Galvestonians. The wagons hauled them through the streets like "hogs from the slaughter pen," Harris wrote.

The date was September 9, 1900–the morning after the unnamed hurricane now known simply as the 1900 Storm or the Great Storm. It remains the deadliest natural disaster ever to hit the United States. The exact death toll was never fully known, but historians estimate the storm killed between 10,000 and 12,000 people; at least 6,000 of them lived in Galveston. The bodies were strewn among the wreckage and debris, in the streets, front yards, and along the beach. Countless others washed out to sea.

The 1900 Storm altered the island's history. Not only did it knock Galveston from its pedestal as one of the wealthiest and most important economic hubs in the nation, it forever shaped the way Galvestonians respond to hurricanes–and not in a good way. For the next 100 years, islanders remained complacent, even defiant, in the face of deadly hurricanes. When BOIs steadfastly refused to evacuate from monster hurricanes, they invoked the legacies of grandparents and great-grandparents who rode out the 1900 Storm and lived to tell about it.

Among the stubborn BOIs who refused to leave Galveston during hurricanes, Pastor William M. Harris' grandson was arguably the most obstinate. Fletcher Harris Jr. was the only son and heir of Fletcher Harris Sr., who was just a boy that harrowing night when thousands of islanders died. Houston television meteorologist Neil Frank, in reflecting on how the 1900 Storm shaped island history, told *The Galveston County Daily News* in 2003:

> I have nothing but respect for BOIs. But there is a culture within the BOIs that is defiant in a sense. They'll say, "My great-granddaddy and my granddaddy didn't run from a hurricane and I'm not running from one either–and why are you running from one?"

Although he didn't name him, Frank's description fit Fletcher Harris Jr. to a T.

Invoking his family's legacy of storm survival, Fletcher proudly stayed on the island during all major hurricanes, including Carla and Alicia. In 1961, Hurricane Carla made landfall as a Category 4 storm that spawned 26 tornadoes, one of which tore apart 120 buildings and killed six people in Galveston. Twenty-two years later, Hurricane Alicia made a direct hit on the island as a Category 3 storm, causing an estimated $3 billion in damage. Fletcher was a big believer in what he called "vertical evacuation," fleeing to higher ground if necessary during a hurricane instead of leaving the island altogether. Like other Galvestonians who had watched hurricanes beat down, but never top, the seawall, Fletcher had unwavering faith in the 17-foot-high structure Galvestonians constructed in the aftermath of the 1900 Storm to protect the city from future hurricanes. He believed, more than anything, that no hurricane could harm him.

But that sense of security, combined with the defiant BOI attitude embodied by Harris, made a dangerous brew, Frank warned in that 2003 newspaper article.

"Texas can't continue to escape hurricanes," he said.

■ THE 1900 STORM is key to understanding islanders' reactions to Hurricane Ike. The two are linked by eerie similarities.

Like Ike, the 1900 Storm formed near Cuba and churned slowly across the Gulf of Mexico. It followed nearly the same path as Hurricane Ike, as it spun closer and closer to Galveston. But, unlike the islanders of 2008, Galvestonians in 1900 had no way of truly knowing the monster that was slowly making its way from the Caribbean to Galveston.

In the years before 1900, Galveston had grown from a small settlement on the Texas coast to one of the wealthiest cities in the country. The city prospered from its natural deep-water channel, which made it the most important seaport in the state. More than 70 percent of the country's cotton crop passed through the port, and 1,000 ships called on the port each year. Galveston was home to 37,000 people, but thousands more passed through each year to vacation or conduct business. The country's rich and famous frequented the beaches, claiming the Gulf of Mexico waters had therapeutic properties.

Dr. Isaac Cline, a highly respected scientist, became head of Galveston's National Weather Bureau in 1889. His office was on the fourth floor of the E.S. Levy & Co. building, which still stands at the corner of Tremont and Market streets. Islanders got their daily weather reports from Cline, who raised various colored flags on the roof to indicate the weather. Cline believed that Galveston was immune from hurricanes because of the mild weather it enjoyed during the late 1800s. Anyone who suggested the island was vulnerable to a hurricane was suffering from "an absurd delusion," he once wrote in *The Daily News*.

Historians still debate whether Cline did enough to warn islanders of the impending danger of the 1900 Storm, but this much is sure: In the early morning of Saturday, September 8, 1900, Cline realized that something was terribly wrong. The barometric pressure on the island had fallen, the wind had picked up, and the tide was almost five feet above mean sea level. Cline hoisted the flag indicating an impending hurricane, hitched his horse to a two-wheeled cart and raced through the city like Paul Revere, warning people on the beach that a dangerous storm was on the way. He beseeched islanders to evacuate to the more solid buildings north of Broadway and sent frantic telegraphs to the National Weather Service office in Washington, until the lines went down in the afternoon. He finally retreated to his house to ride out the hurricane with his family and 50 others who sought shelter.

Conditions worsened as night blanketed the island and the storm surge—uninhibited by a seawall—washed over Galveston, creating a battering ram of debris, at least two stories tall, that pummeled everything in its path. A train trestle broke loose from its moorings and pounded Cline's house until the house broke free from its foundation and began to float. The house rolled over, trapping underwater Cline's wife and almost everyone else in it. Cline managed to escape with his daughters and his brother, Joseph Cline.

At daybreak, few structures remained intact. The damage was phenomenal. Pastor Harris watched the smoke from the impromptu funeral pyres as Galvestonians set fire to their dead neighbors on the beach so disease wouldn't spread.

"I saw the vacant stare of those who had lost their entire families," Harris wrote. "I stood and looked out over a section of our beautiful city where 4,000 homes had stood, where 16,000 people had lived, and saw that it had been converted in a few hours into a waste of desert sand where it was often impossible to find the streets, and where one must have a civil engineer and a map of the city to locate the lot on which he had lived for 20 years. And yet, I find it difficult to grasp the proportions of the calamity, from its very bigness."

■ THE GALVESTONIANS OF 1900 left more than a legacy of survival. They became the forbearers of a steely resolve to rebuild a city that nature all but obliterated.

Galveston Mayor Walter C. Jones called an emergency city council meeting at 10 AM the morning after the hurricane; by the end of the day, he had appointed a committee to start rebuilding.

The Central Relief Committee appointees included a young man named Isaac Herbert "Ike" Kempner. After his father's death six years earlier, the wealthy, 27-year-old financier had been called home from Washington and Lee University to take over the family's cotton and banking businesses and care for his mother and seven siblings. Kempner rode out the 1900 Storm with his family and friends at his mother's house, where the water rose eight feet deep in the backyard. At one point, he tied a rope to his body and, giving the other end to a friend sheltering at the house with him, he ventured out into the flood to find the coachman. Kempner had sent the man to release the family's two carriage horses stabled 30 feet from the back porch, and he hadn't returned. Kempner swam around the stable but found no signs of the man. (The coachman was later found sheltering with the horses on the back porch of an "irate neighbor," Kempner wrote in his memoir.)

As Kempner returned to the house, he noticed that the water had receded by at least two feet. In celebration of the receding water and decreasing wind, Kempner and his friend, Safford Wheeler, set out on foot to spread the good news to neighbors that the hurricane was over. Kempner and Wheeler were welcomed into four or five houses, where they received stiff drinks. This, Kempner wrote, gave them the "spiritual courage" to wade through water, still waist-deep in some places, to spread their good news to the guests at the Tremont Hotel.

"We tried to gain access at the Tremont Hotel, then the largest hotel in Galveston; found the doors tightly locked; no answer to doorbells or our cries," Kempner wrote. "So with wooden creosoted paving blocks afloat in Tremont Street or resting on a sidewalk, we began smashing windows to permit our philanthropic desire to advise alarmed guests that the storm was over. We were promptly arrested by the hotel's night watchman, marched in his custody to the police station some five blocks away . . . No charges, *as yet,* many years later, have been filed against me."

Instead the mayor charged Kempner and the other relief committee members with supervising the island's reconstruction and managing the donations that poured in from across the nation. The city was broke, even before the storm. Kempner and other prominent Galveston businessmen suspected the mayor and aldermen running the city were incompetent, if not corrupt. They lobbied to create a new government made up of a mayor and a board of four commissioners, two appointed by the governor and two elected by the people. Texas governor Joseph D. Sayres appointed Kempner as one of the commissioners. This form of government was approved by the state legislature in 1901, but the Court of Criminal Appeals later forced the city to elect rather than appoint all commissioners.

After the hurricane destroyed the city's tax base, Galveston had no way to pay for its recovery, so Kempner used his personal line of credit. He successfully lobbied the state to allow Galveston to withhold for 20 years the property taxes it would have owed the state. The city used that money to secure bonds for the two civil engineering feats so audacious that Galvestonians could not help but feel that their island would be a fortress impenetrable by any future storm.

In 1901, the city hired three engineers who recommended a project of staggering scope. The city would literally rise from its sad remains, raising the ground 17 feet at the seawall and sloping it downward toward

Galveston Bay. All island buildings had to be elevated with jackscrews, and all sewer, water, and gas lines had to be raised while crews pumped in more than 16 million cubic yards of sand dredged from the ship channel. The same amount of sand today would fill one million dump trucks.

Construction on the seawall began in 1902. Engineers designed it to be 17 feet tall, although later research showed the wall ended up being only 15.6 feet above sea level. The original wall ran from 6th Street to 39th Street. Over 60 years, engineers expanded the seawall for 10 miles, from Boddeker Road on the east to Cove View Boulevard on the west.

"The public defenses against nature came at a high cost, but they succeeded for the most part," historian David G. McComb wrote in *Galveston: A History.*

"Its struggle for survival against nature through the application of technology represents the strongest tradition of Western civilization. Galveston's response to the great storm was its finest hour."

One hundred and eight years after "Ike" Kempner helped rebuild Galveston, Hurricane Ike would test the leadership ability of his granddaughter: Mayor Lyda Ann Thomas.

Thomas grew up studying her family's 1900 Storm memorabilia— books, magazines, and grainy black-and-white photos of the storm's aftermath that grandparents, aunts, and uncles kept scattered through their Victorian homes. Occasionally, I.H. Kempner would talk to the children about the 1900 Storm, but never in detail. Between 1940 and 1950, when Thomas was a child in Galveston, five hurricanes struck the island. Thomas and her family never evacuated.

They rode out the hurricanes in the big, old family houses on Broadway. They filled the bathtubs with water, stockpiled tins of nonperishable food, closed and tied shut the hurricane shutters, lit candles when the lights went out, and they "sat it out," Thomas said.

As she prepared for Hurricane Ike, Thomas pulled out her grandfather's book, *Recalled Recollections,* and thumbed through the pages to remind herself of his contribution to the island in the aftermath of the 1900 Storm. She had already used her predecessors' wisdom to set up a $20 million line of credit the city could access after a storm to help pay staffers and speed recovery efforts. After Ike, she would also attempt to create a recovery committee made up of the island's wealthy and influential. She ultimately had to abandon that plan when the rest of her constituents, more independent than their predecessors, demanded to participate. Although her hand-picked committee didn't get a chance to influence the island's future as her grandfather's had, Thomas supported the 300-member committee that eventually formed to shape the city's recovery. And she spoke constantly, during city council meetings, public appearances, and interviews, of islanders' need to find a unity of purpose and direction. To many, it seemed that Thomas desperately wanted to be remembered, like her grandfather, as one of Galveston's saviors. But her decisions didn't escape criticism. When she left office almost two years after Ike, it was still too soon to tell what her legacy would be. Would she be remembered for calling the evacuation late and keeping people away from home for almost two weeks? Or would future Galvestonians hail her for leading the city successfully through the most extensive recovery effort since the 1900 Storm?

As Hurricane Ike barreled down on Galveston, and Thomas considered how fate continued to place her family in positions of leadership during the island's greatest trials, the irony of the hurricane's name struck her.

"Of all things, of all names that begin with 'I', they picked this one, and, of course it turned out to be one of the worst, representing the name of a man whose whole life was spent making Galveston *better* and *stronger*," Thomas said.

"The deep roots and a long commitment we've all had here made it more important possibly to me than others that we get through this. We've done it before. We did it after the 1900 Storm. So, I knew we could do it again."

Galvestonians felt invincible after the 1900 Storm, a dangerous attitude toward nature's wrath that many would come to regret 108 years later. But that devastating storm also convinced islanders they could recover from just about anything. With the 1900 Storm in their past, Galvestonians would not let a lesser storm keep them from getting up again after being knocked to their knees.

CHAPTER

FIVE

A S THE LIGHT started to fade on Friday, islanders who had watched the water rise all day began to wonder where it would stop. They panicked when they realized how much harder it would be to keep track of its progress in the dark, especially once the power went out. What if the surge started rising faster as the storm got closer? They wouldn't be able to see how much danger they were in until it was too late. Police officers and firefighters had been carrying people to safety out of neighborhoods where water sped past cars whose roof-tops it had already topped. By about 8 PM, the gusts that had steadily buffeted the island all day finally started howling, swinging power lines back and forth like frenzied jump ropes and bending tree branches until they snapped. Rescue teams reluctantly retreated to The San Luis Resort.

But frantic residents continued to call 911, begging for help. All the distraught dispatchers could do was take down their names and addresses and encourage them to carry a saw or axe with them into their attics, if the water got that high. A few determined police officers and city sanitation workers continued to ferry people out of the half-submerged public housing projects, but even they eventually had to give in to the storm's strong winds and rising tide.

Ike's initial assault on the island didn't seem too bad to the people holed up in their houses. The winds were loud and they could hear small tree branches crash to the ground. The surge continued to rise until about two-thirds of the island was underwater. When the calm of the storm's eye arrived, they thought they had endured the worst. But after a 90-minute respite, Ike renewed his attack with a vengeance. Winds, almost strong enough to bump the storm into a Category 3 on the Saffir-Simpson scale, switched direction and whipped the floodwaters into a roiling, white-capped sledgehammer. The waves crashed against houses, shattering windows and bursting through closed doors. For another six hours, the storm beat relentlessly against Galveston's homes and businesses, strewing boats across the freeway and washing the contents of buildings into the flowing streets.

All who kept vigil on the island that night wondered whether Ike would spare anything, including their lives. Those who had evacuated and were watching video footage broadcast by the news crews sheltering in The San Luis Resort wondered if there would be anything left for them to come home to.

■ LIEUTENANT JOEL CALDWELL took one last bite of his dinner, wiped his mouth and got up from the table where three other officers were still eating from the neat buffet of chicken and pasta laid out by the hotel staff. The dining room at The San Luis Resort was filled with the men and women scheduled for the 6 PM shift. It would be the last one of the night. Caldwell, shift commander, hoped he could keep his officers out until at least 9 PM. But he could hear the wind already buffeting the hotel with enough force that he doubted his detail would last that long.

A few minutes before their shift started, the officers lined up in the parking lot to listen to instructions from their captain. Watch out for flying debris. Don't drive through any water. And above all, don't put yourself in any unnecessary danger. The city needs you tomorrow as well as tonight, Captain Henry Porretto told the officers.

As the other patrol cars drove out of the hotel parking lot, Caldwell headed toward the East End in his police pickup. He wanted to drive by his house, to make sure the water hadn't reached its front steps yet. He had to leave his five pit bulls, all rescued from the city's shelter, in the house when he came to work that morning. He just hoped they'd be safe through the night. Satisfied that part of town remained dry, Caldwell headed north toward Broadway.

Over the scanner, dispatchers called out rescue requests. With the rising water filling the streets and strong gusts rattling their windows, the people who had refused to evacuate had second thoughts about spending the night alone. Police officers responding to calls for help discovered they couldn't drive their patrol cars down flooded streets to reach those who needed help. Instead, they parked their cars in relatively dry areas and waded through water to get to flooded houses. They walked out with frightened people, clutching clothes and other belongings as they waded to safety.

One call came in near his location, so Caldwell headed over to the house to check on the situation. A middle-aged woman came out of the front door when she saw him pull up. She came toward him with her hands stretched out and her face contorted with fear. Could he please help her father, she asked. He had bone cancer. He can't stay here tonight, she said. Caldwell never questioned why the woman hadn't gotten her father off the island the day before or to the shelter earlier that afternoon. He just squeezed the button on the radio clipped to his shoulder and called for help. When the patrol car arrived, the elderly man came out of the house slowly. He leaned heavily on a pair of crutches as he walked to the street.

Once the patrol car pulled away from the house, headed for the Ball High School shelter, Caldwell drove north again. Broadway was not underwater yet, but the surge that had started creeping up from the port that morning was less than a block away. At 33rd Street, a man waved him down. Pointing back into the floodwaters at a half-submerged sedan, the man asked Caldwell if he could call a tow truck. My car's stuck, and the window's rolled down, the man said. If I don't move it, the water will start coming in, he said. I only need it towed a couple of blocks, just out of the water, he said.

"That car's gone, brother," Caldwell said firmly. "It's gone. There's nothing you can do now."

But the man kept pointing at the car, its hood already well under-water, and pleading with the officer to call a tow truck. He was dazed, wide-eyed, and confused. Caldwell tried to persuade him to get in the truck and go to the shelter, but the man refused. Caldwell asked him if he would be okay. He said he would and turned back to slosh through the water toward his car, and presumably his home. Caldwell watched him go and shook his head. There was nothing he could do. He couldn't force the man to leave.

A few blocks further west on Broadway, Caldwell stopped to check on one of the bright yellow trucks of the Galveston Island Beach Patrol. Chief Peter Davis and one of his lifeguards stood talking to a police officer. All three of them were looking at a half-submerged minivan two blocks away. They feared people might be trapped inside. Grabbing their emergency floats, Davis and another lifeguard waded into the water and swam to the van. Caldwell and the other officer waited nervously. Davis and his crew had been pulling people out of the water all day. So far everyone had made it out alive. But none of the officers thought that good luck would last. After circling the van a few times and checking a nearby car, Davis and the other lifeguard swam back to Broadway empty handed.

Conditions deteriorated faster than anyone expected. The sun dipped below the horizon, tinting the entire sky with a bizarre, hazy, orange-pink glow. By then, the wind blew with enough force to rock the truck as Caldwell continued to drive west. Stop signs quivered as the water crept higher in the streets. Limbs from the 100-year-old live oak trees that lined the Broadway median crashed into the street. Rain lashed Caldwell's windshield. In the dark, it was impossible to tell where the sky ended and where the water began. Streets that were dry an hour before now looked like rippling rivers. Rescue crews were no longer safe. Caldwell knew he would be putting his officers in danger if he continued to let them patrol. But over the scanner, dispatchers still called out rescue requests. It went against the officers' promise to serve and protect to leave those calls unanswered. But Caldwell also knew they couldn't save everyone.

Reluctantly, Caldwell clicked on his police radio microphone and ordered the officers back to the hotel. It was only 8 PM, an hour earlier than he expected to return. The rescue operation was officially shut down for the night. Caldwell drove south on 53rd Street, toward the hotel. The

16-story tower stood out against the night like a lighthouse drawing refugees to safety, every window filled with comforting yellow light. But as Caldwell looked up at it, the lights suddenly went out. The entire island was now in the dark.

Most of the police officers, lifeguards, and city employees who were helping with rescues followed orders and returned with Caldwell to the hotel, but the 911 calls kept coming. Gene Williamson, assistant superintendent at the city's recycling center, was driving two police officers into one of the city's public housing developments in a dump truck when Caldwell ordered everyone to retreat. They were responding to reports of three children trapped with their parents in one of the apartments. Several feet of water already filled the first-floor units at Oleander Homes, on the north side of Broadway between 53rd and 51st streets. The three men sat silently in the truck's cab for several seconds after hearing Caldwell's broadcast. They looked at each other, but no one had to say anything. They weren't turning back now.

The water was so deep, Williamson couldn't see the road below him as he drove the truck slowly through the entrance to the complex. The truck's weak headlights barely made a dent in the thick darkness around them. From the passenger seat, Officers George Simpson and Javier Rojas told Williamson where to turn. They used the tops of street signs still poking out of the water to navigate. When they got to the back of the complex, Simpson and Rojas climbed out of the truck and came back a few minutes later with the children. They put the youngest, a little girl about three years old, in the cab with Williamson. She was crying and screaming as she looked around, until her eyes focused on Williamson.

"Ike's bad, but you saved me," she said between sobs, repeating the phrase again and again.

With the little girl huddled right up next to him, Williamson drove back out onto Broadway. Two more police officers in a regular pickup truck were waiting to take the children to the shelter. Williamson didn't know how their truck was still running—the water around it was so high the small fishing boat in the bed was floating. They couldn't open their doors, so Williamson climbed out of the dump truck into the waist-deep water and handed the three children to the officers through the window. Before they drove off, the officers told the rescue crew they had three more people waiting to be picked up back at Oleander Homes. Two of them were the children's parents.

Williamson turned the dump truck around and headed back into the deeper water. As soon as they pulled up to the building, the three desperate residents came wading toward them. They carried plastic trash bags over their heads to keep them dry. Williamson thought they would head to the shelter once their passengers climbed into the bed of the truck, but before the officers could close the tailgate, they spotted two more people wading toward them between the buildings. Just as he was jumping out of the cab to help the officers push their passengers up the ladder into the truck bed, Williamson heard his boss's voice come across the radio.

"Three-five-seven, you're mandated to come in."

Williamson ignored the first call and the second. But after the third call, he picked up the radio and told his boss he couldn't just drive away from the people that kept coming toward the truck. As soon as they stop coming, I'll come in, he told him. By then, two other dump trucks had joined the rescue effort. Williamson and the officers with him loaded 20 people into their truck before they were ready to drive out of the complex.

Back at the hotel, Police Chief Charles Wiley overhead snippets of conversation between cops. It seemed that some of the officers remained on the streets even after Lieutenant Caldwell mandated that everyone come in. They were deliberately disobeying orders and no one was reporting it to Wiley.

Only two months on the job when the storm hit, Wiley had a strained relationship with his officers. He started his career policing Galveston's streets when the island was most famous for its illegal gambling joints and prostitution, but he spent most of his career rooting the corruption out of police departments in North Carolina and South Carolina.

When Wiley interviewed for the Galveston job, local police were embroiled in several high-profile scandals. In a span of a few months,

Galveston police officers were investigated for allowing cash and drugs to go missing from the evidence room and blasting a sprinkler head with a pellet gun, flooding the new police station. The police union bucked calls for a civilian review board.

At the end of Wiley's job interview, David Smith, the city's garage manager, said, "I got one question for you chief—Can you fix this place?" "I said, 'Yeah,' and everyone chuckled and said, 'I think he probably can,'" Wiley said.

Wiley's charge to fix the department met strong resistance from the entrenched officers of the department's old guard. Even as the hurricane bore down on Galveston, Wiley continued to bicker with the police union for spreading rumors that the department was refusing to pay officers according to the Fair Labor Standards Act. The act requires municipalities to pay first responders who are restricted from going home a wage equal to 24 hours of work, even if the officers have downtime. Wiley kept telling officers they'd get paid the full 24 hours, but they didn't listen. Frustrated, Wiley asked City Manager LeBlanc to assuage the officers' fears during one of the preshift meetings.

"It irritated me," Wiley said. "I can understand their concern, but I told them several times and they weren't hearing me."

Given his reputation at the department, it was no surprise the cops at the hotel who knew about the officers who stayed on the streets—rescuing people despite the city's order to stop—didn't officially report the rule-breakers to Wiley, even though they had a duty to do so. But, in a way, Wiley hoped they wouldn't tell him.

"Sometimes, you just don't want all the details," he said.

Filled with pride for the brave men who were risking their lives for others, Wiley didn't ask any questions. He didn't want to hear the answers. It was one of the few times in his career that he was okay with officers disobeying orders.

"It was a calculated risk that they took, no doubt about that, but, in hindsight, I'm glad they did it," he said. "Sometimes we do things we know we shouldn't do in hopes that it all turns out for the best. The risk is usually worth the reward."

■ THE DUMP TRUCKS kept coming.

LeeRoy Amador watched as the trucks rumbled to a stop outside Ball High School and new waves of refugees climbed out, clutching babies with no shoes and pets with no crates. Only two animals arrived in a crate: a ferret and a bird. The city promised to provide pet carriers, but Amador knew they weren't coming. Instead of waiting on the city, the Galveston school district police chief ordered district employees working the shelter to transform the freshman hallway into an animal shelter. They dumped over desks, creating makeshift corrals for dogs and cats that might otherwise attack each other.

The former state trooper also realized with growing alarm that he recognized some of the people trudging into the high school: They'd been arrested before. He spotted drug addicts, petty thieves, and some of the island's homeless people. Some of the people plunking down in plastic chairs in the cafeteria were drunk or high, Amador realized. He pointed out the criminals and the intoxicated to Officer Dwight Gaines and the other three policemen working the shelter. "Keep an eye on them," he cautioned.

The babies posed a different set of problems. Mothers, in their haste to leave home, forgot to grab diaper bags. Many babies lacked proper clothing, shoes, and diapers. One infant wore nothing but a diaper and a wet T-shirt. The policemen busted into the teen clinic and pillaged diapers and other baby goods the high school had squirreled away for teen moms.

Just when Amador thought the influx of evacuees was over, someone spotted through the high school's glass-walled entrance an elderly man stumbling up the steep staircase. He fought against the wind as he climbed toward the front doors of the school. Amador and the other officers rushed to the front and formed a human chain, stretching out toward the old man. They grabbed him and hauled him inside and the glass doors crashed shut behind him. The man joined the more than 400 other people now gathered in the cafeteria, waiting for the electricity to die.

■ As SOON AS water started seeping under the Brockways' front door, Merlinda grabbed a metal crate and started packing things she didn't want to get wet. But she didn't have time to save much. The water rose quickly in neighborhoods so close to Offatts Bayou. About an hour later, around 5:30 PM, it already was several feet deep in the house, enough to cover the electrical outlets. The sockets crackled and popped until the television cut off. Emory Brockway assumed the power was out, but just in case, he waded out to the breaker box with a stick and flipped off all the breakers.

"At that point in time we were on an island," he said. "It was just us. We had no information other than what we were experiencing."

By the time Brockway got back inside, the couple's 3-year-old lab mix Wilma was having a hard time keeping her head above water. Even though his wife couldn't swim, Brockway was more worried about the dog. Merlinda was tough, and although the water was swirling up over her knees, she calmly continued to move around the house, moving what she could to tabletops and upper shelves. When Wilma started to paddle, Emory lifted the bewildered animal onto the kitchen counter.

At 7 PM, the water was waist high. Emory kept expecting it to slow down, but it just kept rising. Helpless, the couple watched the grimy, brown tide inch up the wall. By 9 PM, the living room furniture was completely underwater. With the last of the daylight fading fast, Brockway took one more look out the front window to check on his Ford Explorer, parked in the street in front of the house. But it had disappeared under the river now flowing down the street. Throughout the house, the couple heard bookshelves crash down as the water lifted them off their legs just enough to make them unstable. In the kitchen, the washer and dryer started to bob up and down and bang into each other.

Determined not to let the hurricane get the best of him, Brockway had at first watched defiantly as the flood slowly swallowed everything he owned. But as the water got higher, his resolve started to slip. He started to shiver, and he couldn't focus his thoughts long enough to figure out what he should do next. He just kept hoping the water would stop. But it didn't. The refrigerator, which had stood its ground until now, suddenly rose off the floor and shot into the ceiling. It bobbed up and down, leaving gouges in the drywall.

Before Brockway realized how much danger they were in, the water was lapping around his shoulders. He moved Wilma to an ironing board, where he could balance her on top of the water. Merlinda waded into one of the back bedrooms and came back carrying an 8-foot aluminum stepladder. Dazed, Emory looked over at his wife. All he could see was her head sticking up out of the water. She opened the ladder under the entrance to the attic, climbed up and pushed back the square of plywood covering the small hole. It was just big enough for them to climb through.

Climbing back down into the water, Merlinda waded into the kitchen and took several small packages from the top kitchen cabinets—cookies, chips, cans of sardines, dog food, bottled water, a flashlight, a few candles, a box of matches and a cigarette lighter. She went up the ladder again and set them in attic. In one more trip she had placed a large sheet of plywood across the rafters so they would have a place to sit. When she came back down, she urged her husband to climb up to safety. But he would not leave the dog, and he was convinced the animal couldn't make it into the attic, especially with the gap between the top of the ladder and the entrance. She would have to balance on the unstable top step and jump.

"I asked him, 'Do you want to drown?'" Merlinda said later. "I told him to get up there."

Realizing he would probably drown if he didn't do something, Brockway agreed, but only if Merlinda would send the dog up after him. Once he was through the hole, Brockway got on his knees and reached back through for Wilma. Merlinda had the animal pinned against the ladder, trying to get her to climb. The scared dog refused to cooperate at first, kicking and scratching Merlinda as she pushed her from behind. When Brockway reached down and grabbed her front paws, Wilma suddenly seemed to get the idea that they were trying to save her. With a few more pushes from below and some tugging from above, Wilma scrambled up next to her master.

Merlinda climbed up one last time and sat down facing the hole. Brockway switched on the flashlight and pointed it down into the water so they could keep track of its progress. He felt certain all night it would stop, but now he wasn't sure at all. Outside, the wind was howling "loud as hell," Brockway said. Every once in a while, they heard a thud as something flew into the house. Neither of them said much. They just listened. When the wind suddenly stopped blowing, Brockway knew the eye had arrived.

"It was kind of eerie because you knew the rest was coming," he said. "It wasn't like it was all over."

Brockway continued to shine the light into the water below them until he realized the level hadn't changed in quite a while. He was still shivering, so Merlinda wrapped a blanket and a piece of plastic around him. When the wind started to pick back up again, he laid back on the plywood and closed his eyes. Merlinda sat watching for a little longer. But, finally overcome with exhaustion, she lay down next to her husband and called the dog over to join them. All three slept while the winds roared around them.

■ CHIEF AMADOR AND the policemen walked outside onto an elevated ramp at Ball High School to watch the storm's progress. Amador looked south toward the seawall and saw what looked like a flood of water coming from a broken dam, rushing down 43rd Street toward the high school. The telephone poles bordering the streets bent like toothpicks.

He ordered officers to move everyone to the second floor. In the pitch dark of the cafeteria, the officers helped people upstairs, navigating with the glow of their flashlights.

"We're going to die," someone said from the dark. Amador and the other police officers tried to calm the crowd, but they too were frightened, Amador said.

"We didn't know what to expect," he said.

Suddenly, the wind stopped roaring and Amador once again peered outside to see the eye of the storm. The water lapped at the wood shop at the back of the school, its lowest point. Time seemed to slow in the quiet dark, punctuated only by the fires consuming houses just four blocks away. Then, as abruptly as they had ended, the winds picked up again, this time blowing in the opposite direction.

"Look at this!" Amador said.

The water in the streets reversed course. It looked as if a mighty vacuum was sucking all the water back from where it came, Amador said. Cars swept past the school. Amador stared wide-eyed at the water as the wind roared even stronger than before.

■ WHILE EVERYONE ELSE held an all-night vigil, kept awake by the roar of Hurricane Ike's winds, Fletcher Harris slept soundly in his bed in his first-floor condo near the seawall. The eye came and passed, and still, Harris snoozed.

At 4 AM, he awoke with a start. Something was wrong. He was floating.

As he dozed, water filled the first-floor apartment, lifting Harris' mattress and box spring from the metal frame. The papers and files the ex-city councilman kept in stacks on his floor floated about the apartment. Harris scrambled off the mattress into the murky water that swirled around his thin, pale thighs. He remembered his grandfather's wisdom that saved the family during the 1900 Storm: Flee to higher ground.

A two-story townhome abutted Harris' brick condo. He could go there and ride out the storm, high and dry, on his neighbor's second floor.

This was Harris' Plan B—a scheme he'd relayed to his son in Dallas before the storm to assure him he could ride out Hurricane Ike, no problem. But Harris gave his son scant details, not mentioning to Dave that he had no real way of getting inside his neighbor's house.

The neighbors did not leave Harris a key, and the door was locked. Harris grabbed a plaque, upon which was mounted a 10-inch yellow crowbar. The crowbar had a brass nameplate with the words "Fletcher Harris' Hurricane Tool" engraved on it. The tool was a gag gift from county officials, a gentle laugh at Harris' absurd insistence that he would ride out every hurricane.

Harris wrenched the crowbar from the plaque and waded through the water to his neighbor's front door. Using his one good hand, he tried to wedge the tiny crowbar between the door lock and frame. He fumbled in the dark, trying to loosen the stubborn lock. The high winds knocked him down again and again. He cut his arm. He fell on his hip. The door refused to budge.

Exhausted, he gave up and waded into the street, looking for a Plan C. He waded through the water to the street corner and grasped a stop sign with his good hand. He tried to tie himself to the metal post, but it snapped apart in his hand. What happened then, no one knows. Not even Harris. Presumably, he spent the night in the waist-deep water as the storm raged on into the morning. When the sun rose and the winds died, someone found Harris wandering the island, confused, bloodied, muddy, and soaking wet. Whomever found him dropped him at Ball High School to join the hundreds of other islanders who now wanted to get the hell out of Galveston.

Sitting in a hard chair at the top of the front staircase at Ball High School that Saturday morning, Harris looked different somehow, older perhaps. His collared shirt was smeared with muck. Thick blood oozed from a cut on his arm. Unconsciously, he rubbed his bruised hip. His pale face sagged. The characteristic smirk had been wiped away.

"Can you imagine me being so smart-alecky that I thought 'It's just a hurricane?'" he said in a voice so quiet, listeners had to lean in close to hear him. "God has sent me this to teach me a lesson, and a bunch of other people, too. I'm never going to mess around again."

■ **AFTER HE HAD** thought through every possible configuration for tying his family to the tree in the backyard, Steven Rushing left them in the living room, where they watched nonstop television news coverage, and started making a pot of chili in the kitchen. He listened to Lupe and the kids making jokes and laughing while he cooked. They were trying to forget about the water that by this time had made significant progress in its march up the driveway.

Rushing, who had spent his whole life on the water, wasn't afraid of the flooding, but he was worried about the house catching fire if the water got high enough to cause a short in the electrical circuits. Before coming inside for the night, he had watched plumes of dark smoke curl up into the sky from several fires around the island. Only one seemed close to their neighborhood, but it still made him nervous.

Although Rushing knew the wind was picking up outside, he couldn't hear anything through the house's thick walls and strong windows. The family watched Ike's progress through the television, with wind-swept reporters clinging to traffic signs on the seawall and yelling dire predictions over the crashing waves. When the announcers urged anyone in Galveston who was watching to write their Social Security numbers on their arms, Stevie and Tyler started looking through the house for a permanent marker. They were still laughing and they seemed to be treating the whole thing like a big joke, but Rushing began to wonder if they were getting scared.

The longer they listened to the dramatic reports, the more quiet the kids got. When Tyler ran to the bathroom and threw up, his parents realized how worried he was. It only got worse when he couldn't get the toilet to flush. Rushing walked to the back of the house to check the bathroom in the master bedroom. It wasn't working either. On his way back to the living room, he noticed his footprints were visible in the carpet much longer than they should have been. A few minutes later, they started hearing a slight squishing when they walked around the house.

"That's when I knew it was coming in," Rushing said.

Lupe Rushing was too mad to worry about what kind of damage the water was doing to her house. She had wanted to evacuate. She always evacuated. But Steven was determined to stay, and the kids were on his side. She had been outnumbered. But she should have gone with her instinct, she said later. She at least should have taken Tyler and left. But it was way too late for that now.

Worried about what the next few hours might hold for his family, Rushing ordered everyone to put on tennis shoes so they would be less likely to cut their feet if they had to make some kind of escape through the rising water. While Lupe and the kids dug through the bottom of their already soggy closets, Rushing went into the garage and came back with life jackets. He made his wife, daughter and youngest son put them on. The water was now ankle-deep inside the house, but Rushing could tell by looking out the window that it was about a foot higher outside. He knew the pressure in the walls was getting high when the water started shooting like Jacuzzi jets out of the electrical sockets. The power had already gone out, but the generator kept the television going.

When the water rose to mid-calf, Lupe decided she needed to try to save her family memories. She wasn't worried about the furniture–the couple had plenty of insurance. But no claim payout could replace her pictures. Sloshing through the water, Lupe went from room to room, gathering up her photo albums and taking the framed pictures off the walls. With her husband's help, she pulled down the ladder to the attic and carried them up to the highest point in the house, hoping the water would stop rising before it got to the ceiling.

Exhausted from the strain of worrying about what was going to happen to her family, Lupe lay down on the couch with Tyler and Tiffany. She turned her back on the television and the rest of the room, hoping she might doze off. She never did. Before long, she could feel the water soaking through the back of her shirt as it seeped over the top of the couch cushions.

About 1 AM, right before the television announcers said the storm's eye was getting ready to move over the island, the generator sputtered out and the television connecting them to the world outside their sanctuary went black. Rushing decided they couldn't stay there any longer. But instead of heading for the trees in the backyard, Rushing headed for the garage, to see if he could get his fishing boat out. Its center console made it tall enough that he knew if he waited any longer, the water might get too high to float it out through the garage door. He started to go through the door leading from the home's main hallway into the garage, but the water pressure was so high he was afraid to open it far enough to squeeze through. Instead, he broke a window, climbed through with Jason, RJ, and Stevie, and opened the garage door from the outside. The family's washing machine and dryer floated past them and down the street, but the boat stayed tethered to its trailer. They unhooked it and let the trailer roll down the driveway underwater. They never saw where it went. The boat cleared the top of the garage door by less than an inch.

In the living room, Lupe, Tiffany, and Tyler were standing on the couches, trying to stay dry while they waited for the others to bring the boat around to the front door. The two dogs were perched on top of other furniture that was floating. Rushing intended to leave the dogs behind, hoping they would be smart enough to climb into the attic if the water continued to rise. From outside, he yelled to Lupe to pull down the ladder from the ceiling to give them something to climb. In the garage, five puppies huddled in a plastic kiddie pool. He hated to leave them and feared they wouldn't make it through the rest of the night, but there wasn't enough room in the boat for everyone.

Lupe gingerly stepped off the couch onto another piece of furniture that had floated close by. Her husband and the older boys didn't mind wading through the chest-deep water, but she was afraid of the snakes and rats she was sure were swimming through the house in search of safety. Although it was almost pitch black, she could see swarms of bugs floating on the water. But she managed to stay mostly dry by stepping from one piece of floating furniture to the next until she got halfway down the hall. She was too short to reach the attic door handle without help, but the water was so high she grabbed it easily from her floating step stool.

Once the attic was open, Rushing told Lupe, Tyler, and Tiffany to gather by the front door and get ready to come out. The wind had died completely, and he knew the eye had arrived. He guessed he could get to The San Luis Resort in about 15 minutes by boat, but he had no idea how long the eerie calm would last. He remembered Alicia's eye being short, and he was worried about getting caught in the open, in the boat, when the winds picked back up again.

"The only scary part I really had was getting caught in that boat with 120-mile-an-hour winds, and seven of us in that little boat," he said. "I thought for sure we'd be blown away to no telling where. That was the only fear I had."

When he opened the front door, Lupe and the kids waded out, followed quickly by the dogs. Before Rushing could stop them, they had paddled over to the boat and scrambled aboard. They were determined not to get left behind. As soon as everyone was settled, Rushing fired up the engine and headed for the hotel, about two miles away. Not knowing what was under the water or how deep it was, he steered the boat down the center of the roads he had traveled so often by car. With the familiar landscape around them drowned, he had to navigate by picking out the tops of buildings still sticking up out of the water.

In the parking lot of Parker Elementary, they saw an abandoned boat tied to a tree. Jason tried to get it to start, thinking they could use it in case anything happened to his cousin's boat, but the engine wouldn't turn over. Rushing stayed on Stewart Road, planning to turn south on 53rd Street. As they motored past submerged cars, they saw the hazard lights flashing. The windshield wipers on some of them still waved back and forth. Rushing brought the boat close to a few of them, just to make sure no one was trapped inside. But they never found anyone.

The rumble of the boat's motor and the beeping of car alarms in the distance were the only sounds they heard. They narrowly missed a trash bin that floated silently by. Near the intersection of Stewart Road and 53rd Street, they passed by a city dump truck submerged almost to the top of its cab. A few hundred yards later, the boat ran aground. Lupe was ready to make a run for the hotel, but Rushing thought they were still too far away. With the boys' help, he managed to get the boat turned around and headed back down Stewart Road to 57th Street, where he turned toward the seawall. He turned left on Avenue U, cutting through an abandoned neighborhood, where the boat bottomed out again.

This time, the family could see the hotel up ahead. While Rushing tied the boat to a palm tree in someone's front yard, Lupe grabbed Tyler with one hand and Tiffany with the other and started running.

"I'm just screaming for him, and I'm like 'Steven, please hurry!' And he's like, 'I got to tie the boat up. I got to tie the boat up.' And I'm like, 'Steven, we don't know how much time we have! Just please, come on. Come on!'"

Lupe feared at any minute the intermission would be over and Ike would kick up its second-half performance. The sky over the Gulf glowed a weird burgundy that none of them had ever seen. No matter what happened to her husband, Lupe knew she must get her son and stepdaughter to the hotel. Tiffany, three months pregnant and exhausted, had a hard time walking. Clinging to her hand, Lupe begged her to keep going.

"I literally wanted to grab her and put her on my back and run with her," Lupe said.

When they got to the seawall, Lupe turned back to see the other four turning onto 53rd Street and running toward them. She waved her flashlight in the air and quickly got a response from someone else further down the seawall. Lupe assumed it was a television camera crew, but it turned out to be other city employees who had come out of The San Luis Resort to marvel at the eye. Just as Rushing and the boys got to the wall, one of the dogs took off in the opposite direction. Lupe herded everyone else into the hotel, but Rushing insisted on going after his dog. After the kids were inside, Lupe came back out to look for her husband.

When she saw him coming up the stairs with the dog, she burst into tears, overcome by the stress of the last few hours and the relief that they were all finally safe.

"You almost thought you were going to die, it was so scary," she said.

■ AS THE EYE of the hurricane settled over Galveston, Police Chief Wiley ventured out to the front of the hotel. The air was crisp and clean and the skies were clear. Wiley could see stars and hear the squawk of seagulls. It was the third time Wiley had been inside a hurricane's eye. "Most people never get to see that their whole life," he said.

The front of the hotel teemed with reporters who seemed unconcerned or unaware of the pending fury of the hurricane's back half, Wiley said. Wiley, who'd weathered five other major hurricanes in his life, knew the worst was yet to come.

Then the Rushings arrived, drenched and telling stories about wading through the water to get to safety at the hotel. Wiley didn't know Steven, but the image of him—wet and wild-eyed—burned into his brain. He didn't go back to sleep.

"I remember thinking, 'We got to be ready. As soon as the wind started dying down, we got to be the first out there.'"

Unable to sleep and keyed up for what dawn would bring, Wiley set out for his townhome in the predawn hours, before anyone else set eyes on the destruction.

He parked his police Crown Victoria on the street, grabbed a flashlight from his car and climbed the low stairs to his townhome, three doors down from Fletcher Harris' front door. Wiley unlocked his door and pushed. The door didn't budge.

"I knew right then and there, either the wall was gone or we had a massive flood."

He shined the flashlight at the glass storm door. His eyes met a murky water line four feet up the door. Wiley shoved harder, forcing the door open just wide enough so that he could slip inside. The house was slick with mud and smelled funky. A bookcase that had toppled in the high water blocked the front door.

Wiley carefully picked his way through the almost unrecognizable house, shining the flashlight over slimy furniture and the slippery, muddy floor. Wiley and his wife had recently remodeled the place and he knew the damage would break her heart.

He traced the flashlight to the living room coffee table where he'd left his new humidor. The box was missing. Had someone already looted the place? Wiley wondered. But no, as he looked around he found the cigar box lying on the kitchen floor where it had floated from the living room.

He bent over and flipped open the humidor's lid. Inside, two boxes of very new and very expensive cigars were still dry and neatly organized, just as he'd left them.

"It was the happiest I could remember being for weeks and weeks after the storm," he said.

That Saturday morning, as Galvestonians picked through the rubble of the places they once called home, they would learn to find hope in small joys: dry cigars, an unscratched heirloom vase, an intact piece of wedding china, or a mildewy plastic tub full of old family photographs, miraculously clean and dry.

CHAPTER

SIX

KARON TURNER SPENT the evening on the deck of a beach house, watching snakes try to escape the rising water by slithering up the side of the house as bunnies floated by on clumps of grass. Then, in the stillness of the hurricane's eye, she stood and watched horrified as an entire house, its windows and doors still boarded up, floated by upright. The water lapped just below the 21-foot deck of the Crystal Beach house where Karon, her husband Willis, and their friends sought shelter from the storm. Sometime during the night, the rising surge swept away the home's elevator. When Karon opened the door to the elevator shaft, she saw dark water rushing by, as if the Mississippi River ran just below the floor.

Trapped on a vulnerable peninsula bearing the brunt of Hurricane Ike, Karon made the calculations in her head. The storm surge was then 20 feet deep, and a Houston radio announcer predicted another 20 feet of surge would hit Bolivar Peninsula after the eye—that's a 40-foot storm surge in a house barely taller than 40 feet. Karon played out the worst scenarios in her head: They could escape into the attic, but did they have a hammer to claw their way out when the storm passed? If the walls broke loose, could they float to safety atop the pieces of foam insulation? Willis tried to calm her with cool reason. "Karon, that's 40 feet; we're not going to have a 40-foot storm surge," he told her in his low, thick Southern drawl. She worried anyway.

Before cell phone service died, Karon's daughter called incessantly, begging her mother to flee the peninsula that was slowly drowning in storm surge.

"Mother, take the hint—there's not even any media on Bolivar," Samantha said the first time she called. "That should tell you something."

Karon refused. Samantha went back to watching the news, then called again.

"Mother, you need to get airlifted out," she said.

"No, Samantha. I'm not going anywhere. I'm okay."

"Well, put your Social Security number on your arm because you're not going to make it."

Every time Samantha called, she sent her mother into a panic, leaving Willis to calm her with soothing words and his characteristic pragmatism. Then Samantha would go back to watching the news, get frightened again, phone Karon, and start the whole cycle over. The truth was, Karon *was* scared, but she refused to leave because she knew Willis, stubborn as a mule, wouldn't leave. "I knew I would be worse off worrying about him—I would be in [Samantha's] position and I didn't want to be there, worrying about him and what was going on on the peninsula."

The situation worsened as day turned to night and the dark water kept rising and rising, higher than anyone ever expected. As the eye passed over, Karon ventured onto the deck to scope out the scene. In the quiet thick of the eye, Karon watched two or three more boarded-up beach houses sweep by like big boxy boats adrift on the ocean. Fear gripped her, and, unable to watch the ghastly spectacle, Karon turned and went inside, climbed upstairs and lay down on a sofa in the theater room, trying to ignore the panic building inside her. She rose from the sofa and cracked open the door to the attic—just in case. The entire house shuddered and vibrated like a guitar string. Images of tornadoes flashed across her mind.

Curled up on the sofa alone, Karon squeezed her eyes shut and prayed, whispering into the darkness. "Lord, keep us safe."

■ BOLIVAR PENINSULA HAD nothing to protect it from Hurricane Ike's ferocious onslaught. The narrow spit of land—no more than half a mile wide—juts out from the upper Texas coast east of Galveston Island to help form the mouth of Galveston Bay. The low-lying peninsula, just east of Ike's eyewall, bore the brunt of the storm's "dirty side," the side of a hurricane barreling ashore with southerly winds direct from the sea, unbroken by land. The peninsula took the full force of Ike's deadly storm surge. Meteorologists estimate it climbed as high as 20 feet, although no one knows for sure. The saltwater either swept away the tide gauge sensors or else rendered them useless. The peninsula had no seawall or levees to protect it. The surge engulfed it, wreaking destruction so unbelievable that reporters and residents said it looked as if a bomb had gone off.

Too many of the peninsula's residents stayed to brave the storm in their houses. At least 10 people died. Some bodies were found weeks later. Three people remained missing 18 months after the hurricane, according to the Laura Recovery Center, an organization that tracked missing persons reports after Ike.

Those who survived told nightmarish stories of floating for hours in the roiling surf, praying they wouldn't get crushed by pieces of broken houses hurtling toward the bay. When the winds finally died and the surge retreated, Bolivar Peninsula looked like a desert, devoid of trees, grass, shrubs, flowers. Nothing green survived. Rows of houses vanished. The small fishing community of Gilchrist disappeared. A mountain of splintered wood, crushed cars, and dead animals ended up on Goat Island, an isolated marshland cut off from the peninsula by the Gulf Intracoastal Waterway. Search teams later pulled the bodies of peninsula residents from that massive debris pile.

Hurricane Ike was destructive in Galveston. It was apocalyptic on Bolivar Peninsula.

■ THE STUDENTS IN Renee Brawner's eighth-grade science class spent most of their lesson time on the Monday and Tuesday before the storm poring over Hurricane Ike's path and looking at landfall predictions. Brawner and Principal Bill Heuman, a weather bug who always joined the class to talk about hurricanes, viewed the storm as a teaching tool, not a threat. Brawner had been teaching at Crenshaw, the small school with classrooms for all the peninsula's elementary and middle school students, for 11 years. Her passion for marshes, beaches, and wildlife made her a favorite with students.

Many of the peninsula's pastel beach houses belonged to part-time residents who visited several times a year and leased to other vacationers the rest of the time. In older neighborhoods, the houses were not much more than fishing camps, one- and two-room structures elevated only six or seven feet off the ground. But during the last ten years, the peninsula's popularity with wealthy city dwellers had grown, and new subdivisions with big, modern houses grew up on either side of State Highway 87, the road that bisects the peninsula and ends at the ferry landing.

Despite its reputation as a vacation spot, the peninsula had a vibrant, albeit small, community of permanent residents. Brawner and her husband, Brian, a nurse turned charter boat captain, moved to the peninsula from Longview, after falling in love with its laid-back atmosphere. They started in a one-room house in Gilchrist but moved into a newer, three-bedroom house in Crystal Beach a year later. Brawner sat on the deck every afternoon and watched the waves roll ashore as she drank her coffee and unwound from the school day. It was the closest to an earthly paradise she thought she could get.

By Tuesday afternoon, administrators with the Galveston Independent School District, which operated Crenshaw, became worried enough about Ike to start planning for evacuation. They sent e-mails to the Crenshaw staff with instructions to move computers and other equipment to the tops of desks or bookshelves. The school would close Thursday at noon. Brawner read the e-mails without concern. It seemed like they went through similar drills about twice a year, just part of life on the vulnerable peninsula.

When she got a phone call Wednesday evening saying school would not open on Thursday after all, Brawner wasn't surprised or alarmed. She and Brian spent the rest of the night packing and getting ready to evacuate. They planned to sleep in the next morning and have a leisurely breakfast before heading for a friend's house in Wildwood, a small town northwest of Beaumont. When Brian's cell phone rang at 4 AM, Brawner knew it couldn't be good news. After listening for several minutes to the voice on the other end of the line and making a few surprised grunts, Brian started prodding his wife to get out of bed.

"I knew then that something was wrong," she said later. "He never woke me up like that."

One of Brian's fishing buddies had just driven across Rollover Pass, the small manmade channel that connected the Intracoastal Waterway to the Gulf about halfway down the peninsula. The rising tide already submerged the beach side of the pass. Although surprised, Brawner wasn't worried. The low-lying peninsula flooded easily. But older residents always warned new arrivals about getting trapped, and the Brawners knew they needed to move quickly before the Rollover Pass bridge went underwater. Highway 87 was the only way to drive off the peninsula without going across the ferry to Galveston. And once the surf got rough, the Texas Department of Transportation stopped running the ferry, leaving the two-lane road as the only evacuation route.

The Brawners left one of Brian's boats in a storage facility that was supposed to be hurricane proof. They left the other boat and their second truck at a friend's house in High Island, the highest point on the peninsula, on its far eastern end. As they drove farther north, County Judge Jim Yarbrough ordered a mandatory evacuation for peninsula residents. Less than 24 hours later, rising water from the Gulf and the bay met over Highway 87. The ferries made their last run at about 8 PM. Thursday, two hours before they were scheduled to shut down. Anyone who hadn't left by then was stuck.

■ **OUT OF SHEER** luck and with some persuasion, Karon and Willis Turner had caught that final ferry from Galveston to Bolivar Peninsula.

Hurricane Ike caught the Turners off guard. For the early part of the week, they expected Ike to strike South Texas, so they failed to move their most-prized possession, a one-of-a-kind, 45-foot stock cruiser into which they'd sunk their retirement fund, from its slip at the Galveston Yacht Club and Marina. They bought the six-figure boat, which they named *Faith,* in 2005 and sailed it 5,000 miles around the coast to the Florida

Keys with a truck dog named Dirt. The 1960 Matthews cruiser boat with the wooden hull was so rare, they'd never seen another one like it. The boat was to be their retirement home.

The Turners, who run the custom home building company KWT Construction, spent the week before Hurricane Ike came ashore boarding up houses for other people and hauling potted plants inside Karon's nursery and consignment shop, The Barn. When it became clear Wednesday that Ike would strike nearby, the Turners moved their heavy construction equipment to High Island, prepared their hurricane rations, made hasty, last-minute hurricane preparations to their Crystal Beach house, and caught the ferry to Galveston to check on the boat.

Marina workers had already stuffed into dry dock all of the boats they intended to put away. The Turners' boat wasn't in that batch, so they decided at the last minute to take it back to Bolivar Peninsula. They would moor it to the elevated dock of a canalside house they had recently built, they decided. They motored the boat back to the peninsula across the choppy waters of the Intracoastal Waterway, early signs of what was on the way, and hitched a ride back to the ferry and across to Galveston to get their trucks. Willis told the ferry employee: "You need to wait on us. This is the last run and we need to get our trucks back to Bolivar."

Miraculously, he held the boat for them.

They spent Thursday night aboard *Faith*, where they planned to ride out the storm. But by midmorning Friday, September 12–hours before the eye would arrive–the rising storm surge swallowed the dock, the only means of escaping the boat on foot. Rather than risk swimming in the storm surge tainted with household chemicals and raw sewage from cracked septic tanks, Karon decided to bail from the yacht, leaving her husband behind to fend for himself. She would ride out the rest of the storm from the relative safety of the house while he would brave the storm on the boat to try to save it when the hurricane arrived in full force.

They agreed on an emergency signal: Should Karon find herself in trouble inside the house, she would flash her flashlight at the boat. If Willis got in trouble on the boat, he would flash his flashlight at the house.

The Turners had strapped the boat to the elevated dock jutting out from the house, which sat on stilts 21 feet above the ground, allowing the large boat plenty of room to bob up and down with the rising storm surge. The two-story house perched on the edge of a manmade canal on the bay side of Bolivar Peninsula; the Turners figured it was the safest place for their boat because it would be protected from the rising tides and choppy surf.

They were wrong.

■ **Around 6:30 am** Friday, September 12, the U.S. Coast Guard called back to duty the personnel and equipment that had been evacuated to Corpus Christi for safekeeping during the storm.

The situation on Bolivar Peninsula had become worse than anyone expected. The storm surge's early arrival trapped scores of people who tried to evacuate the peninsula too late. Calls for help poured in by the minute.

U.S. Coast Guard Lieutenant John Moran and Lieutenant Junior Grade Dakata Brodie launched the signature orange twin-engine HH-65C Coast Guard helicopter and headed northeast toward Bolivar Peninsula. Neither had worked a hurricane before. They had no idea what to expect. But they had little time to wonder. Almost immediately, Coast Guard dispatchers radioed over the coordinates for three locations where people reportedly were in the water. Moran and Brodie had no information on how many people needed help, what kind of situations they were in or whether they had life jackets. They arranged the coordinates from nearest to farthest, and started their search on the southwest tip of the peninsula near the ferry landing and Port Bolivar.

Meanwhile, another Coast Guard crew searching the peninsula told Brodie and Moran over the radio about five people in a truck near Gilchrist that was being washed out to sea. That crew had been launched out of Ellington Field in Houston at 6 am and was headed back to Houston to refuel when they spotted the black truck floating in the surf. They were too low on fuel to stop and help—could Brodie and Moran check it out?

Brodie and Moran had just finished searching the first of the three locations given to them by the dispatcher. There were at least two other reports they still needed to check out. Talking to each other through microphones embedded in their pilots' helmets, they mulled over the matter. Should they abandon the other two to rescue the people in the truck? That seemed like a bad idea. There was no information about the two victims in the water. They had no clue what kind of trouble those people faced. At least the victims in the truck had something to float in to keep their heads above the roiling surf. They agreed to finish searching the first two coordinates before attempting the truck rescue. It was a tough decision, Moran said, one of many that Coast Guard crew would be forced to make that day.

They hovered low and scanned each location carefully but couldn't see anyone bobbing in the storm surge that was now creeping over the peninsula, swallowing everything. They spun the helicopter around and headed east toward Gilchrist to check on the truck.

By that point, Bolivar Peninsula was no longer a peninsula, but three separate islands poking above the white-capped waves. Brodie and Moran found the black pickup near Rollover Pass, floating on the choppy surf that hid all traces of the road that it had been driving on. The water was up to the bed of the truck. Waves pounded the pickup, breaking over its hood and cab, and filling its bed, where the people huddled into a tight pack. To protect themselves from the shower of sea spray, the group had slid as close to the cab as they could.

Moran and Brodie pulled the helicopter into a hover over the terrified people in the pickup. The rescue swimmer, Shane Moore, prepared to drop down to begin scooping people up.

"You're backing off," Flight Mechanic Matt Russell told the pilots, but they weren't. The helicopter wasn't moving—the truck was. Trapped in a swirling current, the truck was slowly being dragged out to sea.

They had to work fast. Hovering over the pickup, Moran looked out of the nose of the helicopter, peered into the pickup's bed, counted carefully and realized that there were actually *seven* people in the cab: four adults and three children. A Coast Guard's HH-65C Dolphin rescue helicopter isn't equipped to carry so many people. The cramped cabin is already packed with equipment and four people: the two pilots, a flight mechanic and a rescue swimmer. One other person would fit comfortably inside, but *seven?*

The number of people wasn't the only challenge. Winds at that point were 30 to 40 knots—about 35 to 46 miles per hour—and they had to use the truck's bumper as the target landing spot for the rescue swimmer. Coast Guard personnel usually aim for targets three feet or four feet wide, but the crew had no choice this time. The thin sliver of shiny bumper would have to do.

Moore dropped down from the helicopter in his bright red swimming gear and yellow helmet with snorkel and grabbed the first of seven people: a terrified 6-year-old boy. The flight mechanic hauled up Moore clutching the boy to his chest like a baby as they spun in wide circles on the line.

"Swimmer and survivor are coming in," Russell said into his microphone.

Moran turned to look back at the wide-eyed shivering boy and suddenly he realized how frightened the boy must be huddled inside a deafening helicopter with faceless strangers. Moran flipped up the visor on his helmet and shot the boy a thumbs-up. The boy gave him a small, quick thumbs-up in return.

Moore lifted the boy's older sister from the truck and dropped her beside the boy.

"Once she got in, he did better," Brodie said. "She was taking care of him pretty well."

The crew hoisted up the three children from the pickup before the pilots realized they had seven minutes to "bingo," military slang for a designated amount of fuel needed to return to base. The Federal Aviation Agency mandates that all Coast Guard aircraft land with a specific amount of fuel. When an aircraft reaches "bingo," that means the pilots have just enough fuel to fly back, land on the tarmac, and still have enough fuel to satisfy FAA regulations.

Moran heard over the radio another Coast Guard crew headed toward Bolivar Peninsula, and breathed a silent sigh of relief. If they couldn't get to the remaining victims in the truck before they ran out of fuel, at least there was another crew in the area that could finish the rescue, he told himself.

Then, Moran heard the Houston-Galveston sector call out another location of 12 people in the water. His heart dropped.

"I'm like 'holy crap. [The other crew] is going to go do the 12 people in the water and there's no way he'll have space or fuel to come help us out,' " Moran said in an interview.

They were stuck. The only other Coast Guard aircraft was refueling in Houston. If they left, it would take an hour to fly to Houston, refuel and come back. The remaining people in the truck just couldn't survive another hour tossed around in the storm surge.

As calmly as possible, Moran urged the flight mechanic and rescue swimmer to speed up the rescues while not jeopardizing the safety of the rescuer or the victims. What had been a difficult rescue now became even more challenging under the pressure of rapidly dropping fuel levels.

Russell lowered Moore down to the truck to pick up the fourth person, an elderly man. Moore strapped the man to his body. As they stood on the back fender, Moore signaled to Russell to pick him up. Out of nowhere, a huge wave smashed into the truck. Brodie and Moran couldn't see what was happening below them, but out of the corner of his eye, Brodie saw the flight mechanic's hand holding the line attached to the swimmer jerk forward violently. The wave knocked Moore and the old man from the truck and into the water. As he'd practiced in training, Moore rolled underneath the man to protect him from any dangerous things hidden under the water. They rolled back above the surface and, without missing a beat, Moore signaled to Russell to hoist him up.

"I don't even think [Moore] thought about it," Brodie said. "He just did what he had to do and came up and said, 'I'm okay.' "

The daring rescues were Moore's first ever as a rescue swimmer.

"I completely forgot about that," Brodie said. "Everything went so normal, like clockwork, I wasn't thinking about Shane. He had to keep telling me, 'It's my first one!' Seeing how excited he was, seeing his first rescue. It was great. He was enjoying doing his job."

As Russell hoisted up Moore and the fifth person from the truck, Moran, the pilot, called out over the radio: "We're at bingo!" Panic tinged his voice.

"Roger," flight mechanic Russell said. Two more people to go.

In a flash, Russell dropped Moore to the pickup where the waves pounded the truck even harder. Moore wrapped his legs around the sixth person and Russell hauled them up. The pilots told Russell to explain the desperate fuel situation to Moore. Moran saw Russell yell into Moore's ear, and Moore gave him the thumbs up, then Russell dropped Moore down one last time to scoop up the seventh person in the fastest rescue operation Moran had ever seen. As soon as Moore grabbed the victim, and they cleared the truck, the pilots turned the helicopter toward Houston to refuel. Brodie and Moran landed the plane at Ellington Field and taxied in to refuel. They had no time to shut down the aircraft, so they had to do a "hot refueling," or filling the tanks with fuel while the engines are still running. There were just 76 pounds of fuel left in a tank that holds up to 1,930 pounds. Moran sprinted to the bathroom and turned over the aircraft to his commander.

"He looks over at me and is like 'Really?' and I say, 'Okay, sir. You have the controls!' " Moran recalled. "That was pretty crazy."

After a quick break at Ellington, the crew headed back to Bolivar Peninsula, munching on biscuit sandwiches, their first meal of the day. The radio already crackled with requests for help as they ascended.

The other Coast Guard crew—the one diverted to check on a report of 12 people in the water—had left its rescue swimmer on the ground with seven people near the Crystal Beach water tower. Could Moran and Brodie swing by and pick them up?

Moran, Brodie, Moore, and Russell arrived at the water tower, and tried to put the helicopter into a hover, but, because they had just refueled, the aircraft was too heavy to hover. They cut off, flew offshore, dumped some fuel, and returned to start hoisting people up. One of the seven people had a hip injury and was unable to walk. The spot near the water tower was a dangerous area to hover. There were telephone and power lines everywhere, and buildings that blocked movement. The crew hoisted the lady with the hip injury, and nearly backed into a tangle of power lines and trees before Moran and Brodie decided it was no longer safe to hover there. They circled the area and landed the helicopter in a yard 200 yards away. The remaining six people climbed aboard the helicopter, weighing down the aircraft already heavy with fuel. They cleared the trees by only a few feet as they headed toward Gulf Greyhound Park to drop off the victims.

As soon as those seven got off, another call came in: People sheltering at Fort Travis Seashore Park decided they wanted to evacuate after all. The crew decided against refueling–they didn't want the aircraft to be too heavy, again–and set a course for the same fort that sheltered peninsula residents during Hurricane Carla in 1961.

The crew landed at the park and the rescuers tried to muster people who wanted to leave. Only six agreed to leave; Moran watched the others shake their heads defiantly at the rescuers.

"I was surprised by how many people said, 'I'm staying,'" he later said.

The crew dropped off the six at Gulf Greyhound Park and returned to the fort to check, one last time, whether anyone wanted to leave. Nobody wanted to go. Moran, Brodie, Moore, and Russell flew up and down the peninsula, canvassing the area for anyone in distress, but they found no one. Everyone had left or had holed up in their houses to wait out the storm. It was between 2 and 3 PM, and Ellington Field was shutting the fuel pumps there, so they decided to head back to Corpus Christi to wait out the storm and prepare for the next day. The eye of the hurricane was still hours away, and the worst was yet to come. But there would be no more rescuers available until after the storm. Those who refused to leave the peninsula now had no other choice. They would find out just how terrifying a hurricane could be.

■ NIGHT FELL OVER the peninsula and, to Karon's horror, the water just kept rising. The wind smacked the stern of the Turners' boat, and it rocked violently side to side, the loose items inside the cabin sliding and smacking against the walls. Willis Turner and his two companions on the boat could barely keep their footing as it tossed and turned in the violent waves. By midnight, the water had risen astonishingly high–20 feet by Karon's estimates–and was lapping just beneath the main living quarters of the house. The storm surge at that point had lifted the boat so high the bow rails scraped the roof of the dock. Every time the boat smacked the roof, shingles flew off and the bow rails peeled back. Water splashed up over the stern. Hurricane Ike was tearing their boat, their baby, to shreds.

Around midnight, Karon saw, through the driving rain, the flicker of Willis' flashlight. Saving the boat was no longer an option; Willis could only save himself and his friends. He grabbed a rope connecting the boat to the house and the three men pulled themselves inside against the wind and rain that slapped their bodies. Safely on the deck, Willis didn't turn back to see the boat's fate. He climbed into the house and his eyes filled with tears as he walked inside.

"I don't want to see this," he told his wife.

Karon stood in the house with Mike Dunn, one of the men who worked for KWT Construction, and watched the boat through the window. It was hard to see it in the heavy rain and swirling winds, but they kept their eyes trained on a single light mounted to the hull. No more than 30 minutes after Willis, Dunn, and John Utley left the boat, the lines snapped all at once like someone had sliced them all in one swipe. The boat broke loose, bobbed and turned west, bouncing toward the Intracoastal Waterway.

"Well," Karon said to Dunn, "I think it's going to Kemah."

They watched the hull light until it disappeared in the darkness.

Heartbroken, Karon retreated to the house where she occupied her mind by methodically moving all the belongings in the house from the first floor to the second floor, while the others sat around listening to the radio and eating roast turkey sandwiches. When the eye passed over, and Karon stood on the deck watching the houses float by, one by one, all she could think was: "Glad we watched the boat [float away] so we didn't have to watch it be smushed to smithereens." Dunn tried to snap photographs of the floating houses, but they were moving too fast to catch on film. Never once did Karon think there were people around her fighting for their survival.

"I guess we thought we were the only crazy people on the peninsula," she said.

They weren't.

Gail Ettenger, a 58-year-old chemist at ExxonMobil, decided to ride out Hurricane Ike in her bayside house in Gilchrist because her 11-year-old Great Dane, Reba, was too crippled by arthritis to jump into Ettenger's Jeep. JoAnne Burks, Ettenger's neighbor and close friend, told the Associated Press that Ettenger called her hours before Hurricane Ike made landfall to tell her she'd made the wrong choice. Ettenger, her voice shaking with fear, said the water was pushing under her feet and that propane tanks and other household items were floating past the house.

Burks said she suggested Ettenger break into her neighbor's house, a newly built structure that was higher and sturdier than Ettenger's place. Ettenger refused, Burks told the AP, because she could not break into a neighbor's house. That was the last time they spoke. Ten days later, searchers would find Ettenger's body in a debris field in a Chambers County marsh, 10 miles from her house. Ettenger's house was gone but the neighbor's sturdy house still stood. The Associated Press later reported that "amid the muck and remnants of homes, Burks found a pink leather collar. The name Reba was spelled out in rhinestones."

Marian Violet Arrambide, a 78-year-old retired nurse suffering from dementia, lived with her daughter, Magdalena Strickland, 49, and nephew Shane Williams, 33, in a Port Bolivar beach house. Around 6:30 AM Friday, September 12, Strickland called her brother to tell him that they were leaving the peninsula.

"My sister said, 'I'm walking out the door in a hurry. Everything's taken care of. I'll see you in a few hours.' That was it," Raul Arrambide told the Associated Press. Searchers found Williams' body in a debris field on Goat Island October 6, three weeks after the storm. They found Strickland's body in the same area on November 20 and Arrambide's body on December 22.

Karon lay alone on the upstairs sofa, not knowing the horrifying fates of others holed up in houses just walking distance away from their shelter. Terrified for her own life, Karon closed her eyes and prayed for God's mercy. When she opened her eyes again, she saw the face of a little old lady with dark brown hair peering down at her. Karon didn't recognize the woman's face—it wasn't a woman she knew or had ever seen before. She doesn't know if what she saw was a dream or a vision. But as the older woman knelt toward Karon, she spoke to her in a soothing voice that immersed her in feelings of peace.

"She said, 'Everything's going to be okay. Don't worry. Just get some rest,' " Karon later recalled. "It calmed me down and I went to sleep. And I was okay. I was okay."

CHAPTER

SEVEN

SHELL-SHOCKED GALVESTON RESIDENTS emerged from their houses as soon as the winds slowed on Saturday morning. None had ever seen their island so tattered. The water that covered much of the city for more than 24 hours had started to retreat to the bay, but it left a trail of souvenirs stolen from houses, businesses, churches, and schools during its overnight rampage: photo albums, stuffed animals, pots and pans, shoes, military medals, books, and china handed down in families for generations. Over everything, the vanishing flood left a thick coat of slimy mud that disgorged a putrid stench, the tangy combination of mildew and seawater, as soon as the sun came out Saturday afternoon.

People who knew only what happened to themselves anxiously sought news of the rest of the city. On the seawall, small groups of survivors gathered to look at the mountain of splintered wood that stretched from 25th Street to Ferry Road. Unable to hold out through the long night against Ike's pounding waves, Murdoch's Bathhouse, Hooters, and the fabled Balinese Room splintered into a million useless timbers spread across Seawall Boulevard. Onlookers took pictures and stared in disbelief at the suddenly open view of the Gulf.

People whose cars survived drove around gawking at the destruction. Some offered rides to people who wandered up to the usually busy street in hopes of catching someone's attention. Soaked and weary, most of them just wanted to find a way off the island. A gas station at 13th Street and

Broadway had one of the few working pay phones in the city. With cell phone service out, it was the only connection to friends and family on the mainland. Some people standing in line had to beg other survivors for change.

Overwhelmed by how much they had lost, several thousand people grabbed what they could carry and headed for Ball High School, where more state-chartered buses eventually arrived to take them off the island. Waiting for a ride they scorned two days before, storm-weary residents swore they would never stay for another hurricane. Some said they didn't know when they would be able to return.

The amount of destruction shocked even city officials. They expected downed tree limbs and power lines. Friday's early floods taught them to expect widespread damage to houses too. But they weren't prepared for a complete loss of all utilities. Ike's surge topped sewage treatment plants and water pumping stations. Generators powered by natural gas sputtered to a halt when the gas company unexpectedly shut off all service to the island to prevent explosions at ruptured pipes. Galveston had no running water and no source of power. Raw sewage ran into Galveston Bay.

Looking at the destruction was like looking at one of the grainy black-and-white photographs from the 1900 Storm aftermath, pictures of men in suits and hats standing amid piles of debris looking somber and weary. It was as if Hurricane Ike, overnight, had blown Galveston back in time 108 years. Only the broken streetlights and plastic fast-food signs provided reminders that this was today's reality.

That Saturday morning marked a defining moment for Galveston. Islanders had two choices: They could clean up and rebuild like their predecessors did in 1900, or they could abandon a wounded barrier island just as vulnerable to another beating during the next hurricane season. As they surveyed what was left of their city, officials, business owners, and residents wondered: Is it worth it?

■ OVERNIGHT, SCORES OF frightened people trapped in flooded houses called 911, begging for help. They told dispatchers that they would soon have to retreat into their attics because the water was so high in their houses. Unable to send anyone to their rescue, dispatchers helplessly took down names and addresses. They would be the first people rescue crews attempted to find.

As the sky brightened that Saturday morning, the wind continued to howl. Firefighters and police officers pulled on uniforms and anxiously awaited permission to leave the hotel.

Mayor Lyda Ann Thomas called a press conference in the dark hotel lobby. Sopping wet towels covered the marble floor, still slick with water that had leaked inside overnight. Wind lashed the plywood-covered windows. Television crews trained their cameras and bright lights on Thomas' tired face.

The mayor announced that she was allowing city crews out of the hotel to assess the damage and begin the search for the injured and dead. She begged reporters to stay behind while rescue crews picked their way slowly across the damaged landscape. City officials didn't know what the island looked like or how many people might have died overnight. They didn't want reporters to find out first and broadcast the grisly images across the nation.

Few reporters heeded her pleas, instead heading straight to their satellite trucks and SUVs loaded with full cans of gas.

■ PETER DAVIS SPENT a sleepless night in the hot and stuffy ballroom at The San Luis Resort, sandwiched between paramedics too anxious to sleep. Exhausted, he passed out for 45 minutes during the calm of the eye, but promptly woke up when the back half of the storm struck, violently shaking the building. He gave up on sleeping when firefighters rushed into the ballroom, checking the walls for stress fractures.

As the winds died, Davis gathered with the Galveston Police Department's dive team to discuss strategies for rescuing the people trapped in their homes who may have survived the overnight storm surge. The water rescue group prepared themselves for the likely scenario: they would find bodies—everywhere.

Around 8:30 AM, as soon as the winds dropped below 70 miles per hour, the rescuers ventured outside. Davis and members of the police department's dive team drove to Parker Elementary School to retrieve the Beach Patrol's rigid hull inflatable boat, which rescuers left tied to a tree overnight. It was still intact. They flipped it over and launched from the school's parking lot. Steering the vessel west down Jones Road, they floated through yards near submerged houses as they headed toward the Crash Boat Basin, a waterfront neighborhood on Offatts Bayou.

As they approached 103rd Street, Davis caught a whiff of grilled meat. They steered the boat toward the smell and Davis saw junior lifeguards—the young men and women who work summers for Davis patrolling the beaches—paddling between houses in kayaks. The group spent the night in a house elevated atop stilts, watching with alarm as the water rose into the second-floor living room, and then with relief when it began to recede. That morning, the junior guards celebrated their survival with early-morning beers, loud music, and barbecue. "You want some steaks?" one guard offered.

Davis could only stare back, incredulous. He'd expected a kind of post-apocalyptic Atlantis and houses choked with dead; instead the first people he'd found were very much alive and enjoying themselves.

By then, the lifeguards Davis relegated to Santa Fe High School overnight clamored to get to the island to help with the rescues. They flooded in as soon as it was safe to cross the causeway, and immediately teamed up with the Texas Parks and Wildlife crews who had arrived in Galveston with state-issued airboats. They spread out across the watery landscape and started pulling people out of their houses. Most ended up at Ball High School. Rescuers heard horrifying tales from the people they saved that morning. A husband and wife spent the night lying on a mattress in the attic of their single-story house near Offatts Bayou as the water rose higher and higher, until it poured into the attic. For six hours, they clasped each other's hands, waiting for death to come. Beach Patrol arrived instead. Another woman spent the night with her cat sitting on her head as the water crept up as high as her neck before it receded and Beach Patrol officers came to her rescue.

By 3 PM, when the water receded to the point where most people could safely walk out of their homes, Beach Patrol crews had rescued 350 people. That afternoon, Davis realized Galveston had narrowly escaped a devastating casualty count.

"Two more feet of water, and you would have had a lot of people dead," he said.

■ WHEN THE BROCKWAYS woke up Saturday morning, they could still hear the wind buffeting their roof. They couldn't see much in the windowless, dark attic, but grey daylight filtered through the hole in the attic floor they had crawled through the night before. Emory peered down into the kitchen. Only about a foot of water remained in the house. Threading the ladder through the hole, the couple hesitantly climbed down. The refrigerator lay across the kitchen floor, wedged between the wall and the kitchen cabinets on the other side of the room. Some of the cabinet doors stood open. The rising tide scattered dishes around the room, some broken, others miraculously whole. But the living room furniture hadn't moved. The saturated couch stuck stubbornly to the floor.

Merlinda, described by her husband somewhat ungraciously as a packrat, walked through their bedroom and looked at all the things she spent the last 18 years collecting and stashing carefully away. A slimy brown residue covered her knickknacks. Clothes packed into closets dripped onto the boxes and shoes below them. While the Brockways took stock of what they had left, the last of the floodwater drained out of the house and down the front steps. It retreated down Bayou Homes Drive faster than it had risen the night before. Brockway opened the front door and windows—the ones not stuck shut—to air everything out.

A few minutes later, paramedics driving an ambulance came down the street. They offered water and a ride to the shelter, where charter buses would soon start ferrying refugees to shelters in San Antonio. The Brockways took the water but refused to leave their home. Wilma was still in the attic. The couple had no idea how they would get her down. And all Brockway could think about was cleaning out the house before the damage got any worse.

■ **U.S. COAST GUARD** Lieutenant John Moran and Lieutenant Junior Grade Dakata Brodie flew toward Galveston, 300 feet above the shoreline in a rescue helicopter. Their mission that morning: find and rescue any hurricane survivors and document the destruction on the southeast Texas coast. They took off from Corpus Christi as soon as the winds dropped below 55 knots—about 63 miles per hour. They started filming the destruction with the helicopter's onboard camera just outside Freeport.

Waves lapped over the shoreline and around the spindly legs of Galveston's West End beach houses. And though water choked the streets in Galveston's core, the seawall had obviously protected the island from massive destruction. Moran noted that most of the island's buildings still stood. They hovered over Galveston, watching firefighters battle two blazes and scanning the streets for people in need of rescue. But no one seemed to want help. Moran and Brodie watched islanders wade through waist- and chest-deep water, carrying belongings on their heads. Some looked up from patches of dry ground and cheerfully waved at the hovering helicopter.

Finding no one needing rescue, Moran turned the helicopter toward Bolivar Peninsula, where he, Brodie, Matt Russell, and Shane Moore spent Friday morning pulling people from the rising storm surge.

The damage there stunned the crew. Twenty-four hours earlier, elevated beach houses stood defiant against the rising water. Now, entire neighborhoods were gone. Some houses looked whole, but on closer inspection, the crew realized the storm surge blew out whole walls, scattering furniture, cabinets, sinks, and toilets across the peninsula. The tiny towns of Crystal Beach and Gilchrist bore the brunt of the storm surge. In Crystal Beach, Hurricane Ike washed away beachfront houses, leaving no traces of the first two rows of homes that once faced the Gulf of Mexico. The surge ripped apart the inland restaurants and stores at this once-popular spot for weekend vacationers.

Further east, in Gilchrist, only nine houses remained where 1,000 houses once stood. Not one of the nine surviving homes was spared damage. Moran passed reports over the radio to his superiors. "Eighty-five to 95 percent of the peninsula is destroyed," he reported. "Only 10 to 15 percent of the houses are left standing." Even worse, the hurricane cut Bolivar in two places, dividing the peninsula into three small islands. State Highway 87, just south of High Island, remained underwater, and the bridge at Rollover Pass buckled. The peninsula was now impossible to reach, except by boat or helicopter.

Moran secretly hoped to spot someone on the patio of one of the still-standing houses, frantically waving for help. But, he saw no one, and neither did his crewmates. Empty-handed and low on fuel, Moran and Brodie steered the helicopter away from the peninsula to refuel for a second search. As they headed toward Houston, they flew over what looked like an industrial waste site for construction debris. Moran looked down to see shards of broken houses smothering East Bay near Smith Point. Entire roofs, pieces of siding, whole bathrooms, and fishing boats littered Smith Point, where the storm surge deposited whatever had been ripped from the peninsula. The crewman had found the houses missing from Crystal Beach and Gilchrist. Moran had never seen anything like it.

"The amount of damage that was done there . . ." Moran took a long pause, choosing his words carefully. "My thought was: Anyone who didn't get out of Bolivar didn't stand a very good chance."

At one point, Matt Russell, the crew's flight mechanic, thought he saw a body in a pile of driftwood. "Target, three-o-clock," Russell said, and Moran swung the helicopter into a right-hand turn. As he did, the helicopter caught a tailwind. The copter, hovering just 300 feet above ground, quickly lost altitude, dropping 200 feet in 10 seconds before Moran gained control again. The body turned out to be a T-shirt draped across the stacks of debris. "It was a very disheartening wakeup call, just to remember how strong the winds were," he said.

The Coast Guard crew refueled and returned to the peninsula to find five UH 60 Black Hawk helicopters flying side-by-side down the length of the peninsula. The Coast Guardsmen located the Black Hawks' channel. They weren't having much luck either, the pilots told the Coast Guard. They had stopped at Fort Travis, where more than two dozen people rode out the storm, but nobody wanted to leave. The Coast Guard moved out of the way of the Black Hawks, which could search the width of the peninsula all at once.

Moran and his crew managed to pluck three people from the back porch of a beach house in Crystal Beach before the Coast Guard ordered the crew to stand down and turn over the rescue operations to the Black Hawks, which could hoist more people than the small copter. The crew carefully lowered the rescue swimmer down to the deck before sending down the basket that would hoist the three people to safety. But as the crew lowered the basket, a Black Hawk flew by, a little too closely, and the copter got caught in the Black Hawk's downwash. Moore had to protect himself from the wildly swinging basket.

The crew made only one more rescue that day: ambulances couldn't navigate the flooded roads in San Leon to get to a woman who had suffered a heart attack. Moran and his crew retrieved the resuscitated woman from the parking lot of a Jack-in-the-Box fast-food restaurant and flew her to Houston for treatment. By Saturday night, the Coast Guard had rescued dozens of people from Bolivar Peninsula, a surprisingly low number compared to the mass casualties Moran expected when he flew over the peninsula that Saturday morning.

"With the amount of damage done on Bolivar and the amount of people who said they were going to hunker down on Bolivar, I was surprised," he said.

■ AS SOON AS the winds let up, LeeRoy Amador, chief of Galveston's school police department, left the shelter at Ball High School to check on the superintendent and other administrators who had spent the night at The San Luis Resort. He picked up his friend Arnold Proctor, the school district official in charge of business and operations, and set out to assess and document the damage to the district's 13 island campuses. The district's only school on Bolivar Peninsula, however, would have to wait. With the ferry system shut down, and the causeway open only to essential personnel, there was no guarantee Amador and Proctor would be able to return if they left the island.

The men ventured out on the seawall and headed west, dodging bulldozers that had begun moving stacks of debris. They gaped in awe at the devastation. The storm surge had peeled back chunks of pavement from the seawall, revealing the weathered red brick underneath. Streetlights dangled from poles. Concrete picnic tables and benches—popular spots for tourists by day and vagrants by night—lay in broken heaps, pushed across five lanes of Seawall Boulevard. The waves carelessly lifted protective granite and concrete boulders the size of small cars from the base of the seawall and deposited them atop the 17-foot wall. The storm sheared in half the aluminum historical marker at the iconic sculpture commemorating the tenacity of the 1900 Storm survivors. But it left untouched the figure itself: a bereft couple, the mother clutching her child, the father's arm outstretched to an unseen God.

High above his hand, search-and-rescue helicopters buzzed.

Although it was already noon—and the hurricane had spiraled north, wreaking havoc in East Texas and Arkansas—large swathes of the island remained underwater. The deep surge kept rescue crews from searching past 11 Mile Road, even in dump trucks. The dark water of Offatts Bayou lapped over the 61st Street bridge, preventing cars and trucks from reaching Interstate 45. Only the tops of grave markers poked above the lake covering the 61st Street cemetery. The island's main arteries—Harborside Drive and Broadway—remained flooded, and the historic downtown district had yet to drain.

Proctor leaned out of the truck's passenger window and snapped digital photographs as Amador drove past apartment complexes missing roofs and walls, twisted metal awnings, and the tall wooden electricity poles that leaned dangerously over 61st Street.

Everywhere Amador and Proctor looked, they saw ominous signs of a flood of epic proportions. At the district's softball stadium on 83rd Street, debris clung to the top of a chain-link fence, indicating that the water had risen as high as 8 feet. At Burnet Elementary School, 5501 Avenue S, a frightened possum balanced at the top of a gate where it had escaped the rising storm surge. At Parker Elementary School, 6802 Jones Road, a boat rested in the front parking lot.

Amador stopped the truck near a barefooted man standing at the corner of 69th Street and Seawall Boulevard, near the empty Walmart parking lot. His T-shirt and jeans soaked, Jesse Segura asked Amador when the rescue crews would come. He'd spent a horrifying night in his two-bedroom house on 71st Street, fleeing the rising water, and he wanted to leave Galveston as quickly as possible.

All of the seats inside were taken, so Amador offered Segura a ride in the truck's bed. His feet swollen and red, he climbed gingerly into the back of the truck, trying not to put pressure on his waterlogged toes. Segura had decided to ride out the storm at his house because he thought Ike would do as little damage to his place as Hurricane Rita did three years before. As Ike filled his home with water, Segura stacked two mattresses on his kitchen table and tried to sleep. The water rose higher. When it was chest deep, Segura panicked. He waded to the bathroom, climbed on the sink, punched a hole through the drywall into the attic and hauled himself in. He waited there until the winds died down. When the howl subsided, he ventured outside to find help. He slogged through the waist-deep water to find high ground.

"This was a real close call to death for me," Segura said, resting in the truck bed. "I'll never do it again, man. I learned my lesson."

■ BRANDON WADE, GALVESTON'S deputy city manager, knew the power would go out during the storm. But he was surprised when the water stopped flowing in the middle of the night. He thought the hotel's water system might have been damaged or one of the water lines leading to the hotel might have ruptured. He didn't believe it was possible for the entire city to be without water. Although the city's main water pumping station was built just after the 1900 Storm, like many of the city's water and sewer lines, it had never given up in the face of a hurricane.

"I was immediately in denial, complete and total denial," Wade said. "That pump station has functioned valiantly in every storm since 1900. I knew that if we didn't have water pressure at that point, that this storm had been really, really bad."

By midmorning, the wind died down enough for police officers, firefighters, and utility crews to start assessing the damage and searching for survivors. Wade sent Utilities Director Eric Wilson and his crew to the main pumping station with instructions to get the water flowing as quickly as possible. While he waited for Wilson to report back, Wade offered to take the other city department heads to their houses so they would not be distracted during the next few days wondering how much they had lost. He was convinced his house was gone. Waves pulverized the few buildings in front of the seawall, and Wade expected to see similar destruction across the West End. He kept thinking about Gulfport and Biloxi, Mississippi, where Hurricane Katrina wiped wide swathes of beach houses off their pilings.

Mayor Lyda Ann Thomas; Elise Stephens, her assistant; and City Manager Steve LeBlanc also headed out to get their first look at the damage. They drove east on Seawall Boulevard. At 45th Street, piles of granite boulders, washed up from the base of the wall at Fort Crockett Park, almost covered all four lanes. Chunks of the concrete picnic tables and splintered boards from the shade shelters that covered them stuck out between the big, pink rocks. Crews with heavy machinery worked to clear a path through the rubble.

LeBlanc wasn't surprised to see sections of wall missing from the Flagship Hotel. Hurricane Alicia wrought that much damage. He was amazed by what he didn't see. Where the Balinese Room, Murdoch's Bathhouse, and Hooters once stood, only the skeleton of the souvenir shop remained. Nothing but a few pilings sticking up out of the surf marked where the other two buildings had been. But they didn't go far. Almost every plank ripped out of place by the storm washed up into a mountain of soggy wood across the road. The debris pile stretched from 25th Street all the way to Ferry Road. They stopped the car and got out.

"You could smell wood and seawater," LeBlanc said. "I don't think I'll ever forget that."

LeBlanc drove on to Thomas' house, a stately Victorian and 1900 Storm survivor at the corner of 37th Street and Avenue P ½. Based on the damage they saw on the seawall and the number of downed tree limbs and power lines they passed along the way, LeBlanc was amazed they could get there at all. But the water that had risen to about 18 inches in Thomas' yard during the storm had drained by the time they pulled up in front of the house. Her two Labradors ran up to the gate to meet them. Although the mayor had taken her smaller Yorkie with her to the hotel, she left the big dogs to fend for themselves, thinking they would be safe.

She learned later from a neighbor who rode out the storm in the house next door that the dogs spent most of the night on the front porch, which stayed dry. But every once in a while, panicked by the howling wind and crashing branches, the terrified animals dove off into the water and swam around the wrought iron fence, only to return again to the porch.

Once Thomas satisfied herself that her house was unharmed, LeBlanc took her back to the seawall and headed alone to look at his house. On the way, he heard a call on the police radio for a fire in his neighborhood, but they didn't give the address. As he got closer, he could see the smoke. He didn't know until he rounded the corner that it was a neighbor's house and not his own that had burned to the ground before firefighters could get there. The flames never spread, a stroke of luck vital to the whole neighborhood, not only the houses next door. Just a few dozen yards from the burning embers of his neighbor's house sat a tank, carried by the flood from nearby Scholes International Airport. On its side, bright red signs labeled the contents: highly flammable aviation fuel.

As he walked around to the back of his house, LeBlanc could see the water line about three feet off the ground. Debris covered his yard, which faced Lake Madeline. Part of one of his neighbors' boat docks lodged in his lawn. Next to it, fish flopped in the grass. It took him a while to clear a path to the back door and force it open. For a moment he just stood in the doorway surveying the scene. On the opposite wall, a grimy line punctuated with bits of grass and clumps of dirt showed where the water stopped—about three feet off the floor. Sludge covered the floor and ringed the couches in the living room. The family cat, startled by the noise downstairs, ran up to meet him. Given what she must have had to live through during the night, he was amazed she had survived.

Down the street, Wade watched as Planning Director Wendy O'Donohoe and her husband Shawn walked into their house. They had moved in only three months before. O'Donohoe was almost finished decorating the nursery for her second child, who was due in January. Although the house sat across the street from Lake Madeline, the surge coming from the inlet forced open the front door and fun-neled debris into the living room. Trash, tree limbs, and mud mixed with furniture and children's toys. City Attorney Susie Green helped

O'Donohoe dig some of her jewelry out of the mud that filled the main hallway.

"I remember just kind of feeling overwhelmed about how do we even begin cleaning this out, and I needed to get back to my job," O'Donohoe said.

After the O'Donohoes had taken a quick glance into every room, they all piled back into Wade's truck. He would have gone straight back to the hotel, but his coworkers encouraged him to see how far west they could get. They wanted him to take the time to see his house. Wade told them he would drive to the end of the seawall, so they could see the rubble. Based on the damage in town, he was convinced the West End neighborhoods would be demolished.

Piles of sand and tangles of downed power lines covered FM 3005, but Wade managed to get as far as 11 Mile Road. They detoured into Lafitte's Cove to check on another coworker's home. Looking at those undamaged bayfront houses gave Wade hope that his might have survived. The tide was still too high for the group to get there, but they urged Wade to walk the rest of the way. The water was chest deep in the street, but the house, on pilings, was still standing.

"It was shocking," he said. "I still had part of my fence."

Island officials had long considered the West End most vulnerable to storm damage. The seawall lured people into thinking homes in the city's core were safe. Ike reversed the conventional wisdom. Even waterfront houses on pilings did better than houses built on slabs in the city center.

■ THE RUSHINGS CAUGHT a ride out of The San Luis Resort with one of the police officers, who dropped them off in front of their house. Mud covered the driveway and grass. They could tell by the water line on the house that the flood stopped rising about the time they left earlier that morning. The mess inside was worse than they remembered, but the puppies they left behind managed to survive. Furniture that floated overnight ended up in odd places around the house when the water retreated. Sometime during the second half of the storm, the refrigerator flipped over and wedged across the entrance to the kitchen.

Steven opened all the windows and flipped off the main electrical connection while Lupe and the kids stuffed soggy, muddy clothes into black trash bags.

As he had the day before, Steven rode his bicycle to the Moody Gardens parking garage to get the couple's two trucks. The water still stood in places but not too high to prevent Steven from driving them home, one by one. By the time he had the vehicles parked in the driveway, Lupe and the kids had finished packing.

They planned to leave the island for a few days, at least until the power came back on and they could start cleaning out the house. But before driving over the causeway, Steven wanted to stop at the marina and check on his shrimp boat. He thought the *Tiffany Leann* would be safer on land during the storm, but as they drove down Interstate 45, he could tell none of the boats on water or on land escaped Ike's surge. The water lifted yachts and sailboats and pitched them across the road, piling them on top of each other. Their carcasses littered the interstate, a nearby bait shop and boat ramp, and an empty field that separated the marina from *The Galveston County Daily News* building.

Steven had to leave his car about a mile from the marina and walk the rest of the way. Every step he took dealt another blow to his hope of finding his boat in one piece. The marina looked so different than it had 48 hours before that Steven had a hard time figuring out where the *Tiffany Leann* should have been. He checked every stern he could see sticking out of the mountain of boats piled in the middle of the yard. He eventually found his boat's remains in the marina office, crushed under three other vessels.

"There was literally nothing left," he said. "That was devastating to me."

Steven didn't have insurance on the *Tiffany Leann*. As they drove off the island, Lupe wondered how they would recover with Steven unable to work and no money to get another boat.

■ THE FLOODWATER AROUND the 33rd Street water pumping station was still too high for Utilities Director Eric Wilson and his crew to get to it in anything smaller than a dump truck. As they drove past Ball Street and into the pump station parking lot, the truck's wake pushed an abandoned Cadillac into the fence surrounding the Cedar Terrace public housing development. Wilson jumped out of the truck expecting to hear the hum of at least one generator. But silence enveloped the plant.

Inside the building, Wilson found a foot of water in the pump pit. The natural gas generators that should have kept the plant running after losing power sat idle. Wilson assumed they stopped working because they got wet. While he waited for the last of the water to drain, he called Garage Manager David Smith and asked for new batteries to jump-start the engines. His crew changed the oil in each machine and plugged in the new batteries. The engines turned over but refused to start. Texas Gas Service insisted gas still flowed to the plant. Wilson finally had to open one of the valves on the line to prove the gas was off.

Without telling anyone, natural gas supplier Energy Transfer shut down the gas line connecting the island to the mainland as Ike came ashore. With so many pipes along the seawall likely to be broken during the storm, and so much debris floating around neighborhoods to threaten residential gas connections, Wilson understood why it might have been safer to cut all service. But until the gas started flowing again, or until Wilson could get diesel generators large enough to power the plant, his crews had no way to start the water pumps.

The city's main wastewater treatment plant, on Harborside Drive at 51st Street, had diesel generators, and Wilson hoped he would be able to report back to his bosses that at least one of the city's utilities still operated. Ike's surge had risen about four feet above the treatment plant. But Wilson found the generator humming away. The city had 8,000 gallons of diesel stored at the site, enough to keep the plant running for a week. He heaved a sigh of relief as he left plant Foreman Dennis Zajack in charge and went back to the pumping station.

Two hours later, a grim Zajack arrived at the pumping station. He told Wilson that during their first inspection of the treatment plant, the men hadn't noticed a piece of roofing from a neighboring building lodged in front of the air intake for the generator's radiator. Cut off from its air supply, the engine eventually exploded. Wilson had nothing but bad news to take back to the hotel.

■ **MIKE AND WEEZ** Doherty watched Ike come and go from the 5th floor of the Bank of America building at 23rd and Market streets, downtown. The Sealy & Smith Foundation owned the building, and as its executive director, Mike decided he should stay to keep an eye on things. Weez, a member of the Galveston Independent School District board of trustees, chronicled the storm's progress with her digital camera, shining a hand-held floodlight off one of the building's balconies after dark to light up the parking lot below.

After spending most of the second half of the storm in a windowless room, the Dohertys got up early Saturday morning, anxious to check out the damage. Water still covered all the streets they could see. The tall, thin doors lining the front of many of the old buildings around them stood open. At the eastern end of the Tremont House ballroom building, gauzy white curtains billowed out of the broken windows. A flotilla of paper cups and unopened bags of potato chips floated out of Quizno's Sub Shop. A lifeguard tower drifted by. Several Black Hawk helicopters buzzed past them, flying low. When they stopped to hover over a nearby building, the Dohertys assumed they made up part of a search-and-rescue mission.

With the water around them still so high, Weez had convinced her husband not to venture out until noon. Mike wouldn't wait past that.

"We just knew the island had had it, you know?" he said.

Weez packed their car keys, house keys, batteries, cell phones, credit cards, and cash into a backpack. She put everything that couldn't get wet in plastic zipper bags. They used the stairs on the west side of the building because the foyer walls on the other side had collapsed, block-ing the exit. After walking down one flight of stairs covered in mud, the couple stepped down into the cold brown water. It was up to their waists by the time they reached the parking lot. They held hands as they walked slowly toward the street, feeling ahead before each step. They dodged benches and bushes before finally stepping off the curb into Market Street.

While they stopped for Weez to take another picture, a man waded up to them. He was headed for one of the loft apartment buildings to check on his daughter. When Mike said they were leaving downtown, the man asked if they needed money. Surprised, Mike told him they didn't. But the man didn't believe them.

"He said, 'You people need bus money,' " Mike recalled. "We looked pretty rough at this point. He kept saying, 'You people just need to get out of town.' "

Few of Galveston's homeless left before the storm. With the Salvation Army shelter at 23rd and Broadway closed, they had nowhere to go for food. But as the water drained, they began showing up at the boarded building anyway. The Dohertys, covered in mud and soaked, got another offer of bus money and more urging to get out of town as they stood across from the shelter looking at the Rosenberg Library.

Library Executive Director John Augelli first recognized the Dohertys. He and his two staff members walked out of the library for the first time that day as the couple stood on the corner looking at the building. Wide-eyed and agitated, Augelli told Mike, a member of the library board of trustees, that the entire first floor was a loss. The flood submerged the children's collection overnight, and water still stood in the meeting rooms, built below street level. But Augelli worried more about the library's historic books, artifacts and archives on the upper floors. He had no idea how quickly or how far mold would spread. He also had no good way of keeping people out of the building.

"There were a lot of strange characters out on the street right after the storm," Augelli said.

The Dohertys planned to hitch a ride on Broadway, but Mike had a hard time convincing anyone to pick them up. The driver of the first truck they flagged down assumed they were part of the crowd gathering outside the Salvation Army building. He refused to give them a ride but told them to get out of town because they didn't belong. They walked about a block before someone from the University of Texas Medical Branch who recognized them stopped and offered to take them to their home in Cedar Lawn, one of the city's most exclusive neighborhoods.

■ **BY EARLY AFTERNOON,** the winds died down enough for state officials to safely land a helicopter on the pad in front of The San Luis Resort.

Accompanied only by the pilot, Mayor Thomas and City Manager LeBlanc spent two hours flying over the island and Bolivar Peninsula. They first headed west, where they expected to see widespread devastation. Most of the beach was still underwater, and waves lapped at the edge of houses that had been on the beachfront; Ike had sucked a lot of sand back into the Gulf. Some front-row beach houses obviously didn't survive the storm's pummeling, but the West End escaped the widespread leveling that scarred the beaches in Mississippi and Alabama after Hurricane Katrina. Most of the neighborhoods south of FM 3005 sustained some damage, but they were all intact. On the bay side of the island, the city's leaders spotted only a few houses that didn't survive. Most appeared untouched, from the air. Owners who returned weeks later found the walls of their downstairs garages blown out, part of the design that protects the houses from the force of the rushing surge. But the water didn't reach into the elevated living areas.

The helicopter flew low over the houses, looking for signs of life. But the only movement they spotted came from two herds of cattle wandering through the neighborhoods. One herd had gathered under and in front of the Escapes Resort condominium. Most of the West End cattle ranchers sold out to developers years earlier, but those who still owned tracts large enough to support a herd kept the animals to earn an agricultural tax exemption on the property. Everyone who saw the cattle after the storm wondered how they had managed to stay on land when the 10-foot storm surge covered the entire area.

Water still covered some of the neighborhoods behind the seawall when LeBlanc and Thomas flew over. The dry streets were strewn with people's belongings. LeBlanc saw many front doors wide open. He knew from experience what most people would face when they came home. Rebuilding would take months, if not years.

"It reminded me of New Orleans," he said.

■ WHILE MOST OF the island's city and school personnel rode out the storm at The San Luis Resort, a smaller group of officials set up their disaster headquarters at the Moody Gardens Hotel and Convention Center, part of the entertainment complex on the shore of Offatts Bayou that includes an aquarium and exotic animal exhibit. The Moody family opened the first of the complex's iconic pyramids in 1993 and turned the park into one of the island's most popular attractions. Because of its proximity to Scholes International Airport, the city's airport manager and his emergency crew stay at the Moody Gardens hotel during storms. City officials from the small West End city of Jamaica Beach also set up their emergency operations center at the hotel, parking their fire engines and police cars inside the convention center. Little more than a large neighborhood halfway between the island's urban core and its far western tip at San Luis Pass, Jamaica Beach is the only piece of the island that is not part of the city of Galveston.

Jamaica Beach officials had to wait much longer to start damage patrols than their Galveston counterparts. The water around Moody Gardens didn't drain until early afternoon. But by 3 PM, Mayor Vic Pierson and his fire and police chiefs headed toward the West End. Before the storm, nine Jamaica Beach residents told Pierson they intended to ride it out in their homes. He was anxious to find out whether they had survived the night.

Pierson and the chiefs hadn't been at the Jamaica Beach fire station long when one of the refugees walked up with his two Rottweilers to let someone know he was all right. A woman on the same errand arrived on her bicycle. A family of five also survived without injury. The last two residents who stayed had to be rescued by Beach Patrol because the water was still too high around their houses to get to them in a truck. But they all survived. Once Pierson accounted for everyone who stayed, he and the chiefs headed back toward the seawall to get a look at the rest of the island.

At 23rd Street, they decided to head toward downtown and check on O'Connell College Preparatory School, the island's only private Catholic high school. As soon as they pulled up outside the school, at the corner of 23rd Street and Avenue M, a woman came out of a building across the street and told them a woman inside had died overnight. She was the first of four people eventually found dead in Galveston. The chiefs confirmed the woman was dead and radioed the news to the Galveston

Police Department. After taking a quick look at the school, which took on some water but didn't have major damage, the Jamaica Beach crew headed downtown. Pierson wanted to check on the Moody National Bank building, at 23rd and Postoffice streets, where the bank's executive vice president, Mike Christiansen, rode out the storm with his wife and two pets. Pierson, the bank's president, had lost contact with Christiensen at about 10 PM the night before and had no idea how the bank or the sheltering couple had fared.

Pierson spotted Christiansen and his wife, sitting on a retaining wall outside the building, as soon as they drove up. Although the water was still several feet deep in the streets, the couple decided to wait outside the building in hopes that someone would show up to give them a ride. While they were trying to figure out how to get two more people, a cat and a dog into the already full rescue vehicle, a man and a pregnant woman walked up. The woman had just gone into labor. The chiefs radioed Galveston again and asked for an ambulance. Pierson later learned she gave birth to a boy.

In an interview six months after the hurricane, Pierson drew a connection between the dead woman and the pregnant woman a few miles apart.

"Someone's life was over and somebody's life was beginning," he said. "Galveston is not what it's ever going to be, but it's a rebirth. To me, that was a message being sent."

■ AMADOR DROVE TO Ball High School to drop off Segura so he could get food and water and dry off. But as he pulled his truck up to the school, Amador found that the shelter had descended into chaos. In his absence, islanders had arrived from all corners of Galveston to await rescue. They sprawled out on the sidewalk and across the high school's front staircase. Many wore wet clothes. They carried their possessions in trash bags and pushed dogs and cats in grocery carts. They bummed cigarettes from each other and swapped survival stories, absentmindedly petting each other's dogs or rocking small babies in their arms. They all shared the same dazed expression, not even paying attention as frantic paramedics surrounded an injured firefighter. The firefighter, his face twisted in pain, reclined against the concrete steps as medics pulled off his shirt, swung an IV bag over his shoulder, and poked a needle into his arm.

The size of the crowd shocked Mayor Thomas, who stopped by the temporary shelter several hours later. Thomas expected to see many of the island's homeless, but she couldn't believe how many people she knew. She recognized one woman as a volunteer from The Grand 1894 Opera House. The woman clutched a purse, the only thing she remembered to grab when she left her house. Incredulous, Thomas asked the woman why she had stayed. She didn't expect the storm to be that bad, she told Thomas. Like so many others, that woman spent the night in her house, fearing she would drown.

Superintendent Lynne Cleveland arrived to find people traipsing through water that had been driven into the school's front lobby and cafeteria by Ike's winds.

"I was about to die when I saw that water and I saw people walking through that water," she said.

Cleveland found the flooding so disturbing, Amador didn't dare let her look in the soiled classrooms, where pets spent the night, or in the bathrooms, where toilets stopped working sometime during the night and eventually overflowed as people continued to use them.

Cleveland became obsessed with worry that Galveston's hurricane victims, like the victims of Hurricane Katrina in the New Orleans Superdome, would be trapped at the school for days awaiting rescue. Overcome with a desire to clean the flooded campus, she grabbed a broom and feverishly started sweeping water out the front door. While she swept, people from across the island trudged toward the campus, carrying the few possessions they had left.

■ **POLICE CHIEF CHARLES** Wiley tried to forget about the damage at his house as he canvassed the island. Seventeen buildings had collapsed and rescue teams needed to sift through the remains to search for survivors, or bodies. Calls poured in from displaced islanders who claimed their friends, family members, or neighbors hadn't evacuated and now couldn't be reached. Teams of police, firefighters, and other volunteers walked from block to block checking each house for the dead and injured.

Wiley waited several hours to tell his wife about their flooded house. He knew she would "freak out."

"If you want to go look at it, look at it, but it's pretty well messed up," he told her. But she insisted they go together.

"I got to get in here and see what I can save," she told him.

"Don't save nothing," he said. "We're going to get rid of all of it."

She ignored him, grabbed photographs of their daughter and grand-kids and the urn containing the ashes of their beloved dog, and stuffed them in the trunk of his car.

All day, Wiley watched people emerge from their houses, thankful to be alive and anxious to save anything they could. He found one old woman standing in the ashes of a row of townhouses on 75th Street and Beaudelaire Circle that had burned to the ground at the height of the storm. She cried as she sifted through the remains of a lifetime's posses-sions. Wiley stopped and asked her if she was okay.

"Yeah, I'm fine," she said.

"What are you doing?" he asked.

"This is my house," she told him flatly. "I'm looking for some of my heirloom jewelry."

It was the jewelry her husband left her when he died a few years before.

"Is there anything I can do?" Wiley asked softly.

"No," she said. "Thank you." She turned back and continued to sift through the ashes, tears streaking her face.

"That is really, really tragic," Wiley said during an interview. "And that's just one story. There will be thousands like it."

■ ON SATURDAY EVENING, island officials lined up before reporters and television cameras to tally the damage they had surveyed during the day. Their tired, sunken, defeated eyes said more than their words.

The flood covered 75 percent of the island at the height of the storm. There were no utilities. Ten houses burned to the ground during the storm or immediately afterward. Fire crews, limited to the water stored in trucks, had to decide which fires to fight and which to let burn. Seven buildings collapsed after Ike wiped out walls and ripped off roofs. Officials thought the pile of boats at the base of the causeway might have damaged the road, fears state engineers could not put to rest for several days.

Rescue teams found no bodies floating in the streets, contrary to what they expected. Crews accounted for most of the people who had called 911 the night before. But all of the flooded houses had to be searched.

When asked how the island looked, Mayor Thomas described it simply as "a mess," her voice cracking with emotion. Until search and rescue crews could finish their work and the water service could be restored, evacuees waiting anxiously to see the damage for themselves would have to wait.

"We will do everything we can to bring you home as soon as it is safe to do so," she said.

CHAPTER

EIGHT

SCATTERED ACROSS TEXAS, evacuees watched the news coverage of Hurricane Ike with anger and frustration. For days, the same images flashed over and over across television screens: the debris piles on the seawall, the empty spot where the Balinese Room once stood, the wreckage on Bolivar Peninsula, and the blown-out windows in skyscrapers in downtown Houston. "Who cares about downtown Houston?" the displaced islanders wondered. Where was the real news about the neighborhoods where full-time Galvestonians lived? What happened to the historic homes, the public housing projects, the churches, and the schools?

Compounding the frustration, cell phones on the island ceased to work, making it impossible for evacuees to check on their houses. Sick with worry, they packed their bags and made plans to come home, all the while wondering: Is there anything left to come home to?

Meanwhile, city crews struggled to repair basic services. Toilets hadn't been flushed in days. Sewage bubbled out of storm drains and no one could bathe. Without electricity or natural gas, islanders couldn't cook, power refrigerators, or run air conditioners in their dangerously hot and humid houses. Mosquitoes swarmed the city, and the state's health commissioner warned of a growing risk of infectious diseases, including bacteria associated with diarrhea. The flood shut down the island's only hospital, forcing a federal disaster medical assistance team to treat minor cuts and scrapes at the emergency room or at Ball High School. But medics could not treat the seriously ill or injured, sending them instead to hospitals as far away as Houston. The island lacked traffic lights and stop signs, creating a dangerous situation for anyone navigating Galveston by car. And health officials suspected the sludge covering every inch of the island was a mixture of silt, motor oil, lead-based paint, raw sewage, and hazardous materials stored at the port or in garages.

The toxic soup, combined with the growing mold problem and the lack of medical services, created a public health hazard that prompted Mayor Lyda Ann Thomas to declare the island off-limits to anyone except emergency workers, contractors, some business owners, insurance adjusters, and reporters.

Although she was unwilling to declare martial law and force those already on the island to leave, Thomas begged them to go. Only about 1,500 heeded her call. The others stayed and started to pull soggy carpet, drywall, and furniture out of their houses. Those who evacuated before the storm viewed the blockades at the base of the causeway as a punishment. While their neighbors started cleaning up, homeowners barred from coming home could only wonder how high the mold crept up their walls. Would they be able to salvage anything by the time they could come home?

Thomas' decision to block access to the island whipped already frustrated, devastated islanders into a frenzy. Bowing to the growing outrage, the mayor allowed residents to return to the island four days after the storm for what she dubbed Look and Leave. Residents would be allowed to come see their property but had to be gone by sunset. But six hours after she announced the temporary visitation policy, Thomas cancelled it. Emergency responders and state officials got trapped in an eight-mile traffic jam leading to the island, and the Texas Department of Public Safety strongly encouraged Thomas to reconsider allowing people back so soon.

For eleven long days, islanders fumed, fretted, and felt like they were locked in a battle with their own elected officials. A few found ways to sneak past the roadblocks or hitch rides in boats and airplanes. But most could do nothing but count the hours until they could return, knowing every minute multiplied Ike's damage.

■ **LAURA HURT AND** Daya Myers left Galveston on Thursday with an inflatable kayak, their swimsuits, a couple of pairs of shorts and T-shirts, and their two dogs, Gracie and Winston. They headed for Daya's aunt's house near Marble Falls and planned to celebrate the end of a successful summer with a long weekend "hurrication." Fourteen months earlier, the couple moved from Houston, quit their full-time jobs and jumped feet first into their dream of opening a sandwich shop. The Lunchbox Café, tucked into a small corner of one of Galveston's historic buildings just off The Strand on 21st Street, became an instant hit with locals and the lunch crowd from the University of Texas Medical Branch and American National Insurance Company. They hadn't taken much time off in the last year, and this seemed like the perfect opportunity for some rest and relaxation.

The café was built on the loading dock of an old building that had been converted, like most downtown buildings, into storefronts downstairs and apartments upstairs. With five feet separating the floor of the restaurant from the street, Myers and Hurt thought their business would be safe from whatever Ike brought its way. Another storeowner across the street told them her business took on only 8 inches of water during Hurricane Alicia. Even if Ike's surge quadrupled Alicia's, which seemed unlikely, the restaurant would still be high and dry. Before leaving town, Myers and Hurt taped up the café's windows, stacked chairs on tables and moved their small cash register and radio to the top of their refrigerator. Hurt shot some video footage of the inside, just in case they needed to prove what they had to their insurance company.

On Friday morning, they got a call from some friends who had planned to ride out the storm in their downtown loft. The surge was a foot high and rising fast. Worried about their friends and the café, the couple switched on the television in Daya's aunt's living room and started watching a cable news marathon that lasted for three days. Every shot of standing water and early debris on the seawall fed their growing alarm. Hurt, an obsessive journal writer, kept a log of every useful piece of information they heard. They also started getting e-mails from friends and customers, some still on the island. As they all shared what little information they had, a disturbing picture started to emerge. But

Myers and Hurt still held out hope that the café's elevation would protect it from the rising water.

On Saturday morning, Hurt started sending out e-mails to the Lunchbox mailing list as a way to share information with people who had evacuated to places where they didn't have access to the 24-hour live feeds coming out of Houston. Austin's CBS affiliate had turned over its airwaves to the feed from Houston's KHOU, which wasn't as helpful as Hurt and Myers would have liked. The station seemed to switch between shots of the seawall, where Murdoch's, Hooters, and the Balinese Room left gaping holes in the Gulf view, and downtown Houston, where Ike blew out hundreds of windows in the JP Morgan Chase tower. They still hadn't seen one shot of downtown Galveston. Myers tried to comfort frantic friends with assurances that if the downtown damage was worse than what was on the seawall, the news crews surely would be broadcasting from The Strand.

Between checking their e-mail and watching the TV coverage, the couple scoured Flickr and other photo-sharing web sites for pictures from the island. They carefully inspected every photo of downtown that they could find, trying to figure out how high the water had gone. At one point, Myers even held her aunt's magnifying glass up to the screen to see if that made the view any clearer. But nothing gave them concrete evidence of how much damage they might be facing when they came home. The agony of not knowing made the wait unbearable.

■ WHILE HURT AND Myers and thousands of other evacuees searched the Web for information about flood depths and damage in their neighborhoods, people who knew city officials well enough to have their cell phone numbers started making calls. Mayor Thomas' Blackberry rang almost every five minutes once crews set up temporary cell phone towers and service returned on Sunday afternoon. Friends and supporters angrily criticized Thomas for keeping them from their homes for so long and demanded to be let back on the island immediately. If she couldn't do it for everyone, she could at least do it for them, they said. People who spent years currying favor tried to cash it all in at once.

City Manager Steve LeBlanc and Jeff Sjostrom, executive director of the Galveston Economic Development Partnership, also got threatening, cajoling, bargaining phone calls from residents and business owners who thought they deserved special permission to sneak past the roadblocks on Interstate 45. Although LeBlanc denied its existence, word spread quickly that the checkpoint guards had a list of people who would be allowed through. Most of the people on the list owned businesses or had political connections, or, at least, that's how the rumor went. Cleanup crews that showed up at a few businesses Monday morning with power washers, brooms, and mops proved that the disaster perimeter was more porous than officials wanted to admit.

By Tuesday morning, the chorus of irate callers had worn down the mayor's resolve to keep people out until water service could be restored. Officials with the Federal Emergency Management Agency and the state health department stood their ground—the unsanitary conditions on the island made it unsafe for anyone to be there, they told her. Everyone insisted the town couldn't handle an influx of people. They already had reports of people showing up at the John Sealy Hospital emergency room with viruses and infections from the heat and the residue of chemicals and sewage left behind by the storm surge. Health officials feared an outbreak of disease.

"But you could just feel the citizens who were so upset about not coming back," Thomas said.

In opposition to every expert, she finally decided to stave off the angry calls with the daytime entry program dubbed Look and Leave. Property owners would be allowed onto the island at sunrise and could spend the day cleaning out their houses. By 6 PM, they had to leave. A double "L" marked in shoe polish on the rear window of all vehicles coming through the checkpoint would differentiate the Look-and-Leave visitors from the people who had stayed on the island. A strict curfew, started Saturday night, would help encourage people to leave.

Thomas announced her decision at about noon on Tuesday, September 16. People who had already lined up on the interstate, hoping they could sweet talk or bully their way past the checkpoint, got in first. Evacuees staying close by hit the road immediately. The traffic that flowed smoothly for about an hour soon ground to a halt as thousands of people tried to get on the island while they still had enough time to get some work done. The line backed up for eight miles, and drivers refused to follow orders to stay out of the one lane state officials wanted to keep open for emergency vehicles. Texas Department of Public Safety officials finally called the city's emergency operations center and told them they had to abandon the visitation policy.

Although the decision was the mayor's to make, she told the city manager to announce it to the press. LeBlanc, who said later he had opposed the Look-and-Leave policy from the beginning, faced the cameras and microphones without Thomas to back him up. All he could tell them was that the plan hadn't worked. He could only say it would be suspended indefinitely. He didn't know whether the mayor would change her mind.

◼ AS THOUSANDS OF Galvestonians clamored to get back on the island, Dave Harris was desperate to find someone to help get his father, Fletcher Harris, off the island.

It was Monday, September 15, and he hadn't heard from Fletcher since Saturday, when Galveston County Sheriff's Office Deputy Freddie Poor called Dave, on a rare occasion when cell phone service actually worked, and put Fletcher on the phone.

Dave begged his dad to get on a bus and leave town. Fletcher refused. After a brief period of self-pity, Fletcher's cantankerous personality had abruptly returned. Fletcher swatted away a Texas National Guardsman who tried to check his hip, and bickered with another who attempted to coerce him onto a bus. He'd snapped at a drunk man claiming to be an Iraq War veteran, sharply declaring that World War II veterans had it much worse, and scowled at the other refugees who sought shelter at Ball High School. Though he was tired of being at the shelter, he wasn't leaving Galveston.

"What the hell are you going to do?" Dave asked his father.

"I'm 83 and I ain't left yet," Fletcher told him. "My father and grandfather went through the 1900 storm and survived."

"Get on one of those buses," Dave pleaded.

"I'm going back to the townhome to take a nap," Fletcher said, and hung up. Dave redialed Poor's phone number, but cell phone service was down again. Dave waited two days, and, sick with worry, called Poor on Monday to check on Fletcher.

Poor phoned him back around noon. A Texas Ranger cruising the neighborhood found Fletcher sitting in a folding lawn chair in his front yard, still wearing his wet clothes.

"He's not in good shape," Poor told Dave, "But we can't force him to leave."

They opened the doors of the flooded and moldy townhouse to air it out. Later that afternoon, Police Chief Charles Wiley, who lived two doors down from Fletcher in the same townhouse complex, found the old man in the same spot on the front lawn. Fletcher was very pale, had white froth in the corners of his mouth, and had wet himself, Wiley said. "Where can I take you?" Wiley asked. "Where's your family?"

Fletcher tried to argue with him about leaving, but Wiley wouldn't hear it. He summoned one of his officers to Fletcher's house, handed the cop $200 for gas and packed Fletcher in a car headed for Dallas. They met Dave halfway between Galveston and Dallas. Dave traded 25 cases of water for his father, who was by that time in definite need of medical attention. His feet were swollen from wearing wet socks and shoes for days, he had open sores on his legs and feet, and he complained about his hip. His left knee, where he had been hit with shrapnel in World War II, was swollen like a grapefruit.

Dave took Fletcher to see a doctor for a tetanus shot. The hip was fine—likely just bruised when Fletcher fell during the night—but his knee needed attention. Dave's orthopedic surgeon suspected Fletcher's knee was infected. He took X-rays, drew fluid and threaded a small scope inside the knee to view the damage. The doctor found no infection, but removed inflamed, arthritic tissue.

Dave checked Fletcher into an assisted living facility to recover, and on Christmas day, Dave shot a photograph of a smiling Fletcher sitting in front of the Christmas tree with his grandson and Dave. In January, the facility called Dave to tell him that Fletcher had been taken to the hospital. The staff found him shaking and delirious and didn't know what was wrong. Doctors at the hospital found a sore on his right buttock infected with MRSA, a highly contagious staph infection. Harris' condition deteriorated from there. He lost so much weight that his electronic prosthetic hand no longer fit. It was too loose to pick up muscle commands. Relatives and friends had long suspected that Fletcher had dementia, but now it seemed obvious. In March 2009, six months after the hurricane, Dave tried to get a CT scan for Fletcher to confirm what everyone suspected: Fletcher had Alzheimer's disease.

"The lights are on, but it's not as bright as it used to be," Dave said. "He's still got his wit and he's got his humor. He's just not giving people as much crap as he used to."

It seemed unlikely Fletcher would ever return home.

■ **AT HIS HOME** in Austin, Skip Martin started making lists of things to do and supplies he would need to clean out the downtown cigar shop he co-owned with islander Charlie Head. Martin, who worked for computer giant Dell, couldn't get to Galveston before the storm to help move furniture and cigars to the building's second floor, where they would be safe from flooding. He trusted Head had taken care of that, but because he couldn't reach him, he didn't know for sure. On Saturday, Martin tried to find out how much flooding might have filled Hava Cigar, at 21st and Postoffice streets, by searching for photos posted online and reading the accompanying comments and blog entries. Some writers said the water only rose a couple of feet. Others said the entire downtown area had flooded. He didn't know what to believe.

On Sunday, Martin bought cleaning supplies. He planned to drive to the island on Monday to see how much of his store remained. He sent e-mails to customers—Police Chief Charles Wiley, Deputy City Manager Brandon Wade, and Utilities Director Eric Wilson—who might be able to give him some idea of what to expect and whether he could get past the checkpoints. No one could give him a straight answer to either question, so he prepared for the worst. Before he left, he sent another e-mail to Mayor Thomas, City Manager LeBlanc, and Wiley, telling them that if he couldn't get on the island in the next few days he could lose $100,000 in inventory that might otherwise be saved. If Head had been able to move the inventory to upper shelves, the cigars would have survived the storm but would ruin quickly outside of a climate-controlled environment.

"I know a lot of people wanted to get in to looky loo and a lot of people wanted to get in to start cleaning up," he said seven months later. "I was not interested in any of that at all. I just wanted to get in to get those cigars out."

When he didn't get a response to his e-mail, Martin called Wiley and left a message. The police chief called him back late Sunday night. The mayor had asked Jeff Sjostrom to coordinate with business owners to get them past the checkpoints, Wiley said. Martin tried to reach Sjostrom, but he didn't answer his cell phone and his voicemail box was full. After staying overnight in Houston, Martin got up early Monday morning and headed down Interstate 45 toward the island. On the way he got a text message from Wiley. The password to get through the checkpoint was "public-private partnership," the message said.

Martin later insisted the password wasn't part of a secret, backroom deal, as some would claim in the angry weeks following the storm. It provided a legitimate and necessary way for business owners to get back on the island, he said. Martin planned to drive straight to the shop, pick up the cigars, and go back to Houston immediately.

Martin reached the first checkpoint about five miles from the causeway. The Galveston County Sheriff's deputies there hadn't heard of the public-private partnership and gave Martin a hard time for thinking some secret password was going to get him through. But when Martin insisted, the group's supervisor came over to see what was going on. After glancing over Martin's shiny Jaguar and his nice clothes and hearing him explain that he had just gotten a message from Chief Wiley, the supervisor waved him through. Although grateful to be moving again, the checkpoint experience only reinforced Martin's disgust for the Galveston political system. If they thought you were someone important, you got a different deal, he said. He recognized the officers manning the Galveston checkpoint and had no problem getting through it.

When he reached the corner of 21st and Postoffice streets, Martin saw crews already working to clean out The Stork Club, a neighborhood bar, and Rudy and Paco's, one of the island's upscale restaurants and a favorite with the mayor. He figured the public-private partnership must extend to cleaning crews as well as business owners. After calling his landlord to tell him about the cleanup and the password, Martin started moving aside the sandbags his partner had stacked outside the front door of the cigar shop several days earlier.

The smell hit him first, then the magnitude of the destruction. He started walking around the shop clockwise, a ritual that began every return visit. But none of the furniture, pictures or display cabinets remained in their usual places. Ike's convulsing surge had spread them around the store and mixed in a generous helping of mud. He found the bottom four shelves of the store's humidor empty and quickly calculated that Head must have managed to move about half the inventory to the storeroom. But in the dark and humid closet, Martin found only about $30,000 in cigars above the 7-foot-high water line. Boxes of swollen and ruined Camacho cigars packed the lower shelves. Realizing he couldn't do much else, Martin opened one of the dry boxes, unwrapped a Double Ligero, a strong, peppery, $6 Dominican cigar, and lit it.

Standing alone in the storeroom, smoking his cigar, Martin started to cry.

Head and one of Martin's college buddies opened Hava Cigar in 2006. Martin started as a business consultant but soon bought out his friend and formed a partnership with Head. Most islanders didn't give the business much chance at success, but, with each quarter, sales grew. Martin traveled to Galveston monthly to check on operations and get to know his customers. The partners built the business slowly, plowing profits into improvements. They hadn't invested in insurance but planned to before Ike entered the Gulf, putting all policy purchases on hold. Martin knew he would have to pay out of pocket to replace everything that lay in ruins around him. Ike erased almost three years of hard work in less than 48 hours.

At 5 AM the next morning, Martin, Head, and their landlord made for the island in a caravan to start cleaning up the shop and finding out how much they could save. Martin told them getting onto the island would be no problem. But the line of cars waiting to cross the causeway stretched all the way to Exit 15—about 11 miles. It took them four hours to get to the sheriff's department checkpoint. The same deputies who let Martin through the night before turned him around this time. Frustrated and angry, but hopeful that the two jurisdictions eventually would get their policies straightened out, Martin got back in line, with the rest of his caravan behind him. Two hours later, Thomas announced the Look-and-Leave policy and the line started flowing. This time, deputies tried to tell him only residents could come in. Only after more arguing and pleading did Martin convince them to let him through.

Martin and Head spent six hours that day loading furniture and display cases, anything they thought they could save, into the back of Head's truck. They decided to postpone cleaning until Wednesday, anticipating no problems getting back on the island under the Look-and-Leave policy. When they learned it had been cancelled, Martin gave up trying to follow the rules. He contacted a customer who had his own construction company. Although residents and business owners couldn't get through the checkpoints, contractors sped through using the lane reserved for emergency vehicles. Like hundreds of others who had to resort to subterfuge to get to their properties, Martin and Head donned orange vests and hard hats and wrote the name of their customer's company in shoe polish on the side of Head's truck. As part of the company's convoy, they cruised past all the other cars waiting in line.

"All I could think about during all of that was these months and years of patting ourselves on the back about all of our hurricane planning," he said. "I know you can't plan for the level of damage we had, but you would have thought that there would have been a process in place when this happened that they could institute. In a lot of cases, it seemed like all the planning went out the window and it was just reactionary to what was happening."

Although Martin didn't have any problem with people doing whatever it took to get back on the island, he acknowledged the city had a double standard for dealing with businesses. Outraged residents sent fiery e-mails to city officials and to *The Galveston County Daily News,* complaining about the favoritism shown to commercial interests during those first eleven days. While restaurants and retailers set up generators and dehumidifiers to limit the damage to their dining rooms and storefronts, the houses of island residents with no connections to anyone in power quickly festered and filled with mold. Clothes that could have been washed and reclaimed rotted in steamy, waterlogged closets. Officials explained the dichotomy in checkpoint permissions by noting that some businesses, like grocery stores and gas stations, needed to be open before residents could come home. But to many, the unequal response to people begging to come back and save what Ike hadn't destroyed proved that the machinery of influence and politics, running quietly behind the scenes at city hall, was something no floodwater could breach.

■ WITH THE CAUSEWAY once again closed to most people, islanders found creative ways to sneak back home. Evacuees who could borrow or charter boats, airplanes, or helicopters bypassed the blockade and thumbed their noses at the officials who tried to keep them out. Scholes International Airport had the best Look-and-Leave policy on the island, Manager Hud Hopkins joked months later. Hopkins even ran something of a shuttle service, driving people to their houses or businesses so they could see what they would be dealing with when they finally could come home. Some people found no damage. Others ended up standing in front of structures knocked off their foundations. But at least they knew.

When Myers and Hurt heard about Tuesday's Look-and-Leave policy, they knew they could never make it back to the island by curfew that night. So they prepared to drive in from Marble Falls early on Wednesday, loaded down with supplies. They stocked up at Sam's Club with mosquito repellant, Cracker Jacks, baby wipes, gum, and fresh fruit, most of which they intended to give to people they knew had stayed on the island. But when they got back to Myers' aunt's house, they learned the visitation policy had been cancelled.

"That was our breaking point," Hurt said. "Hearing we couldn't come back on the island, that was when we both completely lost it."

"I've been known to exaggerate, but no joke, I thought I was going to have a stroke," Myers said. "I was so angry I could feel my blood pumping."

Although Myers and Hurt couldn't see any way to get back to the island and get a look at the café, Myers' aunt, Dana Martin, had a plan. Without Myers and Hurt knowing it, Martin, a pilot, had been monitoring the Federal Aviation Administration restrictions on Galveston's airspace for several days. Two days after the failed Look and Leave, officials lifted the flight restrictions. Martin offered to sneak Myers and Hurt back home in her Cessna Skyhawk, a single-propeller airplane. She planned to tell inquisitive officials she had clients on board. Myers and Hurt just needed to arrange a ride from the airport to the café.

On their way to Galveston the next morning, they snapped pictures out of the small plane's windows. The damage at the airport stunned them. It looked like a child's toy someone had smashed, Myers said. The crinkled remnants of planes stuck out of the hangars that had collapsed on top of them. The friend that picked them up insisted they go first to their house to clean out the refrigerator. On the way, they stopped for gas—in someone's driveway. The family with the gas had a relative authorized to come onto the island every day. He brought them cans of gas whenever their supplies ran low. They shared what had become a very precious commodity with friends who needed it to power generators or keep cars going. As they left the impromptu gas station, Myers and Hurt encountered another family with a generator-powered washing machine offering their friends and neighbors free laundry service.

The couple's elevated house, in the 2400 block of Avenue N, survived Ike's surge, but the storage space underneath, stuffed with boxes they still hadn't unpacked after moving in the month before, looked like it had taken a couple of cycles in a mud-filled washing machine. After cleaning out their refrigerator, they snapped a few pictures before going to the café. Someone had sent them a photo of the front several days earlier, and they spotted a water line about four feet high. With that evidence to bolster their hopes, they arrived thinking it had escaped damage. But they just hadn't looked high enough in the photo. When they opened the front door, a tomato rolled out.

"I remember thinking, that's not good because that should be in the refrigerator," Myers said.

The shock of seeing the overturned tables, the toppled refrigerator and the ruined equipment kept them from doing any of the cleaning they had planned to do. Instead, Martin started filling trash bags while Myers and Hurt walked to The Strand to take in the storm's aftermath. A skin of fissured mud covered the street and filled the trolley tracks. Some restaurant owners had already rolled stinking refrigerators to the curb so the city's debris management company could collect them. Piles of ruined souvenir shirts, shot glasses, kitschy knickknacks and straw hats dotted the sidewalk all the way to 25th Street. Still, for Myers, block after block of ruin was somehow easier to look at than her own little café.

■ AFTER BILL AND Kathy Moll waded away from their flooded truck with nothing but their cat and Kathy's purse, the couple ended up in a Houston hotel. Although they escaped the rising water that chased them out of their bay front home on the island's West End, they couldn't avoid Ike's misery completely. Their hotel lost power for four long, hot, sticky days. Without television, radio, or the Internet, it was almost impossible to know for sure what was happening in Galveston. But on Tuesday, Moll's son found his father's abandoned truck using satellite images he found on the Internet. The storm surge had pushed it off the road into FM 3005's grassy median, several hundred yards from where the Molls left it.

They didn't make it to the island in time for the short-lived Look and Leave but at his son's house later that afternoon, Moll met up with his ex-wife's husband, who had taken some of his relatives across the Intracoastal Waterway by boat to see their home in the Crash Boat Basin. He offered to take Moll and his son over the next day to check on his house and see if they could salvage anything from the truck. They left from Hitchcock, picked their way across the shallow oyster beds, and docked at a neighbor's house in Spanish Grant. The Molls' house took on only four feet of water during the storm, not enough to reach the upstairs living quarters but enough to ruin everything in the garage and Moll's ground-floor office.

Once they had a chance to look around, they tried to figure out a way to reach the truck, several miles away. Two bicycles left at the house looked promising, until Moll realized the tires were flat. They were about to give up when a Galveston fire marshal drove by on patrol and offered to drive them to FM 3005. The truck, its windows still down in preparation for the Molls' escape, had come to rest next to a Dumpster also washed into the middle of the road by the rushing water. The top layer of boxes and packages the couple had stacked carefully into the truck's cab washed away, along with everything in the bed. But much of the most valuable items remained. The box containing Moll's mother's silver burst open and several pieces were missing. The canvas bag containing their passports and the $2,000 in cash Moll had withdrawn from their account to get them through the evacuation was gone. Ike also claimed a string of pearls and a beautiful diamond necklace Kathy packed into the truck at the last minute. But Moll found the rest of the jewelry and his coin collection buried in the mud that covered the floorboards and the back seat.

Moll had just started to wonder how they would get his salvaged treasures back to the boat when a truck bearing a City of Galveston seal on its door sped by. As soon as it passed them, the truck's driver braked abruptly and backed up to where they stood at the side of the road. Moll expected to get a tongue lashing, or worse, for breaking the city's "no entry" policy. But when the door flew open, Deputy City Manager Brandon Wade stepped out, a wide grin splitting his face.

"Bill! We all thought you were dead!" Wade said, only half joking.

Although he was expected back at The San Luis Resort where the city manager had scheduled a staff meeting, Wade called to say an important matter had come up on the West End. He helped Moll and his son put their tattered boxes and filthy bags into the back of the truck and drove them back to Spanish Grant.

■ THE STREET-BY-STREET SEARCH for the dead continued for days. Search and rescue teams from Texas Task Force One, an urban search and rescue group trained in responding to disasters, went door-to-door, starting on the East End and moving west, looking for survivors and casualties. The city urged those who were anxious about their loved ones to call the city's emergency operations center, staged at The San Luis Resort. As the calls poured in, dispatchers scribbled names and addresses on sheets of paper and handed those lists to the Beach Patrol lifeguards who offered to help do the checks the cops didn't have the time to do.

Beach Patrol Chief Peter Davis and his crew of lifeguards showed up at the hotel each morning to collect a list of the names dispatchers had collected overnight from people worried that their loved ones were missing or dead inside their homes. Davis split that list among lifeguards to search sections of the island. From 8 AM to 6 PM each day, the lifeguards canvassed the city, knocking on doors and passing out supplies to hurricane survivors. If the lifeguards suspected that someone was dead inside a house—or a pet was trapped there without food—they called the police to bust down the door. Lifeguards picked their way through darkened, flooded houses. The work was dangerous. Davis feared two things: that his lifeguards would cut themselves on debris and contract illnesses, or that some outraged homeowner would mistake them for looters and shoot them on the spot. To assuage his fears about the former, Davis convinced the Galveston paramedics to dole out tetanus shots to every lifeguard, but he had no way to stop the latter.

On one run, Davis received instructions to search Cocktails, an eclectic dance club and bar near 24th Street and Mechanic. The caller hadn't heard from the transvestite who lived in the back of the club, and feared he might be dead, Davis said. Davis entered through the front door. He slowly and carefully made his way across the pitch-black, slimy, mud-coated club, yelling "Beach Patrol! Police!" at the top of his lungs, all the while expecting an angry drag queen to burst in and gun him down, he said. He was relieved to discover the man wasn't there.

The death count in Galveston was surprisingly low (only six people died on the island, and of those, only two drowned in the storm surge)— Beach Patrol lifeguards discovered no bodies. They did, however, find a mess of dogs and cats, left behind with little food and water, and hundreds of survivors holed up in their houses without electricity and completely disconnected from the world. Just two days after the hurricane, Davis discovered a man sheltering inside his house with three kids and no food. The man was in shock, exhausted, and disoriented; none of them had eaten in 48 hours, not knowing there was an aid station half a block away, Davis said.

Without phone service, television, radio, or Internet, few survivors knew just how much help had arrived on the island. Davis made "a zillion copies" of a sheet of information cobbled together by Alicia Cahill, the city's spokeswoman, detailing where hurricane victims could find food, water, and limited medical care. He drove into the parking lots of apartment complexes and yelled: "I've got food, water, and information," then waited as disheveled people emerged from their homes. The lifeguards treated minor injuries—like cuts and scrapes—and transported those with more serious injuries to clinics. If people wanted to leave the island, the lifeguards packed them into vans and dropped them off at Ball High School, where hundreds of people were being bused to shelters in Houston and San Antonio. If the survivors wanted to stay, Davis and the other lifeguards made sure they had plenty of water and food. The Texas National Guard passed out boxes containing three-square meals worth of packaged food: dry cereal and evaporated milk for breakfast, ham or tuna salad for lunch, canned ravioli for dinner and plastic tubs of chocolate pudding.

But canned tuna and cold Spaghetti-O's could only go so far—people craved the comfort that came with a hot meal, a rare and precious gift those first days without electricity.

Within two days of the hurricane, five of the Salvation Army's signature red-and-white mobile kitchens rolled into Galveston to begin doling out the first hot meals some islanders had tasted in days. They stood in long lines for a Styrofoam plate heaped with rice slathered in a soupy gravy with bits of chicken. One kitchen parked outside Arlan's Market, the flooded grocery store at 25th Street and Avenue P; the other set up outside Moody Methodist Church at 53rd Street and Avenue U—the unofficial headquarters of the Texas National Guard and other rescue operations. Three other mobile kitchens canvassed the island like ice cream trucks as Salvation Army volunteers broadcast the goods over loudspeakers like ballpark vendors—"Hot foooood . . . Coollllllld waterrrrrrrrr"—enticing hurricane victims from their flooded houses.

By mid-September, the Salvation Army faced serious financial challenges after Hurricanes Dolly, Fay, Gustav, and Hanna took a heavy toll on the organization's resources. Even though the organization continued to feed the victims of Hurricane Gustav in Louisiana and Mississippi as Ike inched toward Galveston, the Salvation Army deployed a fleet of 60 mobile canteens across Texas, placed another 100 on standby, and staged personnel and resources in San Antonio and Tyler, where volunteers started serving meals to evacuees bused there ahead of the hurricane. The evangelical charity also prepositioned supplies such as brooms, mops, buckets, bleach, rubber gloves, and first-aid provisions.

As the hurricane slammed the upper Texas coast and jaunted north–leaving more than four million without electricity–it became clear to Salvation Army officials that Ike was the worst yet that season.

By Monday, September 15–two days after Ike struck Galveston–the Salvation Army had already served more than 20,000 hot meals, sandwiches, snacks, and drinks–and people kept lining up for more. A week later, Salvation Army volunteers had served 1.2 million meals to people lined up at more than 100 mobile canteens throughout the state. As far from gourmet food as it was, hurricane victims savored every bite of the free Salvation Army meals, lifting the plates to their lips to lick every last morsel.

But those looking for a gourmet meal could certainly find one among the many impromptu neighborhood picnics that cropped up around dinnertime throughout the island. At Galveston College, a group of professors who raided the college's culinary kitchen–salvaging fine foods and choice meats before they rotted–fired up a grill and shared with neighbors near the college.

On Galveston's East End, two friends–Pam Houston and Bill Beveridge–organized what would later become legendary picnics. Beveridge salvaged food from the eight Galveston houses he managed for people who only lived on the island part time. He uncovered gourmet wines, pork loin, brisket, mangoes, and enough booze to open a liquor store. He and Houston rode out the storm in one of the elevated, historic Victorian homes. After the storm, they wheeled a grill out to the street and started cooking. When the smells of grilled brisket wafted over the neighborhood, people started showing up. At first, only four people gathered around the picnic table–Beveridge, Houston, and the women who lived next door.

Credit: Weez Doherty

Credit: Weez Doherty

Top: A view from the top floors of the Bank of America building on September 13, about 10 hours after Hurricane Ike passed over the island. The storm surge blew out the windows at the Tremont Hotel, freeing the curtains to billow out in the still gusty wind. Bottom: The salty storm surge from Galveston Bay that filled downtown, flooding stores and drowning abandoned cars, didn't drain completely until Sunday, September 14. This photo of 23rd Street was taken on Saturday, around 1 p.m.

Credit: Weez Doherty

Credit: Dr. Ben Raimer

Top: Three unidentified people walk through floodwaters that still filled 23rd Street on Saturday afternoon. Bottom: Mounds of debris started to pile up outside of homes and businesses as soon as islanders could come home and start mucking out their flooded buildings.

Credit: Dr. Ben Raimer

JENNIFER REYNOLDS/The Galveston County Daily News

Credit: Kathy Modzelewski

Top: Hurricane Ike stripped the popular souvenir shop Murdoch's Bath House to the studs. The owners rebuilt and reopened for business a few months after the storm's first anniversary. Left: One home is completely collapsed and another stripped to the studs on Channelview in Galveston. Right: Thick black smoke clouds downtown, casting an ominous pall behind St. Mary's Church as the Galveston Yacht Basin burns out of control.

Top: Debris from several shops on piers over the Gulf fills Seawall Boulevard for several blocks in Galveston. Bottom: The Phi-Boy, a shrimp boat, washed ashore in the parking lot of Pier 21, coming to rest next to the trolley stop in front of Willie G's Seafood and Steaks restaurant.

Top: A crane sifts through piles of debris tossed out from flooded houses, apartments, and businesses. The mountain of debris in front of the Galveston County Justice Center, at 53rd Street and Broadway, towered over the buildings around it for months after the storm. Bottom: Storm surge from Hurricane Ike destroyed a home on Bayou Shores Drive in Galveston, pushing belongings from inside the home through the garage door and ripping the bricks from the exterior.

Top: Dozens of boats that came to rest on Interstate 45 in Galveston wait to be cleared in the aftermath of Hurricane Ike on Sunday afternoon September 14, 2008. Bottom: Search and rescue crews search the neighborhood at 64th Street and Avenue L in Galveston Sunday September 14, 2008, for residents who tried to ride out the storm in their homes or trailers. The storm surge from Hurricane Ike destroyed the neighborhood.

Credit: Mark Collette

JENNIFER REYNOLDS/The Galveston County Daily News

Top: Debris litters the streets in front of a flooded downtown shop two weeks after Hurricane Ike struck Galveston. Bottom: Debris fills the streets at 62nd Street and Avenue L in Galveston. Storm surge from Hurricane Ike destroyed the neighborhood.

Credit: Leigh Jones

JENNIFER REYNOLDS/The Galveston County Daily News

Top: Hurricane Ike's storm surge swirled around inside houses for 24 hours, rearranging furniture and coating everything with a dirty film. Leigh Jones took this photo of her living room four days after the storm. Bottom: A dry storage area at the Galveston Yacht Basin burns out of control Friday fanned by high winds from Hurricane Ike.

Then someone invited a brother. Someone else invited a friend. Another invited someone she met in the street. Pretty soon, almost a dozen people gathered for Beveridge's daily picnics.

At dusk, the eclectic group of men and women—some who had never met each other before—lounged on porch swings and rocking chairs on the veranda of the Victorian home, chatting and swapping recovery stories as flames licked the edges of a pot of water resting on the grill. As fragrant spaghetti sauce simmered in a pot tucked away under the grill hood, Houston propped her bare feet on a porch railing and exhaled a breath of cigarette smoke that, for a split second, blurred the view of the flooded neighborhood, the broken tree limbs, the empty streets. A neighbor sauntered over and set a tub of fresh cantaloupe next to a vase of fresh yellow tulips. Someone else placed an unopened bottle of merlot on the linen-covered picnic table.

Each day, they met for breakfast, usually pancakes and Cuban coffee or espresso, to discuss the plans for repairing their flooded homes. They met again at dusk to talk about mopping the grime out of first floors, salvaging belongings, and the random acts of kindness by strangers they met throughout the day.

■ CAROLINE DORSETT, DIRECTOR of the Galveston Island Humane Society, expected to see hundreds of hungry animals roaming through the island's neighborhoods on Sunday, when she finally got a chance to drive around and look for them. Many island residents have a casual attitude about pet ownership. Dogs often roam free, sometimes terrorizing neighbors and almost always producing litters of unwanted puppies. Feral cats are equally prolific. But the day after Hurricane Ike slammed ashore, sending animals and people alike in search of higher ground, Dorsett spotted few animals on the streets.

She would have had a hard time helping them at first, even if they had all come running up to her car begging for food. Ike filled the animal shelter with three feet of water, leaving Dorsett with no supplies and nowhere to take any pets she might have found. She could only be thankful she and the board of directors had agreed to evacuate the shelter before the storm. By the time Mayor Thomas decided to call a mandatory evacuation for the island's human population, the 89 animals waiting in wire cages for new homes had been shuttled to safety in Houston.

After her staff tidied up the shelter in preparation for whatever post-storm population it might have to take in, Dorsett locked the door and left. She didn't want anyone to be there as island residents fled the coming storm. The shelter's location on Interstate 45, conveniently on the way out of town, made it too easy for people to stop by and drop off their pets. Before Hurricane Rita, Dorsett unexpectedly ended up with animals whose owners decided to evacuate and didn't want to hassle with any more dependents. She largely avoided that problem this time, but eventually did have to reopen the shelter for several animals her staff forgot at a local vet clinic, where they had gone for treatment. City officials also called Dorsett to the Island Community Center when an elderly woman headed out of town on the chartered buses left her black lab behind.

Dorsett put all 10 animal refugees in the shelter's highest cages, gave them food and water, and hoped they would survive. The next morning, she left the San Luis as soon as possible with Lieutenant Joel Caldwell, a member of the shelter's board of directors, to check on them. Water still covered the freeway access road in front of the building, but the parking lot was dry. Caldwell put on a wetsuit and boots and waded down the street alone. He wouldn't let Dorsett come with him. Overnight, the flood had submerged the shelter's lower cages. But the puppies and kittens in the upper cages stayed dry. The abandoned lab, too big to be put on a shelf, likely got wet, but he was alive. The storm blew out the shelter's windows and ripped off part of its roof, giving the animals enough fresh air to keep them from being completely miserable until they could be moved the next day.

Dorsett and Caldwell took the animals and several more dogs rescued from a vet clinic on 61st Street to another clinic on Broadway and set up a temporary shelter. But with widespread damage on the island, Dorsett knew she would soon need more space to care for the animals people had left behind. Many islanders locked their pets inside boarded houses with extra food and water, thinking they would come home as soon as the storm passed. When they realized how much they had underestimated

Ike, anxious owners called the city's emergency operations center asking for someone to check on their pets.

About a month before the storm, Dorsett had made plans to move the shelter into an old police substation at 53rd Street and Avenue R so the old shelter could be demolished and a new one built in its place. The bunker-style cinder block substation took on some water during Ike, but it was structurally intact. After a quick inspection, Dorsett decided it could be cleaned up and made ready to house animals in a few days. Animal rescue crews from Houston and Denver who arrived on Monday started ripping out carpet, wiping down walls and setting up cages. Although proud of her evacuation plan, Dorsett admitted later she hadn't thought much about recovery. She had no plan for rescuing or caring for thousands of abandoned pets, no room to house them and no system to reunite them with owners who eventually would return. But the Houston Society for the Prevention of Cruelty to Animals, which had sent volunteers to New Orleans after Hurricane Katrina, knew what to expect and what kind of help Galveston would need.

Before Dorsett could even call her contacts in Houston, shelter officials there had requested help from rescue teams all over the country. During the next three weeks, teams from as far away as Los Angeles and New York caravanned to the island with rescue trucks and trailers full of supplies. They even brought their own campers, food, and water, so they wouldn't be a burden on already limited resources. They started rescue missions on Tuesday, as hundreds of residents slipped back to the island under the short-lived Look-and-Leave policy. Directed by requests from owners who couldn't make it back that day, the teams broke windows and busted down doors to save stranded animals. They picked up others wandering the streets. In neighborhoods hit by the worst flooding, they even pulled a few dogs off rooftops. Dorsett expected mostly cats and dogs to come into the shelter, but crews also returned with hamsters, gerbils, guinea pigs, rabbits, and birds. They found an aviary in one house, full of parakeets, cockatiels, and canaries.

Carriage horse owner James "Cowboy" Coffman, whose horses pulled tourists through the historic downtown in picturesque Victorian carriages, left his three animals in their paddock near the port. Trapped between buildings and behind fences, the horses spent the night of the storm swimming around the enclosure, kicking their legs constantly just to keep their heads above water. One eventually tired, or gave up, and drowned. After the water drained, crews found the horse's body pressed against a chain-link fence, rapidly decomposing in the heat. A miniature horse, tethered in the backyard of a house on Bayou Shore Drive, also drowned, unable to break its ties as the floodwater rose quickly up the grassy lawn that sloped down into English Bayou. Its bloated body, barely recognizable as a horse by midweek, filled the neighborhood with a fetid stench until someone eventually removed it.

At one of the badly flooded housing projects, a neighborhood dog was left behind to fend for himself. Residents of Palm Terrace had taken turns feeding the dog they called Duke since the old man who owned him died. But no one thought to evacuate the dog. Duke tried to escape the rising water, but got trapped in a wrought-iron fence surrounding the public housing development. His soggy body remained stuck in the fence for weeks while Palm Terrace residents pitied and mourned him, until someone finally cut the fence and hauled Duke's body away.

Some animals survived the flood but died days later for lack of water and food. A woman flagged Dorsett down one day as she was driving through a devastated neighborhood. One of her neighbors had left a dog tied up in their backyard, the woman said. Someone should check on it, she said. By the time Dorsett picked her way around downed tree limbs to the back of the house, the animal was dead.

Although many people didn't seem to care what happened to their pets, most of those who left animals behind frantically tried to get them rescued as quickly as possible. One family who left a litter of pit bull puppies locked in a bathroom asked crews to break down the door to rescue them. The house had flooded, and one of the eight-week-old puppies died. But three others survived. The rescuers scooped two out of the filth on the floor and plucked one off the bathroom counter, where the rising water deposited it. The volunteers fell in love with the dogs and eventually took them back to New York when they left the island. Dorsett got a Christmas card from one of the adoptive families a few months later, with a picture of the happy dog in his new home. In return, she sent the family a photo of the puppy taken the day it arrived in the shelter, to show them how much its circumstances had changed.

For about three weeks, the rescue teams brought hundreds of hungry and frightened animals to the shelter every day. In the afternoon, volunteers loaded them into trucks and trailers and drove them to Houston, where they went to shelters or foster families. Before leaving the island, each pet had its picture taken and information about where it was picked up entered into a database. Coordinators in Houston uploaded all of the data to a web site so owners could search for their missing pets. Most of the reunions took place in Houston, where families still waited to come back to the island. But Dorsett did get to witness one man joyfully discover his Dalmatian in the shelter, just before it was to be moved to Houston.

She also helped coordinate a 1,400-mile reunion between an evacuee who ended up in New York and the 15-year-old cat she left behind in an apartment. Deborah Snyder intended to take Minnie with her when she evacuated, but the cat disappeared as only a cat can do when she saw her carrier come out of the closet. Snyder called the Galveston Police Department ten days later. Dorsett sent a rescue crew to pick up Minnie the next day and called Snyder as soon as her companion arrived at the shelter. Unlike Snyder, many owners never made an attempt to reunite with their pets. "But there were also a huge number of people who went crazy looking for them," Dorsett said.

Crews eventually rescued more than 2,000 animals from Galveston's streets, apartments, and flooded houses. But only 450 returned to their owners. Others went to new homes in Houston and surrounding areas, where families happily adopted the traumatized and abandoned survivors.

■ As DORSETT SCRAMBLED to rescue pets, the biologists at Moody Gardens worked desperately to save the exotic animals that could survive only so long without the electricity that powered the tightly controlled exhibits where they lived. The staff hadn't evacuated any of the animals at Moody Gardens. Thousands of fish and bats died, trapped in their enclosures. But Greg Whittaker, the attraction's animal husbandry manager, was determined to save others.

While the hurricane rumbled outside, Whittaker lay in his bed, obsessing about the animals and watching the red numbers morph on the digital clock on his bedside table. When the eye passed over, and the winds abruptly died, Whittaker couldn't stand it anymore. He sprang out of bed, snapped on a wetsuit, and tromped downstairs to the front door of the luxury tourist hotel.

He stepped into the black night and struck out toward the glass pyramids that contained all the animal and fish exhibits, wading through dark, chest-deep water. His heart sank when he saw the Rainforest Pyramid. The rising floodwaters breached the glass walls encasing the exquisite collection of rainforest plants, fish, birds, and tree-dwelling mammals.

The water filled the basement of the pyramid like a bowl, killing scores of rare fish, turtles, and snakes too precious or too fragile to display in the public exhibits. Moody Gardens kept its collection of the world's only living two-stripe, white-lip cichlids in the basement. The fish had been wiped out from their African home in Lake Victoria, the world's second largest freshwater lake, and existed only in captivity at Moody Gardens.

The surge nearly breached the neighboring Aquarium Pyramid. Whittaker dashed through the aquarium, making last-minute changes as he anticipated the failure of the emergency generator and tweaking the level of oxygen in the water to save the fish when the power went out. He almost stayed too long.

When he finally stepped out of the pyramids to wade back to the hotel, the back half of the storm slapped him with 100 mile-per-hour winds. To his dismay, the water was rising. Once safe inside the cushy hotel, Whittaker ran into Moody Gardens' General Manager John Zendt. He told Zendt about the flood at the rainforest, and the dire situation at the aquarium. Expect the worst, Whittaker told him.

At 3:51 AM, Zendt made the call: Shut down the emergency generator to prevent the rising water from shorting out the transformers. The electricity died and the hotel went dark. The Moody Gardens staff sat in dark hotel rooms, listening to the wind howl and waiting for it to let up.

When Whittaker and the other biologists waded back to the pyramids the next day to assess the damage, they discovered a hopeful sight among death and destruction. The animal husbandry manager brought with him the fish curator, the manager of the establishment's life support systems, a biologist who worked with penguins and seals, and the resident expert in venomous reptiles. In the Rainforest Pyramid, saltwater filled the freshwater tank, suffocating 4,150 fish, about 80 percent of the exhibit's animals. A grimy sludge seeped into the bat cave and killed two dozen bats. An African bush viper that had twice made news headlines for escaping its enclosure couldn't escape when its life depended on it. It died from stress. But the larger and more precious freshwater specimens—namely the 100-pound catfish—were still swimming, a surprising feat considering that the salinity in the freshwater tanks was about half as strong as regular ocean water.

Even more hopeful, the Aquarium Pyramid did not flood. The electricity died, killing the pumps that aerate the tanks with oxygen, but only three dozen out of the 8,400 fish perished. One chronically ill shark died from stress, but the penguins and seals—visitor favorites—swam quietly in their darkened tanks, oblivious to a rising danger.

Without electricity, temperatures in the exhibits would climb.

The floodwaters rose 14 feet, submerging Moody Gardens' emergency diesel-powered generator and shorting out the electrical switches. The biologists knew they needed to find a way to cool the fish, plants, and mammals most in danger of overheating. Surprisingly, penguins weren't on that list. Predicting a possible power outage, aquarium staff chilled the water in advance of the hurricane to 44 degrees, or 10 degrees colder than the average water temperature in the tank. The chilled water kept the air cool, and the biologists cut down on feedings so that the penguins' metabolism wouldn't rise and cause them to overheat. After three days without electricity, the air temperature in the tank rose from 34 degrees to 58 degrees—still not hot enough to stress the birds. Plus, the biologists had another plan: A refrigerated dairy truck had made its way to the island and was parked outside the aquarium in case the penguin exhibit got too hot. If the birds started to overheat, Whittaker and the other biologists would stuff them into the truck to cool off.

The kelp exhibit, which acted as an "ark" for many of the coldwater animals, posed another problem. Warm water kills kelp, and as the biologists watched the temperature rise, they plotted ways to keep the kelp cool.

The initial plan called for them to punch a hole in the wall and run water hoses from the refrigerated truck into the kelp tank. But no one really wanted to destroy the walls that had survived Ike, so the biologists devised another plan. They emptied frozen fish—shark and penguin food—from a 6-foot deep freezer, connected two 100-foot garden hoses, and coiled the hoses inside the freezer. They then loaded the freezer with ice and rock salt and pumped water through the hoses, into the kelp tank. It worked. The temperature in the tank rose only 1 degree over the next few days until the aquarium's electricity returned.

After five days, the water finally receded from the basement of the Rainforest Pyramid, allowing the biologists to get a first look at the devastation.

They slipped into knee-high waders and snapped on headlamps to check the animals they assumed were long dead. They trudged through a disgusting grime of mud, raw sewage, diesel fuel, and hydraulic fluid that leaked from the elevators.

In the exhibit containing the rare cichlids, a murky water line scored the tank about halfway up, but the fish had somehow lived. The biologists scooped the fish into buckets and carried them to dry ground in the Aquarium Pyramid. On later trips, they discovered even more survivors: a snake that had slithered into a fish tank; endangered turtles covered with black muck; even more snakes slipping across the grimy, oily floor.

A few of the biologists had taken training courses on rescuing animals during oil spills. They quickly set to work swabbing the dirty turtles and snakes with detergent and blotting the oil from their backs and bellies. The others went to work trapping the hundreds of surviving birds and mammals in the Rainforest Pyramid and placing them in crates and cages for transport to the dry, safe Houston Zoo and Downtown Aquarium.

They netted the brightly-colored rainforest birds and enticed the two-toed sloths down from their perches in the tree canopy by moving food closer to the ground each day. A single sloth eluded the biologists for weeks, but they finally coaxed him down with food, then snatched him. He spent his time awaiting a ride to the Dallas Zoo wrapped in a tight, fuzzy ball, glaring with one eye at the Moody Gardens staff members who walked by his new, outdoor cage, once home to tropical birds.

When crews finally cleared the causeway of debris, trucks arrived at Moody Gardens to take the rescued animals to the Houston Zoo, and then on to zoos and aquariums as far away as Fresno, California–their new homes until the Rainforest Pyramid reopened, likely in 2010. The most valuable and most fragile animals were trucked out, but quite a few remained, including the penguins.

The birds stayed in their dark tank for twelve days. When the lights finally snapped back on, they danced, preened, swam, and romped about the cage. Then they started mating. In mid-December, two gentoo penguin chicks emerged from their shells, delighting Moody Gardens staff and becoming the first of many celebrated "Ike babies" to arrive over the coming months.

■ WITHOUT RUNNING WATER, no one could come home. Public Utilities Director Eric Wilson woke up to that reality every day. Although the mayor and the city manager took the blame for the blockade keeping people from their homes, it was really up to Wilson to make it possible for them to return. Ike knocked out power to the city's water pumping stations and sewage treatment plants, submerged pumps and motors, and destroyed generators with flying debris. Wilson and his crews had to rebuild the city's major infrastructure systems as quickly as possible with what little material and equipment survived the flood.

On Saturday afternoon, Wilson sent a text message to a foreman with Boyer Construction, the company working on the new water pumping station approved by the city council months before Ike hit. Did they have a 450-kilowatt generator they could spare, and could they bring it to Galveston? Their answer came right away. They had one in Houston and could deliver it the next day. The generator could get pumps at the airport water station running again, which would at least provide water to the hundreds of city employees, firefighters, and police officers holed up in hotel row on the seawall. The airport station, built above base flood elevation, escaped the surge that overtopped pumps in other parts of town, but its natural gas generators stopped working when the gas supplier shut off service to the island as the storm approached. Wilson sent crews to close every water valve on the island except those on the mains leading to hotel row. The generator arrived at 6 PM Sunday, and 12 hours later, Wilson's crews had it hooked up at the airport and humming away.

The borrowed generator had enough power for one pump, which could push only 3,000 gallons a minute up to the seawall. But on Monday, Texas Gas Service delivered a tanker of natural gas to the 30th Street pumping station, and 108 technicians from the public works department in McAllen, Texas, arrived to help get it going again. Wilson's priority was to get water to the University of Texas Medical Branch and to the county's criminal justice center, where about 1,000 inmates sat in cells with no running water or electricity. But as soon as water started flowing, it ended up almost immediately in showers and toilets and headed back to the out-of-commission wastewater treatment plants. Unless he could get the main wastewater treatment plant running again, raw sewage would continue to flow into the Gulf of Mexico.

On Monday, a reporter for the *Washington Post* interviewed Wilson about the treatment plant woes and the generator that blew up Saturday afternoon. Wilson told him he had ordered a replacement from the U.S. Army Corps of Engineers but it hadn't arrived yet. The story made the front page of the next morning's paper, and, before noon, Wilson received a call from one of the corps' generals at the Pentagon. The story almost got the general fired, he told Wilson. The generator Galveston needed would be there tomorrow, he promised. It arrived at 2:30 AM Wednesday. Wilson's crews had it hooked up and running 90 minutes later.

Although the plant immediately regained some processing capacity, crews spent the next week removing debris from tanks and vacuuming sand out of the water-clarifying basins, which also needed new motors. A specialist had to be called to repair the disinfection system. A week later, the plant finally had full treatment capability, just in time for the water to start flowing again.

On Wednesday, September 17, the *USS Nassau,* a Navy amphibious assault ship, arrived in the Gulf of Mexico from Norfolk, Virginia, to offer several hundred sailors to aid in the recovery effort. The next morning, people driving along the seawall watched in surprise as two of the ship's landing craft drove onto what was left of the beach and unloaded trucks carrying sailors ready to go to work. One contingent headed immediately for the 30th Street water pumping station, where Wilson had just received four new electric motors and a generator big enough to send water coursing through all the mains in the city's urban core. The sailors set to work aligning the motors. Aboard helicopters, they flew parts to the ship, where the parts could be machined to fit the motors.

One week later, with the new motors in place and the generator humming in the background, Wilson's crew opened the valves, and water coursed through pipes that had been dry for nine days. Thomas and LeBlanc began planning for residents to return, and the *USS Nassau* weighed anchor and headed back to Virginia.

■ **WILLIS AND KARON** Turner, the Crystal Beach couple who rode out the hurricane on Bolivar Peninsula, awoke Saturday, September 13, and walked out onto the deck of the house that had been their refuge. As they looked around, surveying the damage, they spotted something in the bay, just past the mouth of the neighborhood's canal. "There sat the boat" just three blocks away from the house, Karon said in her characteristic southern drawl.

"Miracles do happen," she said a year later, her face breaking into a wide smile. "That's the best part of the story."

When their 45-foot stock cruiser *Faith* broke loose and floated northeast toward the Intracoastal Waterway, Karon lost sight of the light attached to the boat's hull and assumed it had either floated away or been smashed to pieces by the debris caught up in the swirling storm surge. Instead, the boat's mooring lines snagged something underwater and swung around, its lights blocked from view by the cabin. *Faith* rode out the rest of the storm wedged against a telephone pole in a marshy area between the canals in the Waterways neighborhood and the Intracoastal Waterway.

"We couldn't believe it," Willis said.

Although only 400 yards separated the Turners from their boat and the yard below was scattered with kayaks washed up overnight, Karon refused to get in the dirty storm surge that still pooled around the house.

They decided to wait until the water receded to retrieve *Faith* from her unholy resting place in the nearby ditch. After haggling with the insurance company and county officials who wouldn't allow them to use the ferry to transport the heavy equipment needed to pry *Faith* from the marsh, Karon and Willis pulled the boat from the muck and floated her to Kemah for repairs. Water had swamped the boat, and the engines wouldn't start, but the hull wasn't cracked and the boat was certainly salvageable. At first, the insurance company wanted to total it and give the Turners a check for $147,000. But the Turners knew they couldn't replace their priceless boat for anything less than $775,000.

"You talk about fight?" Karon recalled. "[Willis] was going to fight to save his boat. He wasn't going to let the insurance company give him any shit."

The Turners spent $220,000 repairing *Faith* and they were still working on her 14 months after the hurricane. They decided, from then on, that *Faith* would spend every future hurricane season docked along the Tennessee River.

When the Turners first emerged from their hurricane shelter that Saturday morning, they thought the damage didn't seem too bad. The houses around them in the Waterways subdivision were intact, minus the breakaway walls on the bottom floors. The house where they rode out the storm lost 10 shingles and everything below the second-story living quarters. They only thought about the death toll when they saw helicopters buzzing overhead. Karon realized that without cell phone service or electricity, they had no way to tell their families that they were okay. They decided to get their faces in front of as many cameras as possible in the hopes that family members would see them alive and spread the word.

The water finally receded enough Sunday for them to leave the house to retrieve their trucks and equipment from High Island. Karon, Willis, and the three others staying with them at the house, decided to move to their employee's house in Crystal Beach on the Gulf side of Bolivar Peninsula. Mike Dunn had generators stockpiled at his house, which was amazingly unscathed—"The steps were even still there," Karon marveled months later. KWT Construction, the Turners' company, built Dunn's undamaged house and the others in his neighborhood that escaped flooding. Those houses testified to the quality of their work and brought the Turners a surge of business immediately after the storm.

The Turners spent that Sunday clearing paths through the mountains of debris just so they could drive around on the peninsula. Unlike Galveston, the unincorporated Bolivar Peninsula didn't have an army of city crews to start clearing debris. The Turners, armed with their company-owned backhoe, took matters into their own hands.

They didn't fully realize the extent of the devastation around them until Sunday, when they made it to State Highway 87 for the first time. Karon couldn't believe what she saw. Their decision to ride out the storm seemed even more unbelievable.

"It was like a bomb went off," Karon said.

It struck Willis as bizarre that he could hear the waves from the highway, and then he realized that the beachside houses that once muffled the sound of the Gulf of Mexico were gone.

That evening, Karon and Willis made their way to Crystal Beach Road to look at their house on the bay side. Though it still stood, the inside was flooded with more than three feet of water. The refrigerator was in the bathroom; furniture from the living room was in the kitchen.

"We didn't take anything," Karon said later. "We were so devastated. It was so heartbreaking and we thought we'd just get out of there and never come back. That was our thinking. At least we had a house. We were fortunate. We were very fortunate."

On Tuesday, Willis asked a Crystal Beach firefighter to pass a message along to Karon's daughter letting her know they had survived the hurricane. She didn't get the message until Wednesday. By that point, worried relatives and friends had already added the Turners to the list of more than 300 missing people from Bolivar Peninsula. Knowing their names were likely listed among the missing and dead, Karon and Willis jumped at opportunities for interviews, thinking that the more people who saw them alive, the better. They did an interview with the Associated Press, which reported in a September 16 article that the Turners decided to ride out the hurricane on their "wooden boat."

"They made us look like total idiots," Karon said, chuckling about it later. "Why would you stay for a wooden boat?"

Most of their family and friends realized they were okay when they spotted Willis and Dunn on CNN. The news crew shot footage of the two working on a piece of KWT Construction machinery, and both wore shirts emblazoned with the company name. Besides, everybody on Bolivar Peninsula knew Dunn never wore shoes, so when they spotted the barefooted man on television wearing a KWT Construction T-shirt, they knew Karon and Willis survived the hurricane.

The Turners had no plans to leave Bolivar Peninsula. They had ample amounts of food, water, and fuel for the generators to power a freezer and a television at Dunn's house, where they watched news coverage of the hurricane. Their trucks and equipment didn't get wet, so they had ways to get around the peninsula. But on Monday, September 15, county officials announced that all people on the peninsula had to leave immediately. Galveston County Sheriff's deputies would escort anyone who refused. Karon and Willis were wary about turning over the peninsula to the first responders. The couple had already witnessed the responders busting car windows, cracking open locked toolboxes in the beds of trucks and jamming screwdrivers in vehicles' ignitions to get them started, all in the name of responding to what they described as a "national emergency," Karon said.

"They were like a bunch of little boy scouts going to war and having a good time and not having to answer to nobody," Willis said. "They would just tear up what they wanted to tear up."

But the Turners had no choice about leaving. They could either evacuate or get arrested. Karon, Willis, Dunn, and their other two companions drove off the peninsula Sunday, September 21 in a caravan. As they left, Karon's heart started racing and she had trouble breathing. She'd had a heart attack before, and she worried that she was having another one in the middle of a disaster zone. She panicked. She stopped a man on the road and asked him to call an ambulance. A nurse coming onto the peninsula stopped to help and gave Karon some tortilla wraps filled with peanut butter and jelly. Karon ate a few of those and began to feel better. When the ambulance arrived, the paramedics discovered Karon's blood sugar was way below normal, and they transported her to a hospital in Beaumont. Karon admitted later that she hadn't been eating properly in the days after the hurricane.

"I didn't have an appetite," Karon said later. "I was in shock or something."

■ IN THE NERVOUS days ahead of landfall, Galveston's City Council declared a state of emergency and put Mayor Thomas in charge of the city. Under the declaration, the island effectively became a dictatorship, with only one person calling the shots. Even the city manager, who normally has the responsibility for daily operations, became merely an advisor to the mayor. Thomas seemed to relish the role of shepherding her people through the island's most difficult trial in 108 years. She ran press conferences, testified before Congress in Washington, and publicly chastised federal officials for not getting aid to Galveston fast enough. Thomas seemed destined to carry on her family's history of storm response and recovery. During television and newspaper interviews, she talked a lot about her grandfather's role in the city's rebound from the 1900 Storm. She seemed determined to play the same part in Galveston's response to another, eerily similar hurricane.

It remains unclear whether the public's criticism of her reentry plan will blemish her legacy. A year after the storm, Thomas acknowledged that even some of her friends still begrudged her decision to keep them away from their homes.

"I paid a price for that," she said. "I have friends here to this day who feel that they should have been allowed to come back sooner. Their houses would have been less damaged. They could have gotten some things out and saved their furniture. But that was not the call I was able to make."

CHAPTER

NINE

ON TUESDAY EVENING, September 23, City Manager Steve LeBlanc gave angry and frustrated Galvestonians the news they had waited for eleven days to hear: The island would reopen at 6 AM the next day. Less than 24 hours earlier, the city's public works crews hooked up the last of the generators and water started flowing again all over town. It was the only thing holding back the homecoming.

Before dawn on September 24, 15 miles of cars, trucks, and SUVs lined up behind the checkpoint at the base of the causeway. When Galveston police officers finally pushed the makeshift barriers aside, the pent-up flood of residents started streaming onto the island. The constant flow of vehicles didn't stop for hours.

Most residents came prepared to clean up. They walked to their front doors wearing rubber boots, masks, and gloves. Some even donned full hazardous materials suits. But they weren't really prepared for what they saw when they forced those swollen and warped doors open for the first time. From the outside, many houses appeared undamaged. The water line wasn't even visible on some. But on the inside, refrigerators lay belly up in kitchens, mud covered the floors, and heirloom furniture was toppled. Mold coated walls, its growth fueled by so many warm days in catacomb conditions behind still-boarded windows.

Fighting despair, they wondered where to begin. Ike had battered their island and their homes mercilessly. Sure, the city had recovered from worse devastation at the turn of the last century, but full recovery now seemed almost impossible. Only 16,000 of the island's 24,000 homeowners had insurance, leaving many to wonder how they would pay for repairs. While homeowners counted the cost of rebuilding, thousands of renters and the 569 families living in Galveston's public housing wondered where they would stay while landlords repaired apartments and houses. With almost all of the Galveston Independent School District campuses flooded, parents wondered when, even if, their children would be able to return to their classrooms.

People came home determined to rebuild. Many set to work right away and never doubted they would put their lives back together. But others couldn't bear the desolation. As they stood looking at their ruined homes and drove around their broken city, they lost heart. About 20 percent of the city's residents decided they wouldn't, or couldn't, rebuild.

The rest refused to give up.

■ SUSAN PARKER AND her husband, Walt, joined thousands lined up on Interstate 45 in the predawn hours of September 24. Friends who had managed to get back to the island before they did and peek through their windows told the couple their furniture appeared mostly undisturbed. But their house on Harris Way was too close to English Bayou for them to wholeheartedly believe the good news. The Parkers pulled up outside their small 1950s-era bungalow just as the sun started to peek over the horizon, bathing the seawall with a warm yellow glow. Susan pulled on black boots and thick orange gloves as her brother walked around to the back of the house. The grass that covered their small front yard crunched as they walked across it. Susan could clearly see a water line across the front door, about three feet off the ground.

Her brother walked in first, forcing the door open with a few hard jabs of his shoulder. The damp, thick stench of mildew rolled out. Susan quickly covered her nose and mouth with the paper mask hanging by a thin elastic cord around her neck. She carried a small camera in one hand and used the other to steady herself as she walked into her living room. Walt hung back, peering through the dark doorway to see what he could.

The doctor guiding him through chemotherapy treatments had warned him against going into his moldy, and possibly toxic, home. As his wife took in the toppled television, dirty floor, and soggy couches, Walt called out encouragement.

"Darlin', I love you," he said, before heading off to check out his auto shop on Stewart Road.

While her brother walked around opening windows to try to air out the house, Susan took pictures and discovered fresh sources of sorrow in every room. Water still filled the cabinet drawers in their recently remodeled kitchen. She let out a plaintive wail after opening one and finding her mother's silver floating below an oily sheen that covered a tray full of soupy muck. Toys littered the floor of her 8-year-old son's room. She knew he would be devastated. But his friends and family had already started sending gift cards to help replace the losses. And the couple had insurance. As Susan snapped pictures of the damage, she had visions of it being repaired.

Only about 67 percent of the city's property owners could say the same. The rest, who mostly lived in poor neighborhoods, could not afford flood insurance premiums that ran close to $1,000 a year for even modest houses. After they got over the shock of seeing the damage for the first time, they began to wonder how they would pay to make repairs. Thinking back to the liberal handouts that followed the government's botched response to Hurricane Katrina, many people expected the government to foot the rebuilding bill. When they learned FEMA aid would max out at $28,800, uninsured or underinsured homeowners began to consider walking away.

The federal government eventually spent $190 million on individual assistance in Galveston County. The money helped pay for temporary housing, home repair projects, and reimbursement for lost possessions. But the 25,381 people eligible for assistance received an average of only $7,491 each, far less than most needed to replace their furniture and repair their houses.

■ THE PUBLIC HOUSING projects echoed with the creaks and groans of wooden doors splintering and giving way. All four public housing

developments north of Broadway—the oldest, lowest section of Galveston—
flooded under at least four feet of water during the storm. That first day
back, the public housing residents were forced to hack their way through
the doors that wouldn't budge because of the piles of belongings the swirling floodwaters stacked against them. They kicked at the stubborn doors
with frustration, sometimes punching holes through the rotten wood.

Some residents came home to find their doors already battered in,
courtesy of the Galveston Housing Authority. The agency sent a crew,
armed with a crowbar and a makeshift battering ram, to sweep through the
projects and smash through every door not already open so that federal
inspectors could check every apartment for damage.

When the doors finally cracked open, they revealed a scene that looked
the same at every unit: refrigerators splayed, face down, on the floor; moldy
couches propped at odd angles; a thick layer of slime coating the floor and
a rotten, sickening stench. Few people found anything they could save.
Jasmine Woods, 12, wrapped a purple Ball High School T-shirt around
the lower half of her face and, on her mother's instructions, navigated the
wrecked belongings in their apartment to save only two things: bedding
and school clothes. The stuff Woods pulled from the apartment filled half
of the smallest U-Haul truck she and her mother could find. At Oleander
Homes, 5228 Broadway, Carolyn Gamble stood outside her apartment
clutching a muddy TV remote. She said she knew from watching the news
that her home was gone, but she had to see it in person to believe it. To
her, it looked like the floodwaters had licked the ceiling. Mold, mud, and
mosquitoes covered all her worldly possessions. Although she estimated
it was all worth no more than $4,000, it was all she had. She packed some
things in a truck, but she had nowhere to take it.

People were angry: angry at Mother Nature for destroying the little
that they had in the first place; angry at city officials for keeping them away
so long; angry at the housing authority for battering in the doors before
they got there, stripping them of their privacy and exposing their wrecked
belongings like nothing more than garbage. Some residents clambered over
the flood-ravaged furniture on their first floor to get to the second floor,
where they furiously chunked clothes and trash from upstairs windows.
Deandre Womack flung wet clothes into his car as his grandmother stood

nearby, watching her grandson's rage. As he slammed the door and got in the car to leave, the grandmother asked him to lock the house. "You can't close the door Grandma—I broke the lock," he said, anger bubbling beneath his words. "They can have what's in there, anyway."

Residents stopped anyone who looked official by virtue of a badge, uniform, or tie to pepper them with the same questions everyone was asking that Wednesday morning: Where am I supposed to live? How long do I have to get my things out? Where is FEMA? Where is the housing authority? Are they going to tear this place down?

Latrice Walker, then five months pregnant, stomped toward the housing authority crew battering down doors. "What are ya'll *doing*?" she shouted. "I live here! You can at least give me some answers." No one answered her. She caught a smartly dressed, white-haired man standing nearby and accosted him with questions. John Williams, the housing authority's maintenance director, had come to supervise the battering crew. He ended up becoming a counselor that morning, the first person to break the bad news to people. "There is no housing," he told Walker. "Trust me. I lost my house on the West End. It's just really bad."

Lack of housing was a big problem for people who had nowhere else to go. The rumor making the rounds that morning was that public housing residents had until Friday—just three days—to remove their belongings. Where they would move those belongings, no one knew. Many of the residents had evacuated to shelters in Austin and San Antonio before the hurricane. They found rides back to Galveston when the buses that dropped them at the shelters didn't return to bring them home. Citing uncomfortable conditions in other shelters, they said they refused to stay in any shelters run by the city. Now, they had nowhere to go. Those who lived in apartments with friends and family, but who weren't listed on the lease, would not qualify for assistance from FEMA. Those who could find hotel rooms needed to have credit cards, and many people on government assistance didn't have good enough credit to own credit cards.

The sights of their flood-ravaged apartments overwhelmed many of the chronically ill, elderly, and disabled people who lived in government-subsidized housing. Lena Lewis, old and fragile with diabetes, stood off to the side as her relatives kicked at the back door of her first-floor apartment in Oleander Homes, until the door splintered and swung open just wide enough for Lewis' niece, Delores Young, to slip inside. Lewis waited at the door while Young shouted back reports of the damage.

"Everything's turned upside down," Young reported. "There's mud all the way through. I'm so used to your floors shining . . . This is depressing. You don't even know where to start."

Young picked her way across the slick floor and around misplaced appliances to open her aunt's front door. Lewis stepped inside, slipped on the grime in her house shoes and promptly walked out, yanking off her rubber gloves and respirator and blaming the rush of emotion on her "diabetes acting up." She clenched her fists and looked away, out over the rest of the flooded apartments. Tears, magnified by her prescription lenses, streamed down her face. Young appeared by her aunt's side.

"I need somewhere to stay," Lewis said, her voice quivering. "I can't live here."

Young grabbed her aunt's shoulder. "You know what Aunt Lena? You can't be in here. It's no good to be here."

Lewis told her niece that she was tired of being a burden. Eighteen people, including Lewis, had been living in Young's house since Hurricane Ike struck Galveston. Young had just learned she lost her job. After Ike, people who had nowhere to live moved in with relatives and friends, crowding dozens of people into tiny living spaces, straining relationships. In one case, 27 family members, including a newborn and two elderly people with heart disease, crowded into one single-family home in La Marque.

There were few things to rejoice about that morning in the projects, among all the devastation and sadness, but when something good did come along, no matter how small or insignificant it seemed, people rejoiced.

Helen Roberson, 77, was too old and fragile to climb through her flooded house, so she caught a man walking by and beseeched him to crawl through her broken home to find the pet bird, Pretty Boy, she'd left behind in the evacuation. He was hesitant at first. Some people claimed they saw a snake next door, and the man didn't want to run into any snake in Roberson's dark house. She kept prodding him until he finally relented, climbed into the sliver of darkness of the cracked door and promptly screamed. Everyone held their breath until he poked his head through the door and held out a moldy stuffed toy monkey that looked like a giant dust bunny. Roberson giggled, the man chuckled, the crowd that had materialized laughed, and then he disappeared behind the door again. After several long minutes, the crowd heard what sounded like faint squawking.

"He's still alive!" Roberson told the crowd around her. "I hear him hollering!"

The man crawled out from Roberson's apartment, carrying a cage littered with seeds and droppings and a distraught Pretty Boy clinging to the corner. Roberson broke into a wide smile. Someone in the crowd called him a miracle bird. Others nodded in agreement. A woman knelt and placed an untouched Bible next to Pretty Boy's cage. She told Roberson she found it in her devastated living room, opened to Psalm 23: "The Lord is my shepherd. I shall not want . . ."

■ As HIS FATHER recovered in an assisted living facility in Dallas, Dave Harris and his nephew made the trip down to Galveston to clean out Fletcher's townhouse and salvage his belongings. When they opened the door, the stench punched them in the nose and then the stomach. They both had to turn away to vomit. Covering their noses and mouths, Dave and his nephew snapped photographs of the apartment: The carpet was invisible below the soggy papers that covered the floor. Dark spots of mold inched up the walls and a stained mattress lay askew across the metal bed frame.

They went to work saving the few things they could from the steaming, sopping mess. They stuffed everything that was salvageable into a dozen 72-quart plastic storage tubs. "That's all he had left," Dave said.

They rescued Fletcher's guns, including his custom-made .45-caliber pistol, his World War II medals and some of his favorite books. But the piles of documents he had stacked on the floor from his days as a city councilman and civic busybody were gone. They also found the generator Fletcher Harris once bragged about to Fox News' Greta Van Susteren, when she asked how he had planned to survive when he rode out Hurricane Rita in 2005. He had never unboxed it. Near that was a case of unopened meals-ready-to-eat, or MREs in military jargon.

Dave brought Fletcher's personal effects back to Dallas, cleaned them, and arranged them around the room to make his father feel more at home. He mounted the war medals behind a glass frame and hung it near his father's bed. He framed Fletcher's Purple Heart. He hung on the wall a proclamation from the city declaring December 20, 2007, "Fletcher Harris Day," and a cap emblazoned with the words: "I Survived Ike."

But all the cheery touches couldn't hide the sadness of what Fletcher's life had become. A calendar tacked to the wall contained only one appointment for the month—an interview for this book for which he never woke up. The two sheets of paper taped above the head of his bed contained instructions for nurses feeding and changing him. His face was gaunt and pinched, and as the television blared in the background, he snored open-mouthed from his hospital-style bed.

Dave said the next time Fletcher would return to Galveston would be for his funeral.

■ STEVEN AND LUPE Rushing left Galveston just a few hours after Ike's winds died down and ended up in New Braunfels, a popular vacation spot in Central Texas. Their hotel quickly filled up with other evacuees. Most conversations struck up in hallways or next to the ice machine started with damage reports but inevitably turned to rumors about what FEMA would do to help storm victims. Some days, good rumors spread from room to room—the government would pay for everything, including their hotel stay. But on other days, the rumors fueled despair—the government wouldn't spend a dime in Galveston.

Lupe Rushing tried to block out the negative and focus on the positive. They already knew how much damage they had, and it was all insured. At least, she thought it was. But when Steven called their insurance company to start the process of filing a claim, the agent told him he only had $10,000 in coverage on the contents of his home. When he had renewed his insurance policies the year before, Steven almost eliminated the contents coverage on his flood policy. He never thought he would need it. But his agent persuaded him to keep at least a small amount, just in case he had a plumbing leak and needed to buy new furniture.

"I wanted to wring his neck," Lupe said, recalling how Steven reluctantly broke the news to her. "I was sick. We didn't know what to think. How were we going to survive? He doesn't have his boat. We have no coverage on our property. Here we are in our thirties. We've worked our whole lives to get this stuff, and it's like, it's gone."

The Rushings had only a small savings stashed away and no idea when either of them would be able to go back to work. It felt like they were starting their lives over from scratch. That's when the emotional roller coaster started, Lupe said. Although Steven kept reassuring her they would make it, she couldn't shake her sadness and fear about the future.

But the couple had no doubts that they would go back to the island, no matter how hard it would be to regain some of what they had lost. Galveston was home. They never considered living anywhere else.

The Rushings stayed in New Braunfels for a week before going back to Galveston to meet their insurance adjuster. Because Lupe worked for the city, they got through the causeway checkpoints without any trouble. The adjuster worked quickly and offered them a settlement the day after he visited their house. Unlike so many others who couldn't file claims until later, when insurance companies started realizing how much the storm would cost them, Steven didn't have to fight to get his money. While other people spent that first official day of homecoming taking inventory of what they had lost and setting aside what could be saved, Steven was taking the last of his soggy drywall and carpet to the curb and sketching out plans to rebuild.

■ TWO DAYS AFTER Hurricane Ike struck, Annette Cooper, 53, grabbed a handful of clothes from her flooded public housing apartment at Oleander Homes, 5228 Broadway, walked 20 blocks to Ball High School and hopped on a bus for San Antonio.

Cooper rode out the hurricane with her 14-year-old son. Her 70-year-old mother stayed in the same public housing development, just a few apartments down. The surge swamped the first floor of their apartments while Cooper, her son, and her mother huddled on the second floor. On Saturday, after the winds let up and the water receded, Cooper ventured out to see if she could find something for the three of them to eat. On Sunday, she walked all the way to Ball High School, where she discovered the buses evacuating people who wanted to leave, then walked all the way back to the projects to grab her mother and son.

"I told my momma, 'We got to get up out of here. We can't stay here.' We didn't have no lights and no water. So we caught that bus," she said.

The bus first dropped them at a shelter in Bandera, Texas. They hopped from shelter to shelter before Cooper enrolled in the federal Disaster Housing Assistance Program, which subsidized rent for hurricane victims. Using that housing voucher, Cooper settled in San Antonio, where she rented a two-bedroom apartment with her mother and enrolled her son in the San Antonio school district.

She never returned to Galveston to salvage the possessions she left behind in her meager apartment. She never returned for a last look at the place before the Galveston Housing Authority tore it down.

"I don't want to set foot on that ground," she said.

A year after Hurricane Ike, Cooper and scores of other islanders still lived in Central Texas, where the buses left them. While Galveston city and school officials held out hope that the thousands of islanders—an estimated 20 percent of Galveston's population—would some day come home, many, like Cooper, said they had no such plans. They refused to return because they had found better lives and better schools, or because, like Cooper, they thought that Galveston was haunted with traumatizing reminders of Hurricane Ike.

Every day, Cooper's mother called Cooper's sister to ask questions about Galveston. Cooper said she blocked out those conversations. She couldn't bear to hear stories about the island she left behind.

"I miss it, you know, to a certain point, but I don't even want to go back there, to be honest with you," she said. "That's something you never want to go through. You work hard for your stuff and you never think you would lose a whole houseful . . . I lost everything in there and I never went back to see it . . . We made it. That's all I can say."

■ As PEOPLE STARTED to clean out their houses, the streets filled with mounds of furniture, carpet, mold-covered drywall, and stinking refrigerators overflowing with spoiled food. The city's debris contractors scooped it up with small cranes mounted to the fronts of dump trucks. All of the trash ended up at two collection sites, where crews sorted it and sent it on to landfills on the mainland. The first site opened at Sea-Arama Marineworld, between Seawall Boulevard and Stewart Road, near 99th Street. Just a day after residents came to the island, the mountain of debris at the defunct water slide park had grown to more than five stories tall. The second site, in front of the Galveston County Justice Center at 59th Street and Broadway, soon eclipsed the sprawling police station, courtroom building, and jail, blocking them from view. Both piles exuded a stomach-turning stench of mildew and rotting food.

The constant debris scooping and sorting operations combined with the film of dried mud that Ike left behind covered the city with a haze that hung around for months. People who had never suffered from breathing problems sneezed, hacked, and wheezed their way through a dry spell that kept any rain from cutting through the heavy dust blanket covering the island. The dust turned out to be the storm's most hazardous legacy. After testing a dozen sites around the island, researchers from the University of Texas Medical Branch decided the "toxic" sludge coating everything didn't include enough harmful chemicals to worry about. Although hazardous chemicals likely washed off Port of Galveston property and out of area garages, they did not stay behind when the floodwaters drained back to the bay, the researchers determined.

While island residents began cleaning out their homes, local officials started to address the damage to public facilities. Port officials raced to get the waterfront cleaned and repaired so its tenants could get back to unloading ships and would not be tempted to take their business elsewhere. Bales of cotton, farm and heavy construction equipment, and several tractor trailers owned by Del Monte Fresh Fruit Co. littered the docks. Both of the port's cruise ship terminals also sustained damage that had to be repaired quickly, lest Carnival Cruise Lines decide to move its operations to a newly built terminal at the Port of Houston, where its ships docked for several months after the storm. The company had two ships at sea when Ike hit. Several thousand passengers who left their cars at lots on Harborside Drive had to find a new way home. All the cars flooded, and after a small regiment of insurance adjusters had verified the damage, tow trucks hauled them to the debris collection site on Broadway.

As soon as residents gutted their flooded houses, they started clamoring for electricity to power saws, nail guns, and sanding equipment. With the help of hundreds of crews from as far away as Georgia and New Mexico, CenterPoint Energy repaired the island's substations and most of its power lines by the time residents returned. But the company refused to restore service to flood-damaged houses unless an electrician first checked the meter for corrosion. Submerged meters might malfunction and spark fires, company representatives told increasingly exasperated homeowners. If the house required a new meter, a city inspector would have to permit the work before a CenterPoint crew would restore the power. Within days, inspection requests inundated the city's building department, which had only three inspectors. Even when the city requested help from inspectors from around the state, the waiting list was several days long, thanks in part to identical requirements from Texas Gas Service. City officials estimated at least 17,000 houses would need the inspections.

Residents soon discovered other sources of frustration as they tried to put their lives back together. Only three of the island's fifty daycare centers had reopened a month after the storm, although most working parents had returned to their jobs by then. Most of the city's traffic signals continued to blink for several months after the storm, slowing commutes and causing accidents when drivers forgot how to take turns at intersections. Mail delivery didn't resume until September 29. Until then, residents had to drive 15 miles to La Marque and stand in long lines to pick it up at a temporary post office set up in a strip mall. The island's two post offices didn't reopen for another month. Although most of the island's major retail and grocery stores reopened quickly, the dearth of employees forced them to cut back on their hours. Restaurants, also suffering from limited employees and supplies, shortened hours and cut back on menu options. Even so, islanders gratefully patronized the businesses that opened and mourned the ones that didn't. Two grocery stores, H-E-B and the Arlan's Market on 25th Street, closed permanently after the storm. Video stores Blockbuster and Hollywood Video also chose not to reopen.

Despite the setbacks, islanders continued to exhibit a resolve to rebuild and resisted the temptation to devolve into self-pity. Many homeowners penned messages of determination on the ruined belongings they had to drag to the curb. "It's only stuff" became a popular mantra, followed closely by "We will survive."

■ HURRICANE IKE SPARED most of Galveston's trees from the cracked limbs and broken trunks that a windy storm usually leaves behind. But just a few weeks after Ike's landfall, the island's majestic oak trees began showing signs that they had not escaped the storm unscathed. Ike surged ashore in the middle of a drought that left Galveston's usually moist soil dry and cracked. The storm brought very little rain to dilute the salty floodwater that saturated the ground. The thirsty trees soaked it up and immediately went into shock. The trees, normally green year round, started dropping their leaves.

Most of the large live oaks that lined Broadway and the historic streets on the island's East End dated back to the early 1900s, when islanders started a reforestation effort to replace the vegetation lost to the 1900 Storm. The trees symbolized Galveston's determination to survive, and no one wanted to lose them at a time when the city most needed their inspiration. Acting on advice from the Texas Forest Service, the city council ordered its parks department crews to start watering the trees daily. Within just a few weeks, a crew with a tanker truck dumped 168 million gallons into the Broadway medians. Forest service arborists cautiously hoped many of the trees would survive.

But by spring, only about 40 percent of the trees had started putting on new growth. The rest remained bare, their naked branches a testimony to the city's loss. In April, teams from the forest service surveyed the trees and estimated about 11,000 on public property and 30,000 on private property would eventually need to be removed. City officials immediately started to wrangle with the federal government over who would foot the bill. The Federal Emergency Management Agency would pay for debris

removal only until April 26. If Congress didn't agree to extend that deadline, the city would exhaust its reserves paying to cut down the trees, a
blow to both its finances and its psyche.

While officials fretted over how to pay for the tree removal, residents
started to protest the death sentence imposed by the Texas Forest Service,
whose experts had started to mark the trees they expected to die. Some
angry residents painted over the marks in an attempt to save the trees.
Others tied wide black ribbons around the trunks of the marked trees.
Residents wanted the city to give the trees at least a few years to recover.
Rumors spread that trees in Mississippi and Alabama didn't leaf out for
two years after Hurricane Katrina washed over them. But city officials
feared the dying trees would become a safety hazard. The city would be
liable if any of the trees fell and hurt someone.

In mid-June, Congress agreed to pay for the citywide felling. The roar
of chainsaws filled the city most of July. Crews ended up removing only
5,000 trees from public property, but the city still looked bare. Chainsaw
artists turned some of the remaining stumps into sculptures. Woodworkers, furniture makers, and specialty lumber companies carried off all the
downed trunks and limbs. Some of the wood even ended up in Mystic,
Connecticut, where historians used it to restore a 167-year-old whaling
ship. Knowing the trees would live on in the items artisans created from
their wood gave islanders some measure of comfort.

■ THE LOOTERS AND squatters who John Augelli feared would ransack
the Rosenberg Library never materialized after Ike's floodwaters receded.
But far more dangerous mold and rot quickly moved in. The historic
library took on a little more than six feet of water during the storm. The
floodwater ruined everything on the first floor, which housed the children's
collection and several meeting and conference rooms. But all of it could be
replaced. Augelli worried most about the library's nationally recognized
museum and archives on the upper floors, which contained irreplaceable
artifacts from the island's history.

While most Galvestonians tried to save what they could of their
own possessions, Augelli and other custodians of the island's treasures

scrambled to salvage pieces of the past. Ike ravaged all of Galveston's historic houses, leaving the most damage at Ashton Villa. The storm filled the genteel mansion's first floor with four feet of floodwater, submerging antique furniture and lapping at the bottoms of priceless paintings. The popular tourist attraction didn't reopen until the Fourth of July, and even then the first floor remained empty. The Galveston Historical Foundation sent everything from the flooded rooms to Michigan for restoration. The foundation expected the entire renovation to cost almost $1 million.

Other historic landmarks—the Bishop's Palace, Moody Mansion, and the Tall Ship *Elissa*—fared better, although they all sustained some level of damage. All of the island's historic downtown churches, some of which dated to the late 1800s, also took on water during Ike. The water damage was bad enough, but Ike also shattered one of the breathtaking Tiffany & Company stained glass windows in Trinity Episcopal Church. Miraculously, the church had started a window restoration project before the storm, and the company hired to bring the glass back to its glittering glory had already taken photographs of every detail of the shattered sections. They got extra help from the Broad Street United Methodist Church, in Columbus, Ohio, which had a matching Tiffany window. The Ohio congregation had recently restored its glass and offered Trinity copies of the rubbings taken of the window to help guide the restoration. In February, artisans in Minnesota began piecing together the shards carefully collected from the church floor the week after Ike blew through.

Three days after the storm, John Augelli finally got in touch with representatives from ServiceMaster, a national disaster restoration company that seemed to have secured contracts with almost all of the major businesses and organizations on the island. Their bright yellow trucks were everywhere. Augelli agreed to pay no more than $700,000 for the company to pump water out of the first floor and start blowing fresh air into the damp rooms. He also hired an air conditioning service company to rig up what was left of the library's HVAC system to start dehumidifying the upper floors. The bill for cleanup, climate control, and temporary power came to just short of $1 million.

"I was just horrified at the cost," Augelli said. "But there was no choice."

Knowing the library couldn't reopen any time soon and facing a rapidly rising repair bill, Augelli laid off half his staff. It took the remaining
librarians almost three months to make the eastern wing of the building
accessible to the public. The library reopened December 7 with access to
most of the books (except the children's collection) and a few computers
set up for free Internet access. Although the library's board members could
have opted to repair all of the building's electrical, telephone, heating and
cooling systems where they were—on the first floor—they decided instead
to move everything up. Nine months after the storm, the work still wasn't
finished, the library still operated on temporary power, and Augelli still
waited for at least some reimbursement from the Federal Emergency
Management Agency.

"I've been a bit surprised at how long it's taken to recover from this
thing," he said. "We took a more difficult path, with the repairs. But if
someone told me eight and a half months into this thing you're still going
to be on emergency power, I would have said, 'No way.' "

■ GALVESTON SCHOOL DISTRICT reopened Tuesday, October 7, even
though parts of the island still lacked electricity and four of the district's
schools remained shuttered because of hurricane damage. Although many
students no longer lived in Galveston, 4,500 children returned to class
that day in a step that islanders championed as one of the first big leaps
toward normalcy. Some traveled from as far as Houston, a 45-minute
drive from Galveston, to return to school. The district had to borrow
buses to pick up children living all across the mainland; the students
came to school without backpacks and lunch kits.

Students and teachers, many of whom also sustained damage to
their homes, spent that first day talking about the hurricane's effect on
their lives as part of a curriculum developed in the aftermath of Hurricane Katrina. The lessons are designed to help children use a natural
disaster as a learning experience. Some teachers assigned essays about
the hurricane, others showed meteorological maps of Ike to teach science
lessons. Another teacher planned an experiment using meals-ready-to-eat
(MREs). The fifth-graders in Leanne Pickens' class drew pictures of their

lives before and after the hurricane. Pickens had the students fold a sheet of paper in half; on the front, they drew three pictures of what their lives looked like before Ike. On the inside, they drew pictures of their present lives. They sketched crude crayon drawings of their homes floating in blue water, dotted with green spots of mold or engulfed in bright orange and red flames. One student drew a picture of the grave of his grandmother who died from a heart attack during the storm.

Typical classroom gossip was replaced by post-hurricane survival stories. The students talked about sleeping on the floor in family members' homes, eating MREs, learning that pets died, and attending other schools while Galveston schools were closed.

Kindergarten teacher Margie Kusnerik, who lost both her home and her school—Burnet Elementary School—in the hurricane, called it "the new normal."

On that first day back, optimism swelled almost everywhere. When asked about Galveston's future, the little boy sitting in Kusnerik's lap thought carefully then said, "They're going to knock the houses down," he said slowly. "And then they're going to build over again."

Kusnerik squeezed him in a giant bear hug.

"That's a great answer," she said.

■ THE LAST WEATHER report Crenshaw Elementary and Middle School teacher Renee Brawner heard before the power went out in Wildwood on Friday, September 12, predicted the storm surge would top out at eight feet. With their Crystal Beach house elevated 15 feet, the Brawners thought they had enough room to escape serious damage. News reports they heard on their battery-powered radio Saturday morning offered only sketchy images of what Ike left standing. According to one report, the storm wiped out everything east of the Big Store, 2385 State Highway 87 in Crystal Beach. That offered some relief. The Brawner's house sat west of the store. But the couple didn't know for sure how their house fared until one of Renee's friends at the U.S. Fish and Wildlife Service e-mailed an aerial photograph of their neighborhood. It was dotted with little white squares. Renee thought they might be blurry images of roofs

until she saw a more detailed image. The white squares in her neighborhood were nothing but concrete slabs.

County officials barred residents from returning for two weeks. Renee
knew some people sneaked back to comb through the sand and rubble
for anything the wind and waves might have spared. It felt like someone
kicked her in the gut every time she picked up a copy of the *Beaumont
Enterprise* and saw a picture of a Bolivar resident gratefully cradling a
salvaged treasure. Renee, a stickler for rules, refused to bypass the roadblocks, even though she fervently hoped they might find something of
their former life to take with them.

"It all just seemed so unfair," she said. "I kept thinking, surely there's
going to be something. It was a three-bedroom, two-bath house. It wasn't
just a little shanty. But nothing, absolutely nothing."

The Brawners came home for the first time on September 26. They
barely recognized their street and could only just make out where their
house had been. The storm scoured a deep sinkhole under what was left
of their foundation, which eventually crumbled into the water. Renee
found some silverware scattered nearby, but it wasn't hers. The sheer
volume of destruction was too much to take in. Officials later estimated
Ike destroyed nearly 3,000 peninsula homes.

"I just felt like I'd had the breath knocked out of me," she said. "You
know how it is when you're a kid and you fall on your back? I just couldn't
hardly speak."

Although the Brawners could have rebuilt, they felt the community they
loved would never be the same. The lack of leadership in the unincorporated
area also discouraged the couple from trying to reestablish their beachfront
paradise, Renee said. Separated from the rest of the county by the mouth
of Galveston Bay, Bolivar Peninsula had always been a little isolated from
its government. Many residents liked it that way. But Ike exposed the necessity for being connected and having strong representation from a local
governing body. Without it, the peninsula's needs just got lost, Renee said.

■ THE STUDENTS AT Texas A&M University at Galveston, the island's
only four-year college, had been in class for just a few weeks when col-

lege President R. Bowen Loftin ordered them to evacuate ahead of Hurricane Ike. Facing weeks of disrupted classes, Loftin decided a week after the storm to temporarily relocate the entire campus, the first such move anyone could remember for an established university. By the time city officials finally allowed residents to return to the island on September 24, roughly 1,500 Sea Aggies had already resumed their course work in College Station at Texas A&M's main campus.

The unprecedented move only added to the strain in College Station, where administrators already struggled to find housing for 48,000 students, a record-breaking enrollment. With dorm rooms and university-managed apartment complexes already full, administrators made a special appeal to students in off-campus housing and alumni living nearby to take in the displaced Galveston students.

Back on the island, school administrators quickly tallied Ike's damage at around $12 million. Most of the small campus' buildings flooded when Ike's surge washed over Pelican Island. The island is a dredge spoils site edged on its southern shore with a crescent of developable land that includes the school, a park, and several industrial sites. But the school's biggest problem was access. The approaches to the bridge connecting Pelican Island to Galveston washed out during the storm. Trustees for the Navigation District, which oversees the bridge's maintenance, made temporary repairs by September 21, but a permanent fix took months to complete.

Fed in part by fears about imminent closings at other island institutions, rumors that the school would never return to the island swirled as the Sea Aggies settled into classes in College Station. When not speculating about the school's possible relocation, jittery islanders fretted its enrollment would plummet as frightened students opted to take classes in a safer environment. But as the state's primary source for marine and maritime training and one of only six training centers for the U.S. Merchant Marine, the school's waterfront location was secure.

On December 14, the Sea Aggies returned to Galveston to graduate 106 seniors and celebrate the end of a long, tumultuous semester. When classes resumed on January 20, only 9 percent of the students opted not to return.

■ **MICHAEL RAINS, A** third-year student at the University of Texas Medical Branch, knew his rented East End apartment flooded during the storm. He knew what to expect when he finally made it back to the island a few weeks later, but knowing about the damage didn't really prepare him for seeing it. Like most of the other medical students, Rains left Galveston a few days before the storm. He packed enough clothes to get him through two weeks in Austin, where he was already scheduled to do a psychiatry rotation. Rains and the other students went through two other storm drills that summer, so by the time Ike came around, they had hurricane fatigue. Rains expected Ike to be like Edouard and Gustav, earlier storms that threatened Galveston before drifting aside. He would spend the weekend with friends and come home. He went through the motions of moving his furniture to the middle of the room, away from windows that might break, and putting his electronics and valuables on the bed and the sofa. But he wasn't really worried.

Sitting in his friend's apartment in Austin, glued to the television storm coverage all weekend, Rains kept thinking about the things he should have taken with him. Not long before he evacuated, his parents brought him all his old pictures, yearbooks, and high school memorabilia. They were cleaning out their attic and thought he should have them. He left all of it in his apartment at 19th and Church streets, along with just about everything else he owned. Although he told himself to expect the worst, he didn't know how bad it was until his landlord called him a week later. The floodwater reached six feet, ruining everything. Rains had nowhere to live and, based on the reports coming out of the medical branch, nowhere to continue his medical training.

Medical branch administrators quickly realized they could not predict when they would be able to reopen John Sealy Hospital, said Garland Anderson, executive vice president, provost and dean of the School of Medicine. The storm flooded every building on campus, including all of the support services housed on the hospital's first floor. With no patients, the third- and fourth-year students, residents, and most of the medical branch faculty had to move off the island, at least temporarily. Most found spots at other medical schools around the state. Others made arrangements for rotations with doctors in private practice, many of whom were

University of Texas Medical School alumni. The first- and second-year students, still in the classroom phase of their training, could only wait and hope the school would reopen quickly enough to keep them on schedule for their board exams in June.

Like most of his 230 classmates, Rains didn't get much time off to think about the storm or what he had lost. He started his psychiatry rotation less than a week after Ike struck and tried not to let his anxiety distract him. But he spent most of his free time dealing with the Federal Emergency Management Agency and his insurance company. Instead of concentrating on his performance, which would determine what kind of specialty he would qualify for after graduation, Rains had to worry about where he would schedule his next rotation and where he would live. Some days, learning took a backseat to surviving.

Rains didn't make it back to Galveston for several weeks, in part because he didn't get any extra time off to deal with the devastation. Ike's surge ruined almost everything in his apartment. The mold and moisture took care of the rest. It took two trips back to the island to finish hauling all of his stuff to the curb where the debris trucks could collect it. When he was done cleaning out his apartment, Rains drove back to Austin. He didn't return to Galveston for months.

"I wanted to spend as little time there as possible," he said. "It was very difficult to know that that part of my life was taken away from me. Seeing the destruction just reminded me. And the more time went by, the harder it was to think about it."

Like the rest of the third- and fourth-year medical students, Rains lived the rest of that school year as a nomad. He spent almost every month in a different hospital and a different city. For most of the year, he lived on friends' couches or in a family condominium in Houston. He carried everything he owned around with him in the back of his car. Rains returned to Galveston for one rotation, in dermatology, but it just wasn't the same.

Without the traditional support systems of fellow students and faculty, Rains feared he would not make the contacts or get the research he needed to remain competitive when it came time to apply for his residency. Toward the end of his third year, He decided to transfer to the University of Texas at Austin. He would still graduate from the medical branch, but he would finish his rotations in Austin.

The uncertainty Ike created was hard on everyone, especially the third-year students, Anderson said. Most lost their housing. Many lost everything they owned. Schools and organizations from around the state raised money to help replace computers and books, but no amount of money could save them from the disruption of their lives. Those who owned houses on the island had to take time away from studying to manage repair projects.

Rains was not the only student to leave Galveston, but most returned to the island for their final year, Anderson said. Ninety-five percent of medical branch resident physicians also returned when the hospital reopened almost a year later. Although all of the students endured great difficulty, it made them more resilient and better prepared for whatever they might face in the future, Anderson said.

"Almost all of us, sometime in our life, will have some very difficult problem to deal with," he said. "This was a real test, and a lot of people will be able to take some inner strength from the fact that they went through a real test, managed to get through it, and did alright."

CHAPTER

TEN

A SMALL GROUP OF reporters from major newspapers in New York and Washington piled out of the back of Deputy City Manager Brandon Wade's truck and looked out across a short beach littered with splintered wood, pilings supporting nothing, broken dishes, and the occasional fork. Ike had plowed over the now pockmarked neighborhood less than 72 hours earlier. Wade ferried the reporters out to the West End to give them a look at the damage there, so they could effectively communicate the island's plight. They had notebooks full of stories about the storm's destruction and the island's desperation. Their articles would have spread news of Ike and the need for assistance to millions of readers around the world.

But their editors weren't interested in hurricane stories any more.

On the morning of September 15, Wall Street awoke to the shocking announcement that Lehman Brothers, one of the nation's largest financial services firms, had collapsed. Hours later, the stock market followed suit. What started as a localized crisis sparked by bad subprime mortgages turned into a worldwide economic downturn that snowballed into a full-blown recession. News crews packed up their satellite trucks while editors in New York and Washington recalled reporters. The aftermath of a hurricane couldn't compete with a worldwide financial catastrophe.

The historic election that sent the nation's first African-American president to the White House eventually eclipsed the economic crisis in the 24-hour news cycle. Barack Obama's cabinet appointments, his strategy for addressing the nation's economic woes, and what kind of dog he would pick out for his two daughters hogged headlines for months.

Island leaders made several trips to Washington during the first few months after the storm, securing early promises of help. President George W. Bush signed emergency legislation giving Texas $3 billion in disaster relief. But the interest in Hurricane Ike ended there. Even former presidents George H. W. Bush and Bill Clinton couldn't get the nation interested in helping Galvestonians recover from what would become the nation's third costliest natural disaster.

Comparisons to New Orleans and Katrina were inevitable. Galvestonians waited for government-issued debit cards that never came. (The government chose not to revisit the debit card program because of widespread abuse of the cards after Katrina.) Officials had to beg for months for trailers for displaced residents, temporary housing that rolled by the thousands into Louisiana, Mississippi, and Alabama shortly after Katrina. Leaders also had to beg for extensions to every deadline set by the Federal Emergency Management Agency for reimbursement for debris removal and infrastructure repair. At the same time, four years after Katrina, the federal government still paid 100 percent of the New Orleans recovery bill.

The nation gave Galveston recovery money but left leaders and residents to clean up Ike's mess by themselves. Islanders felt abandoned, but they responded with the same spirit and resolve that rebuilt the barrier island 100 years before. Although no one else seemed to care whether Galveston recovered, islanders refused to give up on their homes, their businesses, or their city.

■ STATE REPRESENTATIVE CRAIG Eiland, of Galveston, started giving tours of Ike's destruction almost immediately. He mostly acted as a guide for state and federal lawmakers and bureaucrats, anyone who could funnel money to the island. He hosted numerous visits from state senators and representatives. He organized a trip for U.S. Representative Chet Edwards, of Waco, who regularly vacationed on the island with his young family. Edwards was then the senior ranking Democrat on the House Appropriations Committee, an important place to advocate for recovery money.

Eiland wanted to make sure everyone with the influence to bring goodwill and money to Galveston got an eyeful of its littered streets and saturated buildings. When producers from ABC's *Good Morning America* called a week after the storm and asked him to give a tour to one of their camera crews, he quickly agreed. The show's advance team also asked Alicia Cahill, the city's spokeswoman, for help with logistics. Cahill arranged for the crew to stage a live shot on the West End. She also helped organize a helicopter tour with Deputy City Manager Brandon Wade for on-air personality Robin Roberts, who was supposed to anchor the post-storm coverage. Roberts and Wade were to fly along the coastline to film the damage.

Good Morning America scheduled the show for September 22. But less than 48 hours before the satellite trucks would have broadcast Galveston's plight around the country, the show's producers called to cancel. The bigwigs in New York decided to stick with the story of the ballooning financial crisis, the producers told Eiland and Cahill. With banks failing and the stock market sucking retirement accounts dry, the national news programs weren't interested in hearing about a storm and a small town in Texas.

■ THIS PROBLEM OF being forgotten was nothing new to the storm-battered barrier island. Months after the catastrophic 1900 Storm, Galvestonians tried desperately to remind people the island still needed help.

First Baptist Church Pastor William Mercer Harris gave a speech to a congregation of Baptist pastors 14 months after the hurricane that killed 6,000 Galvestonians, including many congregants of both the black and white Baptist churches. Harris beseeched the state's Baptist leaders to hold up their promised end of the bargain: raise $15,000 for the recovery of the hurricane-damaged churches.

He wouldn't think the pastors needed reminding of the horrific devastation the hurricane wrought upon Galveston, he started off saying, but then he recalled a conversation he had with a "very prominent man" at the Southern Baptist Convention in New Orleans in May 1901. It was then eight months after the storm, but just days after a devastating fire in Jacksonville, Florida, that wiped out 146 city blocks, destroyed more than 2,000 buildings, and left 10,000 homeless. The fire, which came to be known as the Great Fire of 1901, is still considered the largest metropolitan fire in the south.

The prominent man said to Pastor Harris: "Brother Harris, you had a terrible time in Galveston . . . You had nearly as bad a time as they had in Jacksonville," Harris recalled in his speech.

"I said 'Yes, we had nearly as bad a time as they had at Jacksonville. There were, according to the outside estimate, 25, who lost their lives in the Jacksonville fire, and that was a terrible thing. At Galveston, there were 7,000 that went out with the tide. I think we had nearly as bad a time as they had at Jacksonville."

"Well," the man retorted. "I did not mean with reference to the loss of life, but with reference to the destruction and loss of property."

"Well, we had nearly as bad a time in that respect," Harris said. "At Jacksonville, they lost 1,800 houses. At Galveston, we lost 4,000 houses. At Jacksonville, they lost $12 million worth of property, with $5 million of insurance. At Galveston we lost $17 million of property, with no insurance. We did have nearly as bad a time at Galveston as they had at Jacksonville."

That conversation taught Harris a sad lesson, one that Galvestonians would forget 108 years later when the nation, once again, turned away as islanders set to rebuilding on their own.

"Anything like accurate and vivid memory with respect to even the greatest calamities soon fades from the minds of men," he told the gathered Baptists.

■ ON SEPTEMBER 16—THREE days after Hurricane Ike made landfall—President George W. Bush flew to the island to survey the destruction in his home state. He met with Mayor Lyda Ann Thomas and City Manager Steve LeBlanc and asked them what they needed to speed the city's recovery. He spent about 45 minutes listening to them describe the damage and reassuring them that the federal government would do everything it could to help put Galveston back together.

As LeBlanc walked with the president back to his waiting helicopter, someone else asked Bush what he planned to do about insurance giant AIG. LeBlanc, out of touch with anything that wasn't happening in Galveston, had no idea what they were talking about. U.S. Representative Sheila Jackson Lee, a Democrat from Houston, who was part of the entourage, seemed surprised when LeBlanc asked her what was wrong with AIG.

"Oh, haven't you heard?" she said. "The stock market crashed."

LeBlanc could only groan as he realized what the financial crisis would mean for Galveston and its recovery. In just a few days, islanders lost their homes and much of the city they loved. How many more would now lose their savings? LeBlanc couldn't check his own retirement account for several days. By the time he did, it had lost more than half its value.

LeBlanc added his dwindling retirement to everything else he lost that week. In Galveston, the imploding economy took second place to Ike. But everywhere else in the country, the financial crisis was the only crisis. Congress had 56,000 people clamoring for hurricane relief and 300 million begging for economic relief. It wasn't even a fair fight.

"With the double whammy of the storm and the economy, Galveston was lost," LeBlanc said. "We, unfortunately, did get forgotten."

■ HURRICANE IKE JUST couldn't compete with Hurricane Katrina. Both storms devastated historic cities on the Gulf of Mexico with widespread and unexpected flooding. But the similarities ended there. Katrina killed more than 1,000 people, the destructive power of its winds and waves compounded by human error and gross negligence. Round-the-clock news coverage of shell-shocked families searching for lost loved ones and abandoned survivors in desperate need of food and water broke the collective heart of the nation. People opened their checkbooks and gave generously. As they had after the Asian tsunami in 2004, former Presidents George H. W. Bush and Bill Clinton teamed up to raise money for Katrina victims. In just a few months, the Bush-Clinton Katrina Fund brought in $130 million.

Three years later, the presidents joined forces again to raise money for Ike victims. They visited the island on October 14, touring the city and meeting with FEMA and city officials in the morning before ending their visit with a walk on the beach. They stepped around splintered pilings and whole sections of wall torn from nearby houses as they made their way to the waiting throng of television cameras and reporters. Standing at the end of Pabst Road, its pavement and underlying utilities smashed into little chunks of plastic pipe and asphalt, Clinton declared the destruction as bad as anything the two had seen after Hurricane Katrina. But he acknowledged few people in the rest of the country realized that.

"I don't think the American people know how much you still need here," Clinton told the reporters.

Despite the challenge of capturing the attention of a nation distracted with its own financial woes and the upcoming presidential election, Clinton said he felt confident in the fund's ability to raise enough money to make a significant contribution to the area's recovery. If people could still afford to contribute to political campaigns, they could afford to donate to storm relief efforts, he said. Bush and Clinton followed their press conference with an exclusive interview with Greta Van Susteren of Fox News, who broadcast that night's show beneath a leaning beach house.

The renewed interest in Ike sparked by the two presidents lasted only a few days. Donations came in but dried up quickly. After six months, the presidents had raised only $2.2 million. By the summer, the fund's managers had stopped hoping for an unexpected influx of cash and declared an end to the fund-raising campaign. Everyone was disappointed, the fund's spokesman acknowledged in local media reports. He blamed the fizzled campaign on the dismal stock market and the pervasive fear of financial collapse.

■ DESPITE THE APPARENT lack of public interest in Galveston's fate, neither President George W. Bush nor Congress backed away from the pledge to help the island recover.

At the end of September, Bush signed a disaster relief package that included $3 billion for Texas. The U.S. Department of Housing and Urban Development funneled the money to the state, which in turn sent it to regional organizations to divide between the storm-ravaged cities and counties. The funding came in two allocations, eight months apart. Galveston got $267 million in the first round and expected to get $190 million in the second round, although federal officials still hadn't approved the allocation 18 months after the storm. The money would go a long way toward giving the city completely new drainage, sewage, and water systems. It would also help rebuild some of the damaged houses.

The federal funds gave city worker Gene Williamson hope for Galveston's future. If the city spent the money right, it could be rebuilt better than it was before the storm, he said.

After rescuing dozens of public housing residents from the rising water the night the storm surged ashore, Williamson spent the next few weeks working nonstop to clear debris off the streets, get fuel to city vehicles, deliver portable toilets, and repair damage at the water and sewer plants. Williamson's house escaped the flood, but enough water seeped into the garage to ruin all of his tools. With no help from FEMA and no insurance, Williamson had no way to replace them. Before working for the city, Williamson had owned his own locksmith business. He had planned to reopen it in his retirement, so he and his family wouldn't have to rely only on his city pension. Without his tools, the business plan seemed like a pipe dream.

But Williamson refused pity for himself and the city he passionately loved. The entire world forgot Galveston, and no one knew what it really suffered. But that didn't stop Galvestonians from rebuilding, he said.

"The people in Galveston are puttin' it together," he said. "We're all helping each other. We're not saying, 'Poor me, poor me.'"

CHAPTER

ELEVEN

AFTER THE 1900 Storm, University of Texas President William L. Prather sent word to the school's regents in Austin that the unprecedented devastation at the medical branch campus made it necessary for the school to remain closed for the rest of the fall term. The response from Regent Beauregard Bryan came by cable: The University of Texas stops for no storm. One hundred and eight years later, the medical branch's students, staff, and faculty adopted the historic telegram as their rallying cry. But, for months, it was more wishful thinking than reality.

Hurricane Ike's floodwaters closed the medical branch emergency room and hospital for the first time in history, scattered students and residents, and gave some state lawmakers the excuse they had been looking for to close the campus for good. The storm filled the first floor of almost every building on campus with about four feet of salty, corrosive surge, causing $1 billion in damage and lost revenue. With doctors unable to see patients or perform surgeries, the hospital bled cash. Administrators soon realized they would be forced to lay off thousands of doctors, nurses, and support staff, many of whom had just lost everything they owned to Ike.

In Austin, University of Texas System regents, who oversee all the schools in the system, looked at Galveston's repair bill and started to question the wisdom of investing any more money in a vulnerable facility on a barrier island. Rumors swirled that the regents intended to use Ike as an excuse to move the school to Austin, something island leaders had feared for years. Instead of sending a clear message of support, as their predecessors had in 1900, regents gave vague promises of assistance, all of which hinged on what state legislators agreed to contribute to the recovery effort. Without knowing what lawmakers would do until well into the spring, medical branch President Dr. David Callender announced on November 12 that regents had authorized him to cut 3,800 of the 8,000 jobs on the island campus. Many islanders believed the layoffs signaled the beginning of the end for the medical center, which they relied on for care, jobs, and the community's economic stability.

But the layoffs galvanized island leaders to fight for the campus. Elected officials, business owners, and residents with no direct connection to the school joined medical branch students, staff, and alumni to lobby the state legislature for recovery money and operating funds. They barraged lawmakers with phone calls and filled their e-mail inboxes with pleas for support. White-coated students spent a day in the capitol meeting with representatives from their home districts. Local legislators bargained, wheedled, and called in favors until they had enough votes to restore the medical branch to its pre-storm health. On the last day, almost at the last minute, of the 2009 legislative session, the medical branch and the island finally got the message they had waited eight months to hear: UTMB stops for no storm.

■ ON SEPTEMBER 25, state Representative Craig Eiland of Galveston led fellow legislator Tom Craddick, then Speaker of the House, on a tour of the University of Texas Medical Branch campus. They carefully walked around boxes of sodden records and plastic trash bags full of disintegrating insulation. The buildings, tethered by giant plastic tubes to dehumidifiers the size of semi trucks, looked like patients on life support. Almost all of the campus's 80 major buildings took on water during the storm. In some buildings the water line reached only three feet. In others it got closer to six feet. Campus maintenance crews quickly calculated 1.3 million waterlogged square feet, about 20 percent of all buildings.

Ike's surge inundated John Sealy Hospital's pharmacy, blood bank, oncology department, and cafeteria. It filled the basement of the hospital annex building, destroying the electrical distribution system for five buildings, including the Children's Hospital and John Sealy's operating rooms. It sloshed into 130 elevator shafts and overtopped the control center for the pneumatic tube system that doctors, nurses, pharmacists, and technicians used to distribute medicines, test results, and patient orders throughout the hospital. The disaster response cleanup crew of 400 that started pumping out water and setting up the giant dehumidifiers quickly swelled to 1,400 workers in full-body protective suits, swarming the campus to preserve as much as possible. UTMB poured $160,000 a day into diesel for portable generators to power the massive fans set up in almost every doorway. But the condensation that covered the floors and walls and filled the buildings with an eerie indoor fog soon crept up to floors that hadn't taken on any water, ruining computers and electronic diagnostic equipment.

Medical branch officials initially estimated the damage and lost revenue would come to $700 million. A year later, the figure had risen to $1 billion.

Craddick's tour lasted just 30 minutes. Eiland, a Democrat, hoped it would be enough to earn the powerful Republican's support during the legislative session that would begin in January. He already knew he would be bringing a big recovery bill with him to the capitol, and he would need statewide, bipartisan support to get it passed. But UTMB had been a political football for years. Even with a wave of storm sympathy, Eiland knew it would be difficult to get all the money UTMB would likely need to make a full recovery.

"We had been fighting the perception for years of UTMB not being justified in its existence on a barrier island," he said more than a year after he gave Craddick the tour. "Ever since Tom Craddick had been Speaker, [the medical branch] had not been funded fairly or fully."

Medical branch leaders had for years fought rumors that the University of Texas Board of Regents wanted to move the medical school to Austin, where it would be closer to the state's flagship university and, some speculated, less dependent on state assistance. Slowly starving the

Galveston campus of funding was one way to make the move a necessity, those who feared the move said.

The medical school, Texas' oldest, was founded in 1891 with a mission to treat the state's poor. Almost 120 years later, with Texas among the nation's leaders in uninsured residents, the medical branch had no shortage of poor patients needing care. Revenue from paying customers couldn't cover annual losses that had grown to an average of $20 million. Medical branch officials approached the legislature every two years to make up the difference. But lawmakers had grown tired of giving the medical branch access to so much state money. They wanted the medical branch to lobby regional governments to set up a hospital district to help offset indigent care costs, a funding mechanism used by every other regional medical center in the state. But island leaders had always counted the contributions of the Sealy & Smith Foundation, which built and owned many of the medical branch buildings, including John Sealy Hospital, as the local share of the campus funding. Galveston voters also balked at paying for patients that came from as far away as west Houston, where the boundaries of a taxing district likely would not reach. Local politicians, who knew the extra tax burden would be a tough sell to constituents, continued to resist it. For the past 15 years, as long as Eiland had been in office, state lawmakers, medical branch officials, and island leaders had maintained an uneasy standoff over who would pay the bill for the regional health care the medical branch provided.

In response to local opposition to the taxing district, the state gradually decreased its contribution, forcing the medical branch to lay off hundreds of faculty members in 2006 and start making plans to change its patient mix by bringing in more paying customers. The medical branch would have to learn new ways to operate more efficiently, Dr. Kenneth Shine, executive vice chancellor of health affairs for the University of Texas System, told angry medical branch faculty members in January 2007. When Ike struck almost two years later, many island leaders feared it would be the excuse legislators needed to force the facility to move, in whole or in part, to Austin.

■ IKE WOULD BE Dr. David Callender's first brush with a hurricane, and he had a bad feeling about it. Regents tapped Callender to lead the medical branch only 15 months earlier, enticing him away from the University of California–Los Angeles Hospital System, where he was CEO. Callender replaced Dr. John Stobo, who couldn't recover from the unpopular lay-offs and other cost-cutting measures forced on him by the state funding shortage. Callender rose to the top of a long list of presidential candidates in part because of UCLA's impressive financial turnaround during his tenure. Callender turned UCLA's $18 million annual operating loss into a $70 million operating margin in just three years. University of Texas regents had high hopes for what he could do in Galveston.

Just six weeks before his emergency operations officer made her recommendation to evacuate John Sealy Hospital, Callender unveiled his plan to turn the medical branch's estimated $35 million deficit into a $20 million profit in 10 years. His plan didn't include layoffs, something he promised he would avoid at all costs when he took charge of medi-cal branch operations the year before. But two months after he watched Ike ravage the campus that he hoped to transform into a model of fiscal responsibility, Callender was forced to recommend cutting almost one-quarter of the institution's employees in a last-ditch effort to keep from running through all its cash reserves.

"We had to think about ways we could survive, maintain campus activities, continue the cleanup and restoration, think about the cash flows associated, and get through until we could get an emergency appropriation from the legislature," he said.

Callender hoped to persuade state legislators to give the medical branch some cash to temporarily cover cleanup expenses that quickly ballooned to $120 million. He had access to only $160 million in unre-stricted reserves and very little hope of being able to reopen the hospi-tal, which normally provided more than half the institution's revenue. His counterparts at Tulane and Louisiana State University, both of which faced similar situations after Hurricane Katrina, told him not to expect FEMA funding or insurance policy payouts anytime soon. The situation was crippling, Callender said. The UT System and the state's legislative budget board offered the only possibility for short-term salvation.

Callender appealed to the University of Texas regents, system administrators, state legislators, Governor Rick Perry, and Lieutenant Governor David Dewhurst. For a while it looked like the medical branch might be able to get an emergency appropriation from the state to help stem the flow of money draining out of its accounts, but the legislative budget board eventually decided it couldn't hand out any money, even on a temporary basis. The UT System also declined to step in with a loan. No one wanted to risk emergency funds on a bet the legislature would fully fund recovery on the Galveston campus. The medical branch would have to get by on its own until lawmakers returned to Austin in January.

■ NO MATTER HOW many times they tallied the cleanup and payroll expenses, medical branch administrators always came up with the same conclusion: Without making major cuts soon, the cash reserve account would be empty before the end of the year. Within two weeks of Ike's landfall, Callender decided layoffs were his only option. No one wanted to go through more downsizing, especially those who had survived the previous three years of reductions and reorganization, said Dr. Ben Raimer, senior vice president for health-care policy and legislative affairs. Raimer had been at the medical branch since 1969, when he arrived as a young medical student. He eventually traded in his pediatric practice for a string of administrative positions at the medical branch, finally landing at the head of the legislative affairs team in early 2008. It would fall to him to coordinate efforts to persuade lawmakers that the medical branch deserved a massive cash transfusion. But until January, they had to stop the bleeding through layoffs.

"That would be the only way we could get back on our feet," he said. "That's a very undesirable thing to have to do. But given the choices, it was probably the only practical solution."

In the temporary command center set up on the seventh floor of the administration building, the debate about layoffs immediately progressed from if, to when and how. But island leaders, stunned that the medical branch would deal the community such a painful blow before it had even staggered back from Ike's pummeling, couldn't move past the "if." As soon as she heard what Callender had planned, Mayor Lyda Ann Thomas called State Representative Craig Eiland, giving him the details in what he described as an expletive-laden diatribe. After Eiland called Callender to confirm that 3,800 jobs sat on the chopping block, he called Lieutenant Governor David Dewhurst, who had just heard the news from State Senator Steve Ogden, chairman of the finance committee. Ogden, a conservative, far-right Republican from Bryan and graduate of the University of Texas' rival, Texas A&M University, seemed the least likely person to come to the medical branch's rescue. But Dewhurst and Ogden agreed that it would be unforgivable for the UT System to leave so many people jobless after all they had suffered from the storm, especially with the state sitting on a $5 billion surplus and a $6.8 billion "rainy-day" fund.

Dewhurst and Ogden persuaded Callender to postpone the layoff announcement, originally planned for October 6. But they couldn't promise the state would come through with any cash, the only thing that could prevent the job cuts. Callender, Raimer, and other medical branch administrators met with Perry, Dewhurst, Ogden, and other top lawmakers a week later to talk about options. The meeting provided encouragement but little else. Medical branch administrators left Austin without the money they so desperately needed. In an attempt to give employees some warning about what was coming, Callender announced the medical branch would continue to issue paychecks until at least November 1, eventually extending the deadline to November 14. During an October 28 visit to Galveston, Dewhurst and Ogden insisted layoffs weren't imminent, but most employees expected the announcement was.

It came on November 12, after the UT Board of Regents met behind closed doors in El Paso in a meeting that critics said violated the spirit, if not the statute, of the state's open government laws. Despite all their promises, the state's top legislators had been unable to come up with any money to bolster the hospital. The UT regents also declined to put up any cash, leaving Callender with few options. To help soften the blow, the medical branch continued to pay employees until mid-January, giving them another year's credit toward their state retirement benefits and time to look for new jobs. Dr. Kenneth Shine, then interim chancellor of the UT System, traveled back to Galveston with Callender to break the news to the medical branch staff. Most took it better than island and county officials. The layoffs would do more damage to the community than Ike had, County Judge Jim Yarbrough and Mayor Lyda Ann Thomas complained bitterly in local media reports. Thomas, usually self-controlled and diplomatic, couldn't control her anger and frustration when she confronted Shine later that day.

"I said, 'How in God's name could you and the regents, at a time like this, come down here and put 3,000 people out of work,' " she recalled a year later. "And then I said, 'You know what, Dr. Shine? You should be ashamed of yourself.' "

Most community leaders feared the job cuts would touch off a landslide of economic decline from which the island would never recover. Business owners who counted medical branch employees among their best customers started to wonder whether they should bother trying to reopen. Many feared the layoffs were just the beginning of more reductions at the medical branch. It seemed obvious the University of Texas regents hoped to take advantage of a devastated city to relocate the medical school to Austin, Thomas said. Without the school and its constant supply of students and residents needing instruction in all specialties, John Sealy Hospital likely would become a community hospital with only 200 beds. Its Level 1 trauma center, once ranked top in the nation, would be a thing of the past.

At the time, the layoffs seemed like the worst thing that could have happened. But in hindsight, that painful decision probably helped secure the institution's future more than anything else, Eiland said. The layoffs got Ogden's attention and made him a much-needed ally in the upcoming legislative session. The regents' willingness to fire people who in many cases had just lost everything to Ike raised the powerful senate finance committee chairman's suspicions, Eiland said.

"He felt, I think, that there were many ulterior motives there," Eiland said, referring again to the long-held suspicion that the regents wanted to move the medical branch off the island.

■ POLITICAL MANEUVERING AHEAD of the 2009 legislative session turned out to be just as important for the medical branch as midsession lobbying. Speaker Tom Craddick, powerful but unpopular, had maintained a tight rule on the Texas House of Representatives since 2003. A bipartisan coalition that included Eiland tried to oust him from his leadership position in 2007 but lacked the support to get it done. Voters returned 76 Republicans and 74 Democrats to the statehouse in the November 2008 election, giving Craddick's opponents the numbers they needed to send him back to the floor. Eiland threw himself into the effort, knowing that he would have a strong ally in a new Speaker if he helped get him elected.

"I always knew I could get the Democrats' support to help UTMB," he said. "What I needed was a Speaker that would allow that to happen."

House members unanimously elected San Antonio Republican Joe Straus to succeed Craddick, a promising sign for Eiland, who immediately set to work getting seats on important committees for as many friendly legislators as possible. He wanted, he said later, to make sure Galveston had friends in high places. He had no idea at the time how successful his efforts would be. On February 11, Straus reached across the political divide and selected Eiland to be his speaker pro tempore, the second-highest leadership position in the house.

But Eiland barely had time to celebrate what was a significant milestone in his political career. As he accepted the congratulations of his fellow legislators, medical branch administrators prepared to get the results of a study that they expected to set the course for the institution's future. Callender hired Atlanta-based Kurt Salmon Associates to evaluate the medical branch's financial situation and make recommendations for the optimal path to recovery.

The same day Straus appointed Eiland speaker pro tem, giving him an even better platform to lobby for the medical branch and Galveston, Kurt Salmon Associates recommended the medical branch move all its in-patient care, except what it provided to inmates in the state prison system, to League City. Eiland and local leaders, shocked by the unexpected blow, howled in protest. They immediately started a campaign to discredit the study's findings.

Knowing the fight over the medical branch was all about money, Eiland focused his critique on what it would cost to move the majority of its operations to the mainland. His arguments became the basis for the funding plan he would take to the legislature a few weeks later.

Eiland built his plan around two key financial components—investment and leverage. The $3 billion campus was too valuable to abandon, especially considering how much money both the UT System and the state would lose by doing so. The consultants recommending the mainland move estimated it would cost about $1 billion to build a new hospital and clinic facilities in League City. Where would that money come from? The medical branch expected to get about $650 million in recovery funds from the Federal Emergency Management Agency, but only $125 million could be spent on the mainland. Walking away from repairs to the island campus would mean sending about $525 million back to Washington, Eiland reasoned.

Regents also would lose the considerable investment of the Sealy & Smith Foundation, which had poured $600 million into the campus since 1922. In 1881, Texas voters approved a referendum selecting Galveston, known then as the "Wall Street of the South," as the site for the state's medical school. But when island patriarch John Sealy died three years later, leaving $50,000 for unspecified charitable purposes, the school still hadn't been built. His wife Rebecca and brother George decided to use the money to build a hospital. Their investment prompted the state to build the medical school's first building, a stately structure known as Old Red that now sits in the middle of campus.

Sealy's children, John Sealy and Jennie Sealy Smith, continued to support the hospital, even repairing it after the 1900 Storm. The siblings also built a women's hospital, which the state paired with a nurses' residence. Sealy and Smith started their foundation in 1922 with a mission to fund construction and maintenance of hospital buildings in Galveston and provide health care for the city's residents. They both died childless, leaving the bulk of their estates to the foundation. By 2008, its assets had grown to about $750 million. Previous foundation board members had grown adept at using the money at their disposal to gain influence with

UT regents, making sure they gave the medical branch the attention it deserved.

"They would give money, but they would leverage it," Eiland said. "They would leverage the money for power and position within the UT System, whether it was making sure friendly regents were appointed or whatever. Since that time, the Sealy & Smith Foundation had kept to its mission, but people in Austin and the UT System didn't know about them and took them for granted."

Until Kurt Salmon Associates released its report, the foundation had stayed on the fringes of the fight over the medical branch's post-storm future. But as soon as the consultant gave regents an excuse to move the hospital, the board woke up, Eiland said. The foundation agreed to put money into Eiland's recovery plan, but only if others did the same. Less than a month before the storm, the foundation had offered to put $125 million toward a new surgical tower that would help bring more paying patients to the island. The board of regents rejected the offer, in part because several members opposed investing any more money on a vulnerable barrier island. Under Eiland's plan, the foundation reiterated its willingness to pay for part of the tower's construction. It also offered $30 million to renovate patient rooms in John Sealy Hospital and another $45 million for other improvements.

"We wanted to show that we believed in the future of Galveston and the future of UTMB," Mike Doherty, the foundation's executive vice president, said.

The foundation hired a lobbyist to add to the pressure in Austin to support the funding plan. Doherty and other foundation board members testified before the house and senate finance committees and reminded regents their mission was about rebuilding in Galveston. They made it clear the foundation would not give any money off the island.

With the foundation's $200 million pledge and FEMA's $650 million in repair funds, Eiland hoped to persuade the regents to kick in $125 million for the new surgical tower. He also needed their commitment to keep the medical branch on the island, otherwise legislators would be unlikely to contribute anything to the recovery effort.

The regents would consider both the Kurt Salmon Associates recommendations and the Eiland plan during their March 10 board meeting. Before taking their vote, four regents held a public meeting in Galveston to gather input from the community. For three hours, the regents listened to 47 people cajole, implore, and threaten them not to walk away from the island. Almost everyone spoke in favor of the Eiland plan.

The tide of support for the medical branch, already growing daily, got another unexpected boost as the regents considered their options. Eiland feared any plan to save the medical branch would face strong opposition from two regents—H. Scott Caven Jr. and Robert Rowling. But thanks to issues completely unrelated to the medical branch, both men left the board before the end of the legislative session. The governor chose not to reappoint Caven when his term expired February 1. Austin politicos speculated that Perry wanted to punish Caven for supporting Senator Kay Bailey Hutchison, his rival for the Republican nomination for governor in 2010. Rowling, who also served as head of the University of Texas Investment Management Co., resigned after members of the senate finance committee questioned that board's decision to pay bonuses after taking massive losses in the stock market. The new regents Perry appointed to replace Caven and Rowling had much more sympathy for the medical branch, Eiland said.

When the regents met to decide the fate of the Galveston campus, they emphasized their admiration for the community's efforts to rally around the medical branch. Seeing Eiland's plan as a viable option for the future, they agreed to fund their share—$125 million for the new surgical tower. But their support hung on a commitment from the state for the $140 million needed to match FEMA's funds. They also decided to end the standoff over a hospital district while they had their chance. Before they would spend a dime on the hospital tower, the regents wanted local leaders to commit to creating a steady, tax-funded revenue stream for the hospital.

Confident that island and county leaders would not oppose the hospital district with so much at stake, Eiland turned his attention to getting the plan, now known as House Bill 6, through the legislature, an effort he felt sure would be his biggest challenge yet.

■ **WHILE EILAND WORKED** to create a funding plan the legislators could support, Dr. Ben Raimer worked to convince them the campus was worth saving. Raimer, leader of the medical branch lobbying effort in Austin, spent the first two weeks of the legislative session backpedaling to undo some of the damage medical branch administrators had done to their own recovery effort in October and November.

"We used the word 'devastated' probably one time too many," he said. "People thought 'devastating' was something you couldn't recover from. We didn't say we had a bad flood down here. It was all couched in terms of a hurricane. And to people's minds, a hurricane means things got blown down, blown away. It was Berlin after World War II or London after World War II. I think we were our own worst enemy at first in describing it as a devastated campus, because it wasn't."

Raimer realized he had to convince lawmakers the damage wasn't so bad it couldn't, or shouldn't, be repaired. He organized tours for anyone willing to take time away from the capitol to get a look at the damage firsthand. Whereas Craig Eiland's early tours focused attention on the destruction, a bid for sympathy, Raimer's tours highlighted the parts of the campus that Ike left unscathed. Instead of comparing the damage to what the New Orleans medical community experienced during Hurricane Katrina, Raimer started comparing the medical branch's condition to that of Houston's Texas Medical Center after Tropical Storm Allison in 2001. The unexpected rainfall Allison dumped over the bayou city filled streets and buildings and poured into the basements and first floors of several major hospitals, leaving behind more than $2 billion in damage. But state lawmakers never considered closing them or moving the medical center to higher ground.

Raimer also reminded lawmakers how important the medical branch was to the state's medical community. Using U.S. Department of Education statistics, he reminded them that the medical branch ranked first in the nation in graduating underrepresented minority students, first in the nation in Hispanic graduates and tenth in the nation in African-American graduates. Although the students it recruited ranked only 80th in overall grade point average, they had ranked first in Texas on the national board exam for five years in a row. Why throw that away? Why break up the team that makes that possible, Raimer asked legislators. For many years, the medical branch had done what was right, before it became politically correct, in recruiting minorities and students from poor, rural communities, Raimer said. That tradition paid off as administrators and supporters made their appeals to legislators from far-flung parts of the state who otherwise might not have cared about the school's fate.

"That was powerful to me in dealing with people like [Juan] 'Chuy' Hinojosa and Royce West, both minority senators," Raimer said. "They understood real, real quick the importance of UTMB's recovery because of that historical tradition of educating minority students."

On March 17, 120 students wearing white coats and nurse uniforms arrived in Austin to add their voices to the appeal for the medical branch. They represented the full diversity of the campus, driving home the point Raimer had made for the previous two months. They met first with legislators from their hometowns and then with House and Senate members who would connect with their life stories and experience.

Galveston's community leaders planned to follow up the students' visit with one of their own, but House Bill 6, known as the "Save UTMB bill," unexpectedly hit a snag.

The bill, which passed out of the House Appropriations Committee with unanimous support, would have given the medical branch $300 million in recovery funding, $50 million shy of Eiland's goal. But the bill drew on money in the state's "rainy-day" fund, a move unpopular with Republicans who otherwise wanted to support Eiland's efforts. Sensing either defeat or a bloody battle if he continued to push his bill forward, Eiland set it aside and started looking at alternatives.

The new relationships he had fostered with the state's Republicans, including the governor, proved invaluable. Although Perry had been in office for nine years by the time the 2009 legislative session rolled around, Eiland admitted he had not spent much time building rapport with the governor. Until Ike struck, he viewed the head of the opposition party as an adversary. But Perry seemed genuinely interested in helping the medical branch and Galveston recover. Eiland started meeting with the governor every two weeks, giving him updates on recovery progress. Those chats eventually overflowed to other issues, and as Eiland's leadership role expanded, Perry looked to him for analysis of debates in both the House and Senate. Eiland spent so much time in the governor's office he had his own chair, a spot reserved for him no matter how large the gathering or who else attended. Eiland and his family, temporarily living in Austin until their Galveston home could be repaired, even started attending church with the Perrys.

A week after he had hoped to see House Bill 6 passed, Eiland struck a deal with Perry and Straus to roll most of the medical branch funding measures into the House Appropriations Bill, which would pull the money from the state's general fund. More than 200 islanders drove to Austin on April 16 to witness the vote. Almost filling one side of the gallery, they sported buttons that said, "UTMB: We stop for no storm."

Many feared the vote would be close, but when legislators pressed the buttons at their desks, only five lights on the vote display board glowed red. The bill passed 141–5. The Galveston delegation roared.

Steve Ogden led the charge for medical branch funding in the Senate, where some measures had to be shuffled around to win support. The supplemental budget that passed May 27 included only half of the money the medical branch needed. After consulting with Eiland, Ogden suggested the other half could come from tuition revenue bonds, which would not cost the state anything to issue and therefore wouldn't encounter much opposition. Eiland declared himself satisfied with the solution, but legislators had little time left to merge the two main budget bills and get the reconciliation bill passed by both chambers before the end of the session on May 31.

The budget bill passed in plenty of time, securing for the medical branch $150 million in recovery funding to be used to match the FEMA reimbursement, and $566.5 million in general revenue funding, $109 million more than it got for the previous two years. But with legislators distracted by a last-minute fight over new voter registration laws, time ran out for the budget reconciliation bill, leaving the medical branch without the $150 million in tuition revenue bonds for the surgical tower. The only way to resurrect the bond package was to tag it onto House Bill 51, a measure drafted and championed by Dallas Representative Dan Branch to provide university research funding.

For three days, the last of the session, Branch resisted any effort to modify his bill. He had worked on it all session and was reasonably sure it would pass as written. With an added and unrelated measure tacked on, the bill might hit a snag in the Senate. From his perch in the gallery, above the House floor, Raimer watched one member after another approach Branch's desk to whittle away his opposition. To help make Branch more comfortable, Eiland and Raimer took the bill, with the bond package attached, to the Senate, where Judith Zaffirini secured the five conference committee votes needed to guarantee its passage in that chamber. Assured of the Senate's support, Branch relented and agreed to add the medical branch bond to the bill.

With less than five hours left in the session, Eiland and Raimer thought they had just squeaked by. But because Corpus Christi representatives didn't think Branch's bill included enough money for the Texas A&M campus there, they tried to block its passage. Raimer immediately got on the phone to UT System administrators, who called their counterparts at the Texas A&M System and persuaded them to back off. The Corpus Christi delegation withdrew its objections, but the bill still had one opponent who didn't seem at all inclined to back down. Angered that the University of North Texas didn't get as much from the bill as she thought it should, Representative Yvonne Davis, of Dallas, was withholding her support.

In a last-ditch effort to save the bill, Raimer called Murry Matthews, legislative director for influential African-American legislator Al Edwards, of Houston. As the son of Galveston's former city manager, who then worked for the medical branch, Matthews had a keen interest in seeing the bond package pass. He called Edwards and asked him to talk to Davis.

It was 10:30 PM.

As Raimer watched from the gallery, Edwards approached Davis and put his arm around her shoulders. Raimer could see her nodding as Edwards talked. As soon as he walked away, Davis approached the Speaker's table and withdrew her objection, clearing the way for a vote. Edwards later told Raimer he urged Davis to understand that it was not her night. If she hoped to have another night in the future, she would gracefully walk away from a fight that gained her nothing.

Thirty minutes after Davis withdrew her objection, a group of legislators surrounded the podium for the bill's reading. Eiland stood at Branch's side. The rest of the group included Democrats and Republicans from all over the state. Their presence sent a message to the rest of the representatives—don't you dare vote against this bill. Only four members did.

"It's just funny how individuals made so much difference," Raimer said six months later, as he looked at a picture of the group taken just before the vote.

Against all odds, the medical branch got everything it asked for at the beginning of the legislative session. In five months, the combined efforts of legislators, administrators, and supporters pulled it back from the brink. Eiland acknowledged later he didn't really think everything would go so well.

"It wasn't free and easy, but we got everything we needed and asked for," he said. "It was a remarkable deal how it all ended up."

■ As soon as Eiland's battle for the medical branch ended, County Judge Jim Yarbrough's began in earnest. Both the UT Board of Regents and the legislature made money for the new hospital tower contingent on the creation of a taxpayer-funded revenue stream. Technically speaking, that meant the county had to find a way to fund indigent medical care for families and individuals making 100 percent of the federal poverty level. Before Ike, the county funded medical care only for residents who earned up to 21 percent of the poverty level, the minimum contribution required by state law.

County commissioners all said they supported creating a hospital district to come up with the money, although they made it clear they still believed the Sealy & Smith Foundation contributions should count toward the lack of local tax money going to the hospital. But the legislature had the county over a barrel. Without the hospital district, the new tower wouldn't be built. Without the new tower, the medical branch didn't have enough room to return John Sealy Hospital to its pre-storm, 550-bed strength. Patient rooms on the upper floors had to make way for the pharmacy, blood bank, and other vital services moved from the first floor to prevent future flooding. The new tower offered the only guarantee the medical branch wouldn't downgrade to become the state's only community medical college, County Judge Jim Yarbrough warned during a heated workshop meeting in August.

Yarbrough didn't think the county could afford not to form a hospital district, but he didn't like it. And he knew voters wouldn't like it either. County commissioners had to agree to put the hospital district on the ballot in November, but it was up to voters to decide whether they wanted to tax themselves to help pay for the medical branch's restoration. Galveston residents probably would approve the new taxing entity, but it would be a much harder sell in the north county, where more conservative residents opposed tax increases in general. The vote would be close, and Yarbrough knew the measure had a good chance of failing, which would erase any lingering sympathy among state lawmakers for the medical branch and the Galveston community.

Just weeks before the deadline to order the election, Yarbrough decided he couldn't risk it. He and a majority of the four commissioners decided instead to raise property taxes. Because storm damage lowered home values, commissioners could raise the tax rate without increasing most homeowners' tax bills. Conservative activists might oppose the county's decision to raise taxes, but they couldn't do anything about it at least until the next election.

■ MEDICAL BRANCH SUPPORTERS, including Yarbrough, fully expected the UT System regents to move forward with plans to sell the revenue bonds and build the new tower as soon as the legislature's demands were met. But the regents hesitated. They wanted to see whether the medical branch would still have legislative support, and funding, in 2011. Until then, they refused to commit to the new hospital tower. The delay and apparent waffling frustrated people who depended on the medical branch's return.

Eiland, acting as a liaison between the community, the regents, and the legislature, tried to strike a conciliatory note. Based on past funding problems, he could understand the regents' reticence. But he assured everyone he fully expected legislative support for the medical branch to hold steady. At the same time, he urged regents to move forward with as much building as they could afford, to help ensure lawmakers' commitment.

"What I want is to have so much construction, so much investment in UTMB, that they can never turn away again," he said.

Eighteen months after Hurricane Ike, the regents had yet to approve their portion of the funding for the new surgical tower, and medical branch administrators still hadn't figured out where to move the first-floor clinic and office spaces flooded during the storm. John Sealy Hospital and its emergency room were open, although not with the same number of beds or quite the same level of care. The inpatient psychiatric facility at Rebecca Sealy Hospital remained closed, but Shriners Hospital for Children, a nationally recognized burn treatment center, had reopened. Full recovery for the island's medical community would take much longer than most people wanted. But the medical branch was on the mend, something that seemed impossible in the weeks following the storm.

CHAPTER
TWELVE

GENELL SIMMONS SAT sobbing on the curb outside a shelter set up under a large white tent. In her lap she clutched a Ziploc bag full of papers and medicines. Hot tears rolled down her puffy face. The 58-year-old woman tugged at the neck of her white T-shirt, trying to shield her pain from the people gaping at her from behind the chain-link fence that surrounded the Red Cross facility.

Simmons' apartment in the public housing developments flooded during Hurricane Ike. The Galveston Housing Authority condemned the property and threw up a tall fence around the complex, leaving Genell and her husband, James, homeless. In late October, more than a month after the hurricane, the two walked to the temporary tent city shelter, set up in an elementary school playground, in search of somewhere to stay. Shelter officials turned them away at the gate because they had stopped accepting new refugees several days earlier. Deflated and hopeless, Genell fell to the curb and cried.

Like thousands of other Galvestonians, the Simmons had nowhere to go after Hurricane Ike flooded them out of their homes. Ike damaged at least three-quarters of the island's residences and almost all of its apartment complexes. Hotel rooms and apartments from Galveston to Houston quickly filled with displaced residents and recovery workers. The Red Cross provided temporary shelter in the tent city until federal funding dried up in late October. All but about 200 people managed to find somewhere to stay by then. The state shuffled the remaining refugees into a new shelter operated at Scholes International Airport by a statewide social service agency. It remained open only long enough for case managers to get residents into more permanent living arrangements.

The Federal Emergency Management Agency insisted that the island and surrounding communities had plenty of rental properties available to house the displaced. But Galveston landlords complained that they couldn't fix their damaged buildings because they were still fighting with insurance agents or stuck in long lines to obtain city permits for repair work. By the time the weather started to cool, only a handful of apartments had vacancies each week and rent skyrocketed. With housing options scarce, city officials asked hundreds of islanders still waiting to come home from shelters in Austin and San Antonio to stay put. Although Mayor Lyda Ann Thomas publicly pleaded with the Federal Emergency Management Agency to give Galveston 500 two-bedroom trailers for its neediest residents, it took the agency six months to provide just 54.

Hundreds of islanders celebrated Thanksgiving and Christmas in hotel or motel rooms subsidized by FEMA. It was a miserable existence. Entire families slept in single bedrooms. They cooked dinner in microwaves while their children played in parking lots. Every time an assistance deadline approached, the federal government threatened to toss them out. When FEMA did finally stop paying for hotel rooms, people who still had nowhere to go were shepherded into a federal housing program that subsidized rent for hurricane victims. But problems plagued that program too.

A year after Ike swept islanders out of their homes, about 20 percent of the city's population had not returned. Many who had didn't know whether they could afford to stay. Moving to other communities proved to be a blessing for some, especially those who had a hard time finding work on the island. But not everyone rejoiced at the city's changing population and demographics. Ike hastened the island's transformation into a resort community, a change resented by many who hoped to see Galveston return to its roots as a thriving port and industrial town. With blue-collar jobs scarce and housing costs increasing, few besides retirees, doctors, researchers, lawyers, and people looking for vacation property could afford to live in Galveston.

■ EVEN BEFORE ISLAND residents came home to find their houses unlivable, city officials knew Galveston faced a serious housing shortage. The storm flooded 75 percent of the island and took a heavy toll on its rental properties. Although only the first floor of most apartment complexes flooded, management companies kicked residents out of second- and third-floor units, too, so that repair crews could work unhindered. Most of the complexes that didn't flood sustained heavy wind damage. The gaping holes in their roofs allowed the scant rain Ike did bring to saturate otherwise undamaged apartments. And when the Galveston Housing Authority condemned four public housing developments reserved for the island's poor, it left 569 families with nowhere to go.

The Federal Emergency Management Agency tried to soothe fears about housing scarcity by assuring islanders flooded out of their homes that the government would put them up in hotels until they could find somewhere more permanent to stay. Agency officials working from a state emergency operations center in Austin insisted that communities near Galveston, including Houston, had enough hotels to accommodate everyone who needed a room. But less than two weeks after the storm, the 35 hotels closest to the island all had "no vacancy" signs hanging in their lobby windows. And only 2 percent of Houston's hotels had vacancies. Some islanders had to go as far away as Katy, on the west side of Houston, to find a room.

Mayor Lyda Ann Thomas asked FEMA to set up temporary mobile home parks for displaced residents, but officials refused. Expansive trailer parks set up in Louisiana and Alabama after Hurricane Katrina remained open more than two years later. Agency officials did not want to get stuck with another long-term housing program in Texas.

Left with few options to offer residents who came home to houses caked with mud and covered in mold, Thomas and City Manager Steve LeBlanc scrambled to open a shelter that would at least keep islanders off the streets. With so much of the city crippled, LeBlanc hoped to keep the shelter on the mainland, where residents would at least have access to open stores and some semblance of normalcy. But neighboring communities all declined LeBlanc's requests for assistance, as did the operators of both of the city's convention centers. LeBlanc told reporters both buildings had too much storm damage that needed to be repaired. Critics charged that neither Moody Gardens nor Landry's Restaurants, which operated the facilities, wanted to turn them over to the island's destitute. Representatives from both companies denied the accusations. Landry's officials claimed they wanted to reopen the center to conventions, which would help boost the island's economy, as soon as possible.

LeBlanc finally asked the Red Cross to set up a temporary shelter under a massive tent pitched behind Alamo Elementary School on 53rd Street. The tent, similar to those used by the army in Iraq, could hold as many as 500 people, each one getting a cot and about 170 square feet of semi-personal space. It would never be considered luxury accommodations, but it beat sleeping on the street or in mold-infested houses, LeBlanc said.

The shelter opened on Thursday, September 25, the day after the island reopened to residents. That night, 42 people came through the gate. By Sunday, that number had ballooned to 210, and people just kept coming.

The Red Cross maintained a tightly controlled environment and restricted media access beyond the gates, unless reporters gained permission from officials who hovered by their sides during the entire visit. Shelter residents, who wore paper identification bracelets at all times, had to check in at the shelter's only access point every time they entered or exited the tent. Even with the sparse conditions, few people found reason to complain. The charitable organization provided hot showers, served meals three times a day and offered a place for people to do their laundry. Some shelter residents returned to the tents only to sleep while other Galvestonians visited only during the day to rinse off under hot water or wash their dirty clothes.

Before the Galveston school district reopened, a team of teachers organized daily visits to the shelter to give children the sense of normalcy of regular schooling. On three cafeteria-style plastic tables in the shelter canteen, students of all ages studied together, read books, played games, and colored. Louise Powell was in charge of the teachers hired at the beginning of the school year to work at the district under a federal grant that provided tutoring and after-school activities for children in high-poverty or low-performing schools. Powell called the shelter tutoring sessions the "hurricane school" or "the school without walls." Her teachers planned before the storm to start tutoring sessions to help struggling students; instead, the teachers, many of them new to Galveston, found themselves working at a tent city in the aftermath of a hurricane. The tutoring sessions made it possible for students in the shelter to keep up with their studies while the schools were closed. But they also gave parents a chance to clean out their homes, trek to La Marque to get their mail, meet with insurance adjusters, and run errands, without further exposing their children to the island's problems.

The Red Cross Shelter quickly filled with people who had evacuated before and after the hurricane to shelters in Austin and San Antonio. Hundreds of Galveston residents, mostly people who lived in public housing, boarded buses hours after Mayor Lyda Ann Thomas ordered the mandatory evacuation on Thursday, September 11. They spent the first few chaotic days sleeping on the floors of school basketball courts until cots arrived. Then they moved to the Austin Convention Center where they waited on friends and relatives to provide news about Galveston. They carried a few belongings with them in trash bags; after the hurricane, that was all many people had left. Some returned on buses to Galveston after the Austin shelters closed; some caught their own rides back. They said they were anxious to return, but when they arrived in Galveston, they discovered they had nothing to come home to.

LeBlanc expected to need at least two more tents to shelter residents who had nowhere else to go, but in the end, only 450 people checked into the shelter on its busiest night. Most of them came from the city's public housing developments. Two of the six properties managed by the Galveston Housing Authority escaped major storm damage. The mid-rise residential towers reserved for the elderly and disabled remained open. But four other properties, home to 569 of the island's poorest families, had major damage. Housing authority officials condemned Magnolia Homes, Cedar Terrace, Palm Terrace, and Oleander Homes. Officials ordered tall chain-link fences installed around all four properties and gave residents two weeks to claim any belongings they left behind.

Tensions between shelter and neighborhood residents quickly grew. Less than two weeks after the shelter opened, a homeowner shot a shelter resident he claimed had trespassed onto his property and refused to leave. The man wasn't seriously injured, but the incident alarmed city officials, who feared riots would break out if the shelter stayed open. Three days after the shooting, LeBlanc announced the shelter would close on October 26, when the federal government stopped paying its operating costs. But faced with the likelihood that many shelter residents would end up on the street, LeBlanc appealed to the state's Division of Emergency Management to open a new shelter. This one, operated in a tent set up at Scholes International Airport by the National Guard, stayed open for three weeks. Case managers for Baptist Child and Family Services, a nonprofit organization with state contracts for disaster response, helped all 300 people who first checked in find new places to stay before the shelter closed on November 10. If people thought the Red Cross shelter was tightly regulated, the Baptist-run facility was even more restrictive. Curfews and rules were strictly enforced, and anyone caught violating either one was forced to leave. When the shelter finally closed, people were more than ready to get out.

■ FRANJETTA JONES MANAGED to get a hotel room in Galveston in early October. She had a voucher from the Federal Emergency Management Agency that paid for the small room she shared with her two children, but she didn't know how long the money would last. Federal officials initially said the free hotel stays would end on October 11. The agency extended the deadline for two weeks just days before its expiration. Families who had nowhere else to go prayed the deadline would slide again, but officials continued to insist people needed to find more permanent accommodations.

On October 27, hundreds of the 1,474 displaced residents staying in Galveston hotels found eviction notices taped to their doors. Latina Vallery escaped the October evictions but got her notice early on November 13. The manager of the Super 8 motel, where she had lived for the last month, told her she had to be out by 11 AM. Vallery planned to keep her room for another week. By then, her landlord promised to finish repairs on the house she had rented before the storm. While she frantically shoved her few possessions into bags and prepared to leave, Vallery called her FEMA caseworker to find out why she had been disqualified for assistance.

Hotel managers, alarmed at the number of people suddenly disqualified, also called the agency to find out what had gone wrong. But federal officials didn't take a closer look at the problem until Mayor Lyda Ann Thomas called the regional coordinator and demanded an explanation. The notices turned out to be a mistake. Vallery and others finally got word at 9 PM that night that they could return to their rooms. Thomas publicly criticized the agency for the last-minute evictions and errors that only added to islanders' stress. During a meeting with David Paulison, the agency's top administrator, she strongly suggested the agency give people more notice before kicking them out of the only shelter they had.

In late October, the U.S. Department of Housing and Urban Development started issuing Disaster Housing Assistance Vouchers to help cover rental costs. The temporary housing program, administered by the Galveston Housing Authority, was supposed to last 18 months but, as expected, the federal government extended the program at the last minute.

At first, the vouchers covered the entire rent payment, as long as it fit within federal rental rate standards. But after six months, the vouchers decreased by $50 each month until the renter eventually paid the entire bill. By the start of 2010, most people who could afford monthly rent payments were dropped from the DHAP program, but almost 2,000 Galveston County families continued in the program. Those so-called hardship cases, people whose meager incomes couldn't cover the rent of the apartments in which they were living, didn't have any other viable options for affordable housing. Some of the families came from the demolished public housing developments.

With each new voucher it issued, the housing authority provided a list of rental properties available on the island. But families looking for new homes found flood-damaged floors and carpets that hadn't been replaced, broken windows, missing drywall, and rusted appliances in many of the available properties. Overwhelmed by the number of units opening each week, housing authority officials stopped mandating interior inspections, which allowed unscrupulous landlords to skimp on storm repairs. Despite the substandard conditions in many properties, desperate families snapped them up.

Not all landlords agreed to accept the housing assistance vouchers, equating the program and its participants with standard, income-based housing programs. To help weed out the "riffraff" and recoup some of their storm repair costs, some landlords agreed to take the vouchers but required tenants to pay large security deposits not covered by the assistance program. Others jacked up the rent so high the voucher only covered part of it.

As landlords finished repairs and more apartments and houses became available, the skyrocketing rent started to come down to more reasonable levels. But few properties could be rented at their pre-storm rates. To increase the number of properties available to storm victims participating in the rental assistance program, the federal government set voucher values higher than the island's average rent. Tenants could pay the rate increase, as long as the program continued. When it ended, the island's renters, which made up more than half of the pre-storm population, found themselves paying more for housing than many of them could afford.

■ WHILE RESIDENTS STRUGGLED to find affordable housing, City Manager Steve LeBlanc and Mayor Thomas continued to ask the federal government for mobile homes, requests put off with a variety of excuses. FEMA officials at first said the mobile homes could not be installed in a flood zone. When they finally gave in and overruled that policy, it took another three months to find land suitable to hold a large group of trailers. They wanted to put 140 trailers in front of the Galveston County Justice Center. But county commissioners nixed the plan in late November, claiming a developer had expressed interest in buying the property. But several commissioners also said a trailer park at the justice center, with its prominent Broadway frontage, would not project a positive image to island visitors.

FEMA also had to abandon several proposed sites on the mainland after community leaders refused to allow the trailers to be installed.

La Marque Mayor Larry Crow said his city needed to take care of its own first. And Hitchcock Mayor Lee Sander said he feared once the trailers arrived, they would never leave. The agency finally got permission from the Galveston Independent School District to install 54 trailers on a soccer field at 83rd Street and Stewart Road. But the temporary trailer park didn't open until March 12, six months after the storm. Although 961 families remained in hotel rooms paid for by the federal government, only 29 qualified under the agency's rules to move into the trailer park. The rest of the trailers remained vacant until October 2009, when FEMA started removing them.

Thomas described dealing with the federal agency, with its rigid policies and cumbersome requirements, as one of the most frustrating aspects of the island's recovery. Wading through bureaucracy took too much time, she said. After its muffed response to Hurricane Katrina, the agency viewed Ike as an opportunity to do things right.

"And doing it right meant that it took [an] even longer time to help our people than I think was necessary," Thomas said. "Because if you remember, after Katrina, hell, the government gave all those FEMA workers credit cards. By the time they got here, they had a bad reputation. So they were trying to clean up their act, and in doing that, they took an inordinate amount of time in Galveston to get the money flowing to us."

■ WHILE DISPLACED RESIDENTS struggled with ever-shifting deadlines and confusion over hotel rooms and shelters, conflict simmered over what to do with damaged public housing units. By the time it reached a full boil, it would expose a ferocious racial tension that surprised many who proudly proclaimed Galveston as a tolerant city.

On September 23, the Galveston Housing Authority condemned all four public housing projects set aside for poor families. Harish Krishnarao, the authority's executive director, promised that none of the residents would be permanently displaced. But more than a month after the storm, he couldn't say when, or if, the damaged properties would be repaired.

Federal inspectors didn't visit the sites to assess the damage until the end of October. Two weeks later, Krishnarao told the authority's board of trustees that the damage would cost about $14.5 million to repair. But he would not say when the rebuilding would start. Public housing residents anxious to come home couldn't understand why Krishnarao continued to be vague about his plans for the local agency charged with providing housing for the city's most vulnerable residents. African-American community leaders began to suspect Krishnarao wanted to tear down the damaged developments and replace them with single-family homes. Such a move could drastically alter the demographics on the island's north side and dilute the voting strength of a district designed to elect an African-American representative to city council. It would also leave some families with no place to live.

According to housing authority statistics, more than a third of the island's pre-storm population of 57,000 lived in poverty. Eighteen percent of city residents lived in extreme poverty, earning less than $10,000 a year. About 2,200 families received federal housing subsidies before the storm, with another 1,676 on a waiting list. After Ike's three-pronged attack on the poor—rising rents, job losses, and unexpected expenses—local social workers feared the need for assistance just to sustain daily life on the island would only grow.

At the end of November, Krishnarao finally admitted he intended to emulate Biloxi, Mississippi's post-storm rebuilding plan, using federal tax credits to replace the damaged developments with new, mixed-income communities. Biloxi's strategy included a homeownership program that swapped out public housing rental units for single-family homes, just as Galveston's north side community leaders feared.

Desperate to slow Krishnarao's plans and get public housing residents home, making it harder to displace them later, community activists appealed to U.S. Representative Sheila Jackson Lee, of Houston, for help. Jackson Lee, known for her affinity for media attention, swooped down on the island on December 3. Although she had no constituents in Galveston, she announced the formation of a task force of pastors and community leaders who would work to shape the future of the north side, including the resurrection of public housing. Jackson Lee pointed to New Orleans, where officials demolished all but one public housing development after Hurricane Katrina, and said she did not want Galveston to share the same fate. Playing to a crowd of supporters waving signs and shouting encouragement, Jackson Lee announced she had convinced Krishnarao to agree to repair two of the four damaged developments to provide temporary housing for displaced residents. The other two developments could be rebuilt, and once residents in temporary situations had new homes, the first two developments could be addressed.

Although Krishnarao emphasized the added cost of repairing buildings that might eventually be torn down to make way for new developments, he moved forward with the Jackson Lee plan. Housing authority board members agreed at the end of January to demolish Oleander Homes and Palm Terrace and temporarily repair Cedar Terrace and Magnolia Homes to bring displaced residents home as soon as possible.

The demolition plans hit a snag in early March when Lone Star Legal Aid, an advocacy group that offers free legal services to the poor, filed a complaint with the U.S. Department of Housing and Urban Development. The complaint alleged the housing authority wanted to circumvent the federal process for demolition and use emergency procedures instead. Lone Star Legal Aid wanted to make sure Krishnarao's rebuilding plan didn't reduce the number of public housing units available to residents who couldn't qualify for a homeownership program. Although Krishnarao denied claims he wanted to avoid federal scrutiny, he agreed to include the same number of apartments in the rebuilding plan if Lone Star Legal Aid would withdraw its complaint. The group agreed.

By mid-March, more than 100 families had signed up for one of the remodeled apartments at Cedar Terrace. On March 24, Krishnarao asked the Galveston City Council for $60 million to help fund his rebuilding plan, which included replacements for all damaged public apartments and about 2,000 new townhouses, duplexes, and single-family houses. The plan had unanimous support from the housing authority's board.

Any broad community support Krishnarao might have had for rebuilding public housing vanished after that meeting. An online petition started by the housing authority's opponents quickly attracted more than 2,000 supporters. In comments on the petition web site, they labeled public housing residents as drug dealers, prostitutes, and lazy mooches living off hardworking taxpayers. They blamed public housing residents for the island's crime, bad schools, and shabby appearance. The rhetoric soon turned racist.

Anxious to stem the tide of opposition that threatened to sink all his plans, Krishnarao returned to the city council two weeks later and said he probably would need only $30 million of the city's federal disaster recovery money. But he stuck by his claim that the island needed to quadruple its subsidized housing. Krishnarao got a lukewarm reception from the council and a warning from the city's planning department. The housing authority did not consult the city before agreeing to repair two of the damaged housing developments. Had the housing authority done so, it would have learned that it had to meet the city's requirements for rebuilding in a flood zone: Repairs to any structure could not exceed half of the structure's value. Otherwise, the property would have to be demolished. Krishnarao was stuck.

On May 1, unable to stand the heat of fierce public opposition, the housing authority board abandoned plans to build any new subsidized housing on the island. The agency's agreement with Lone Star Legal Aid required it to replace all 569 storm-damaged units, but it would not make plans for new units. Although the board agreed with Krishnarao's assessment that the proposal for additional housing had become an unnecessary distraction, several members abandoned it reluctantly. Housing authority Commissioner Raymond Lewis made it clear he intended to raise the issue again. "I just want to make sure this is not off the table until the end of time," he said.

Two months later, the housing board had to backpedal again on rebuilding plans after the city's planning department decided the two damaged developments could not be repaired unless they were elevated to meet current building codes. Although all other housing in the city had to meet the same standard, public housing supporters accused the city of blocking attempts to bring the poor back home. Lewis tried to put a positive spin on the setback, telling former residents the rebuilding process might move faster with all four of the developments being constructed at the same time. The board pledged to do its best to have the new housing ready in 18 months.

Without opposition, they might have met that goal.

Energized by their success at getting the agency to back away from plans to increase public housing beyond the four developments, opponents went on the attack. They accused the agency of mismanaging properties before the storm, allowing them to become magnets for crime and disruptive behavior. They questioned the wisdom of rebuilding any public housing in a place so vulnerable to hurricanes and floods. Surely public housing residents would be better off farther inland, safe from storm surges and closer to better schools and a variety of jobs, opponents reasoned. They wanted the agency to abandon all rebuilding plans. If that wasn't possible, they hoped to persuade the agency to rebuild less housing than it had before the storm. Wary of the growing sentiment against the agency, the city council set aside $25 million of its federal disaster recovery money for the public housing rebuilding effort but refused to release the money until Krishnarao provided a detailed plan for each of the four developments.

Desperate to find a compromise between the agency's agreement with Lone Star Legal Aid and its opponents' demands, Krishnarao proposed a design process that would incorporate public input. On June 16, 2009, the housing authority hired Civic Design Associates, a Houston-based firm, to create a layout for three of the four sites. The board had already approved a plan for 20 duplexes at Palm Terrace, a continuation of pre-storm redevelopment on a neighboring site. Civic Design Associates hosted three public meetings in late July. The architects gave participants the opportunity to draw up their own plans and submit suggestions for the new developments. The resulting designs included townhouses and low-rise apartment buildings, off-street parking and private yards. Although the density of each site varied, all the required units were included.

By then, all of the old, barracks-style buildings had been demolished. Grass grew where buildings once stood, and public housing opponents had even less interest in seeing the open space redeveloped for the island's poor.

In September, two weeks after the city marked Ike's one-year anniversary, the island's largest neighborhood association adopted a resolution questioning the rebuilding plans. Members of the Galveston Alliance of Island Neighborhoods hoped to persuade the agency to reduce density on the existing sites and scatter public housing throughout the island. The scattered-site concept, which gained popularity with national housing advocates in the mid-1990s, put families in existing neighborhoods where they would be surrounded by other working families and not face the stigma of living in a subsidized community. With so many of the island's neighborhoods emptying out because of the post-storm population loss, alliance members hoped the housing authority could take over some of the abandoned houses.

Krishnarao planned to present his rebuilding strategy to the housing authority board for approval on October 19. But opposition again forced delays. The island's neighborhood groups wanted the agency to take more time and get more public input before deciding how to rebuild. Opponents accused the agency of trying to force an unpopular and irresponsible plan on a city still struggling to recover.

Seeking compromise for what he hoped would be the last time, Krishnarao postponed his presentation and scheduled three public meetings. He also unveiled new designs for Magnolia Homes, Cedar Terrace, and Oleander Homes. Each site would have fewer units and more than one-third of the replacement housing would be built as scattered-site units.

It was exactly what opponents had requested, but they still weren't happy.

The first public meeting, held on October 19, devolved into a shouting match between housing supporters, mostly African-American, and opponents, mostly white. It was the first skirmish in what developed during the next few months into an ugly racial fight that attracted the attention of two well-known advocacy groups for the poor: Texas Appleseed and Texas Low-Income Housing Information Service. When Texas Appleseed attorneys in November penned a letter to the U.S. Department of Housing and Urban Development, opposing the state's plan to spend a second round of federal disaster recovery money, they singled out Galveston and its ugly racial tensions over public housing as reasons why the Department of Housing and Urban Development should question the state's promise to further fair housing. The opposition to rebuilding Galveston's public housing, Texas Appleseed complained to HUD, was an egregious example of race-based housing discrimination.

The fight only got nastier. Housing authority commissioners in December approved a plan to replace the 569 demolished public housing units by rebuilding 70 percent of them on the existing footprints, and scattering the rest throughout Galveston. Critics of the housing authority—who had by this time formed organized groups—lashed out at the plan, saying it segregated public housing residents and violated HUD standards. They called on the housing authority to spread public housing throughout the county, or not rebuild public housing at all. Opponents of the agency accused Krishnarao and commissioners of being "poverty pimps" and they lodged complaints with HUD about the housing authority and its practices. They circulated another petition, this one calling on residents to demand a vote before the city spent any local, state, or federal dollars on government-subsidized housing. They lobbied the planning commission to deny the housing authority the right to rebuild until it presented a more palatable plan, but planning commissioners approved the plan anyway.

On February 25, city council members met to decide whether to release the $25 million in federal dollars to the housing authority to jumpstart rebuilding of public housing. Scores of people packed city hall to testify for and against the housing authority's plans. Proponents of rebuilding packed council chambers; opponents congregated in an adjoining room. Officials from the city, the housing authority, and a regional organization charged with distributing the federal dollars to Houston-area municipalities all warned city council members that HUD was watching Galveston closely to make sure the city wasn't discriminating against its poor. They all hinted that if the city continued to delay allowing the housing authority to rebuild its developments, the federal government could strip away the millions of dollars it set aside for Galveston to rebuild hurricane-damaged houses and infrastructure. Releasing the money to the housing authority for rebuilding was critical for Galveston and the rest of the region to continue to receive federal dollars, said Jack Steele, executive director of the Houston-Galveston Area Council.

Opponents of the housing authority dismissed those insinuations as scare tactics and urged council members to delay approving the housing authority's plans until the agency came up with a better plan, one that didn't include rebuilding the projects north of Broadway. The meeting turned ugly; opponents and proponents of public housing snapped at each other openly, accusing each other of racism and not caring about Galveston's poor people. After nine hours of public testimony and deliberation, the council voted 5–2 in favor of the housing authority's plans.

Housing authority commissioners breathed a sigh of relief, but this was just the beginning of a rebuilding process that would take years to finish. The agency still had to give the plan to HUD officials, who would examine it to make sure it met all federal guidelines. Architects must be hired to draw up plans. Only after HUD gave the plan its stamp of approval could the housing authority begin rebuilding housing for the poor—as long as no one challenged the plan in court.

Eighteen months after the storm, it seemed unlikely public housing on the island would be rebuilt by Ike's second, or even third, anniversary.

■ WHILE THE ISLAND'S poor waited to come home, more than 1,400 homeowners waited for the city to start spending the $104 million in disaster relief money earmarked to repair and rebuild Galveston's damaged houses. The city's program offered the only hope many had for returning to their ravaged homes. Although state and federal officials approved the spending plan ten months after the storm, the money didn't get released for another two months. It took the city several more months to hire a contractor to manage the projects. It took so long to wade through the state and federal requirements for both applicants and construction crews that none of the work had even started eighteen months after the storm.

In the first months after Hurricane Ike struck Galveston, advocates for the city's poor and homeless prophesied that Galvestonians struggling before the storm—the indigent and the homeless, the working poor and public housing tenants, the elderly and disabled—would have the hardest time rebuilding their lives. Never did that seem more true than in the spring of 2010, as thousands of poor hurricane victims continued to wait for help from government bureaucrats whose hands were bound by their own red tape.

CHAPTER

THIRTEEN

J OE ENRIQUEZ LIVED less than 100 yards from English Bayou, a man-made inlet in the middle of the island. Hurricane Ike filled his modest three-bedroom house with almost six feet of storm surge. Enriquez had insurance, but not enough to elevate the house, a mitigation measure he feared the city would require before he could rebuild. Enriquez, living temporarily in an apartment in Texas City, drove to the island almost daily to visit the city's permit office and check for new versions of the residential property assessment map.

Every building in Galveston showed up in green, yellow, or red on the big printout posted outside the planning department. Green properties could be rebuilt. Red properties had more than 50 percent damage and had to be brought up to current flood codes, which most often required elevation. Yellow properties remained in limbo, waiting for federal assessment teams to determine whether their damage passed the 50 percent mark.

While he waited for permission to rebuild, Enriquez grappled with his insurance company. Like thousands of others, his settlement offer came in well below what contractors estimated it would take to put his house back together. More than 800,000 property owners in the Houston-Galveston region filed insurance claims after Ike. Anxious to curb their losses, insurers fought even the most obvious claims. When checks did finally come in, mortgage companies snatched them up and refused to release the money until homeowners could prove the repairs would be done right. Banks said their rules protected the value of their assets, but many believed lenders invented the delays as a way to keep insurance proceeds in their accounts, earning interest.

As problems with insurance companies, lenders, and the city dragged on, "for sale" signs started popping up all over the island. Investors and speculators swooped in to snatch up good deals. Homeowners took what they could get and walked away, grateful to avoid the hassle of rebuilding. Those determined to make repairs had their pick of a swarm of contractors who converged on the island from all over the country hoping to make some easy money, often at the expense of storm victims. Many contractors left jobs half finished and vanished. Some never even started work before making off with hefty deposits.

By the beginning of November, the city released the final version of its damage assessment maps. About 1,500 houses, mostly in the city's poorest neighborhoods, had to be elevated before they could be rebuilt. But most of those homeowners had no insurance. They had to depend on federal disaster relief funds to make repairs. More than a year later, they still waited for the money to arrive.

Enriquez finally got permission to rebuild six weeks after the storm. He considered himself lucky to escape the elevation requirement. Like many others, Enriquez believed Galveston would go another 100 years before seeing another Ike. City officials, who lowballed rebuilding cost estimates to reduce the number of elevations, seemed to agree. Unlike their predecessors, who responded to the last devastating storm by rebuilding to limit the next storm's damage, Galveston officials in 2008 chose expediency over mitigation.

■ AFTER RETURNING TO Galveston, islanders spent the first few weeks cleaning out their flooded houses, figuring out what they could salvage, and looking for a place to stay until they could move home. But by early October, lines started forming outside the city's planning department. Homeowners wanted to rebuild, although not everyone wanted to reinvest in property that could flood again. Still shell shocked by the destruction and magnitude of their losses, many homeowners talked about raising their houses before making repairs. They didn't know how they would pay for the work, but they couldn't imagine rebuilding without doing something to make them less vulnerable during the next hurricane season.

With the island's flat landscape so close to sea level in most places, many homeowners knew their battered houses did not meet current codes. Almost the entire island, everything but a narrow strip along the seawall, was in a floodplain. But with three-quarters of the houses built before 1975, most dwellings sat below the current base flood elevation level set by FEMA. In the city's urban core, the base flood elevation was about 11 feet above sea level, just a few feet off the ground in some areas and seven or eight feet in others. Conjuring images of the 1900 Storm recovery effort, when crews raised almost all houses left standing and pumped millions of gallons of dirt onto the island to raise the ground under them, homeowners felt sure the city's leaders would find some way to get them out of harm's way, and help them pay for it. Wasn't the federal government still shelling out billions of dollars to shore up the levees in New Orleans, a city built below sea level, they reasoned?

Within a week of the storm's landfall, Planning Director Wendy O'Donohoe had sent a few top staffers out to do what she described as a "quick and dirty" damage assessment. Everyone—city leaders, state officials, FEMA representatives, and data-hungry reporters—wanted statistics. How much of the island flooded? How many houses had damage? How much would it all cost to repair? Planning department staffers, bused in from the mainland to get through the roadblocks quickly, surveyed the entire island in just a few days, identifying the areas that needed more analysis to determine how bad the damage really was. The next phase of assessment, a "windshield survey" that took seven teams of inspectors four weeks to complete, evaluated every neighborhood based on overall damage.

In early October, the city turned its damage assessments over to a team of FEMA inspectors, who conducted the residential substantial damage estimate evaluation required by the agency's National Flood Insurance Program. City officials asked the federal government to conduct the evaluation, rather than assigning the task to the planning department, to make the process go as quickly as possible. But even with the federal help, some homeowners still had to wait until mid-November to find out whether they could rebuild, a delay that earned the city council hours of angry harangues from frustrated residents every time it met. Mayor pro tem Danny Weber, a self-styled man of the people, angrily told federal officials the city might just move forward without the assessments if the agency's inspectors couldn't move faster. But doing so would have risked residents' access to the federally subsidized flood insurance program, which held almost all flood insurance policies on the island. To limit the number of future payouts, the agency required cities to follow some kind of assessment process to make sure heavily damaged houses were raised above base flood elevation or removed. Municipalities that didn't comply might get kicked out of the program, leaving residents to buy insurance on the open market at much higher rates.

Federal inspectors used a damage assessment formula that compared the destruction to an estimated cost of repairs. Houses with damage that would cost more than half their value to repair would be labeled "substantially damaged" and would have to be elevated or torn down. Houses with less damage could be rebuilt on the ground and would not lose their flood insurance eligibility. Although FEMA provided the formula, it was up to the city to set the rebuilding costs. High rebuilding costs would push more houses into the substantial damage category. Elevated houses would be at less risk for flooding during the next Ike-like storm, but based on the number of homeowners without insurance, city officials knew many people would not be able to afford to lift their houses onto pilings or build new ones. Residents who couldn't afford to make repairs might just walk away from their houses and the island, leaving the city dotted with gutted, rotting, useless properties weighing down the tax rolls.

"There was so much pressure to keep that cost low," City Manager Steve LeBlanc said of the damage estimate formula. "If we set the bar too high, it would be unachievable and we would have run people out of town. Did we miss an opportunity? I don't know. We pushed it as far as we thought the community could handle."

The city's planning department divided houses into six categories, based on their quality before the storm. Low-quality houses were assigned a $45 per square foot rebuilding cost. Repairs to excellent-quality houses were estimated at $70 per square foot. Using those numbers, the assessments came in much lower than contractor bids and insurance settlements, but O'Donohoe defended the numbers and the results.

"We knew it could definitely cause people not to be able to rebuild, or allow people back to properties that had a lot of water," she said. "We knew there were properties that had a lot of water, but still the structural elements of the house weren't compromised."

No matter how low the city set rebuilding costs in the damage assessment formula, the poorest neighborhoods north of Broadway would have the highest number of substantial damage rulings. The area had some of the highest flood levels in the city, and the mostly small, ramshackle houses weren't worth enough to balance out the repair costs. Fancier houses, even those sitting on slabs on the shores of Offatts and English bayous were worth so much, nothing short of a structural collapse would make them substantially damaged.

In many cases, the houses most likely to flood again were rebuilt. Sitting in his newly remodeled living room, the sunlight glinting off Lake Madeline reflecting on the ceiling, LeBlanc acknowledged his home was no safer from future damage than it had been before Ike. He had thought about not rebuilding, but this was home, he said. What about next time? He just shrugged.

Relatively few people criticized the assessment process for being too lenient because most people wanted to rebuild without taking on the hassle and extra cost of future flood mitigation. But almost everyone acknowledged the process was too porous to have much value beyond bureaucratic paperwork. Once the assessments were complete, property owners could get their substantial damage ruling changed by bringing contractors' estimates for the repair work to the city's planning department. Most commonly, people whose houses had substantial damage brought estimates that showed the work wouldn't cost as much as the inspectors thought, lowering the total percentage of damage. But, anxious to get access to the extra $30,000 the National Flood Insurance Program would pay to help offset elevation costs, some homeowners brought estimates that showed the work would cost much more than inspectors estimated.

The obvious ease with which the assessments could be changed angered residents who had to wait in long lines at the permit office just to go through what seemed to be a meaningless exercise. Why didn't the city just save everyone a lot of trouble and aggravation by letting people get on with rebuilding without the need for assessments or permits, they wondered. O'Donohoe acknowledged the system allowed people to manipulate the numbers. But it was a federal requirement. During meetings with FEMA representatives and Mayor Lyda Ann Thomas' testimony before Congress, city officials did what they could to convince Washington bureaucrats the assessment system needed some changes.

"We're hoping the process continues to be updated and modified," O'Donohoe said.

■ CITY OFFICIALS RELEASED the first map dotted with red, green, and yellow on October 16, clearing the way for the first wave of homeowners to start making repairs. But the inspectors hadn't made it as far as Bayou Homes Drive, Emory Brockway's street. The Brockways finished gutting their house within days of crawling down from the attic, where they holed up during the storm. They wanted to start rebuilding immediately, but all of the lots in that area were still colored yellow. Although he had asked for a FEMA trailer, the stubbornly independent survivor refused to leave his property for a more comfortable hotel room that the federal government would have paid for. He scoffed at the people out to get all they could from the taxpayers. Brockway believed people should take care of themselves as much as possible and only seek help out of absolute desperation. Even then, they should take the minimum amount of help they needed.

The sooner he could start making repairs, the less time he and Merlinda would have to spend on the air mattress in the corner of their shell of a living room. Like others anxiously awaiting their fate, Brockway made the trip to the city's planning department almost daily to peer at the large maps spread out on top of one of the glass display cases that normally got attention for the historic police department artifacts it held. Within the first week of map releases, Driftwood Lane, which runs along Offatts Bayou perpendicular to Bayou Homes Drive, turned from yellow to green. Brockway had high hopes his street would be next. The city released updated maps every few days, but Brockway's house, and those of his neighbors, remained yellow.

Although federal requirements called for every house to go through the residential substantial damage estimate assessment, inspectors did not visit every one. Based on the average values and the amount of known damage, the inspectors cleared some neighborhoods for repair immediately. Because the city's most influential and wealthiest residents had their homes in most of the quickly cleared neighborhoods, rumors of special favors spread rapidly among the increasingly frustrated homeowners who left the permit office disappointed every day. In reality, most of the city's high-dollar property just didn't have enough damage to trigger FEMA's substantial damage ruling. The inspectors didn't need to look at those houses to know that.

For Brockway, with nothing to do but pace around his gutted house smoking and thinking about the work he could be starting, the wait seemed interminable. The map revealing his home's fate wasn't released until November 5. Brockway fully expected to get the green light to make repairs. He was shocked to see his lot and 23 others on the street colored an infuriating, unbelievably bright red. He had two options—find a way to raise his house, which was built on a slab, or prove to the city the house had less damage and was worth more than the inspectors thought. It took Brockway a month to get an appraiser to come to the house and certify it was worth more than the value listed by the central appraisal district. That was all he needed to go from red to green. The planning department staff members didn't even question the appraisal before filing it away and giving him permission to start making repairs.

"The city of Galveston is the biggest farce I have ever run across in my life," Brockway said three months later. "My house was put in the red zone. It cost me $250 for a public appraiser, that I paid for, to take a piece of paper down to the boys in the planning department at the city. And you know what? They didn't even look at it."

■ JOHN GIOVANNINI APPLIED for a building permit on October 1. Four weeks later, he was still waiting to get it, although inspectors cleared the single-story house for repair almost immediately. Giovannini and his wife Judy moved to Galveston and bought their property on Gerol Drive, across Lake Madeline from the city manager's house, in 2004. Its previous owner had modified it for wheelchair accessibility, making it the perfect place for the couple to live out what they expected to be a comfortable and gentle retirement. They evacuated ahead of Hurricane Ike and came home during the Look-and-Leave policy to find about 18 inches of water still sitting in the house. Giovannini measured the highest water line inside at 4.5 feet. The highest line outside topped that by another foot. He couldn't believe the city's leaders would let him rebuild.

Like other homeowners frustrated into a frenzy by some part of the recovery, Giovannini became a regular during council meeting public comment periods. He continually berated council members for refusing to make the difficult decisions that would in the long run protect islanders from enduring the horrors of a Hurricane Ike again. He reminded them how effective their forefathers' mitigation measures after the 1900 Storm had been for the last 100 years and begged them to follow that example by requiring all 75 percent of the city that flooded this time to elevate.

"A joint effort to raise us up now is an idea whose time has come," he told the council in mid-November. "If you want to encourage us to leave, just refuse to continue to take mitigation action . . . All I see from you is indecision and no action that will help keep the middle class here."

Giovannini, a psychiatric social worker by training and a stickler for wise fiscal management by nature, saw the city on a direct course for what would be a manmade disaster the next time a wall of water washed ashore. Everyone would realize then that the damage could have been prevented. Allowing so many people to rebuild in harm's way, subsidizing their risk with taxpayer-backed insurance, was fiscally irresponsible, Giovanini argued. He refused to do it. People who didn't understand his mania about elevation told him a storm like Ike would never happen again. He just rolled his eyes.

While his neighbors started making repairs, Giovannini began a long argument with city planners over exactly how much his house was damaged. The contractor estimates he got pegged the damage between 59 percent and 72 percent. He asked the city to produce the inspection report for his house showing it was less than 50 percent damaged. The document didn't exist, of course, because the house hadn't actually been inspected. Two months after Giovannini filed his permit request and submitted his contractor estimates, the planning department finally agreed the house had too much damage to be repaired.

As soon as he got his substantial damage letter to submit to the insurance company, Giovannini filed for a demolition permit and started looking at plans for a new house, on pilings. He thought about just walking away, but he couldn't afford to.

"Real estate is our asset," he said. "We would have left if we could have. We were actually looking to move before the storm, but we couldn't sell the house."

■ **JOE AND GLORIA** Enriquez bought their house on Bayou Shore Drive in 1987. They never worried about how close it was to English Bayou, just across the street. Although swanky houses fronted the water on the southern end of the street, the houses around Enriquez were all valued at less than $100,000. With the exception of those few waterfront properties, the neighborhood had gradually become an enclave for the city's middle-class Hispanics. Some even referred to the area as "Little Mexico."

Ike pushed about five feet of surge from the bayou into Enriquez's house. While he waited for the city to decide whether he could rebuild, the retired custodial superintendent slowly tore down the drywall and scraped up the laminate floor tiles. After working construction and maintenance jobs his whole life, Enriquez had a good idea what it would cost to replace everything in his home after he gutted it to the studs. Unlike some of his neighbors, Enriquez had insurance. His adjuster proposed a payout totaling about 86 percent of what the Galveston Central Appraisal District said the house was worth. But Enriquez felt sure it would cost more than that to make all the repairs.

For 46 days, Enriquez worried about what he would do if the city said he had to elevate. He tried to remain upbeat for his wife, who had taken the hurricane's fallout so hard her doctor prescribed antidepressants. He constantly tried to assure her they would make it through, no matter what happened. But he wasn't really sure.

On October 29, the city released the inspection reports for Bayou Shore Drive, clearing the Enriquez house and almost all others on the street to rebuild. Enriquez couldn't believe his luck. Now all he had to do was figure out how to make up the difference between his insurance settlement and the repair cost. The insurance company paid him $40,000, but the lowest bid he'd gotten from a contractor was $58,000, which was $3,300 more than the house was worth.

Almost as soon as Ike's winds died down, contractors swarmed to the island from all over the country. A handful legitimately wanted to help and do good work. But the rest made up a ragtag crew of shysters and charlatans interested only in swindling a quick buck before hightailing it back out of town. It was hard to tell the difference when a man with a tape measure clipped to his belt showed up at the front door and offered to put everything back faster than the homeowner thought possible. Promises of being back home in time for Christmas tempted more than a few homeowners to make a bad choice of repairmen.

Hoping to cut down on the number of out-of-town contractors taking advantage of trusting homeowners, especially the island's elderly residents, city officials ordered all contractors and tradesmen to register with the planning department, provide a surety bond, and show proof of liability insurance. Officials begged residents to do business only with contractors on the list. But the registration requirement only proved that contractors could put up the money for a license, not that they could be trusted. The registration didn't include any kind of background check or customer service survey.

Enriquez decided to hire subcontractors to do most of the work on his house, hoping he could save some money supervising the job himself. The crews made good progress at first. He and his sons even did some of the work, spending weekends laying a decorative blue and yellow Mexican tile throughout the living and dining rooms. But by the end of the summer, the contractor hired to hang drywall, replace trim, and install cabinets had disappeared. He left the job unfinished, owing Enriquez a $4,000 refund the disappointed homeowner didn't really expect to get. A year after the storm, the family still couldn't live in the house and Enriquez had run out of money.

The mortgage company still had $5,000 of the insurance proceeds it refused to release until Enriquez completed a checklist of repairs. But the work the lenders wanted done didn't make much sense. They told Enriquez to finish the kitchen cabinets, install all the doors and hang the finishing trim. The checklist said nothing about working bathrooms or gas and electrical connections, the very thing the family needed to move back home. Enriquez did a little work on the house every day, using the money he earned from a part-time job to buy materials. Some days, when he was really feeling down about the future, he just sat on an air mattress on his living room floor and watched a small television plugged in to an extension cord snaked through a window. It wasn't the retirement the 65-year-old had envisioned.

"I've worked all my life, you know," he said. "I figured retirement was going to be a lot better than what it is, with Ike coming along. I retired in May of last year, prior to Ike coming. I told my wife we would be fine, that everything was going to work out. And then, boom, this hits us. That really set us all back."

Although the worry lines around his eyes betrayed his discouragement, Enriquez always came back to his rallying theme: We're going to make it, one way or another. He followed the confident declaration with a wide smile, as if to prove he really wasn't worried. Sitting behind her husband in the small mobile home FEMA finally installed on the property in May, Gloria's eyes welled up with tears. He puts on a brave front, she said.

■ THE ISLAND'S NORTH side, home to much of the African-American community, used to be a tight-knit neighborhood of middle-class, working families. With the Port of Galveston to the north, cotton warehouses to the south, and the Falstaff Brewery in the middle, the neighborhood offered proximity to most of the island's good-paying, blue-collar jobs for more than 50 years. The community boasted a church every few blocks, but Central High School was its crown jewel. The school, founded in

1886 for the city's African-American teens, was the first of its kind in Texas. The school operated out of several different buildings, settling on the campus at 31st and Sealy streets in 1954. The north side's proud graduates walked across its stage for 14 years, until Galveston integrated its schools in 1968.

Not long after its students left the neighborhood to attend Ball High School, the jobs started to leave as well. The factories and warehouses shut down, the brewery's vats sat empty, and business at the port hit the low it had been sliding toward since the 1900 Storm. In the 1970s and 1980s, the four public housing developments on the north side became a haven for drug dealers, gangs, and violent crime that gradually engulfed the rest of the neighborhood. The north side became known as a place no one went voluntarily after dark, unless they lived there.

By the time Ike struck, the neighborhood had cleaned up its dangerous image, thanks to major improvements in the housing authority management, but its derelict aesthetic remained. Many of the old timers had moved out or died, leaving their houses to children who had long since left Galveston for better opportunities. Willie Ruth Scott stayed. The spry 72-year-old lived with her daughter, Wendy, in the house her father built in the 3400 block of Ball Street in 1954. The neat, single-story, ranch-style house, surrounded by a chain-link fence, sat back from the road, giving Scott plenty of room for beds of bright flowers.

Scott almost didn't evacuate for Ike. It was the first time she could remember leaving ahead of a storm. She rode out hurricanes Carla, Alicia, and Rita in her father's house. It never flooded. But this time, her worried children made her go. She left with one change of clothes, expecting to come home after spending the weekend playing cards at her son's house. She ended up staying there for three months, until FEMA could install a mobile home on top of her once vibrant flowerbeds.

Ike's surge rose all the way to the rafters. Scott, stuck without power or television in Houston, had no idea how bad the damage was. Even when her children brought her back for the first time two weeks later, she still thought the house had escaped because it was standing. It wasn't until they opened the door that she realized the extent of the destruction. She had just bought a new air conditioner and had new wood laminate floors installed, a present to herself to celebrate her retirement from the University of Texas Medical Branch.

"It just goes to show you can't make plans," she said months later while flipping through photos of the mud-covered floors, walls, and ceiling.

Scott didn't have insurance. It was too expensive for someone on a fixed income, her daughter said. Like thousands of others, Scott was depending on charitable groups or federal disaster assistance money to put her house back together.

A group of local activists who knew how much help many people would need after the storm formed Galveston County Restore and Rebuild before most homeowners had even gutted their houses. With $2 million in private donations, about half coming from Houston Mayor Bill White's Gulf Coast Ike Relief Fund, the group paid for building materials and organized volunteer construction crews to make repairs for people like Scott. By the end of 2009, the organization had rebuilt 154 homes.

Church-affiliated groups also traveled to the island from all over the country to help with the rebuilding effort. And about 10,000 college students spent the post-Ike spring break painting, cleaning, and replanting. Galveston didn't attract the star power New Orleans mustered after Hurricane Katrina, something many islanders resented. But the thousands of average Americans who spent their vacations ripping out moldy carpet, swinging a hammer, and wielding a paint brush did more to boost the city's morale than a visit from Brad Pitt or Sean Penn.

As in New Orleans, and just about any other disaster zone, volunteer assistance came much faster than government assistance. In the weeks following Ike, President George W. Bush pledged $3 billion in disaster relief for all areas ravaged by storms in 2008. The biggest chunk of the money would go to Galveston, $267 million in the first round of funding and $190 million in the second. But it wasn't until March that city leaders learned how much they would get to spend rebuilding houses for people who had no other way to make repairs. They started making plans to spend the first round of funds dedicated to housing, $160 million, in April, but had to wait until the storm's first anniversary to find out whether the relevant state and federal agencies approved the spending plan. The wheels of government seemed to turn especially slowly to people like Scott who waited to move home. Thanks to federal red tape and additional state requirements, city officials did not expect the first construction job to start before April 2010, more than 18 months after the storm.

Many people complained bitterly about the delays, none louder than City Councilman Tarris Woods. With most of the north side's residents still away from home, Woods lost his voting base. But no amount of criticism or accusations of a racism-inspired purge of the African-American community—claims made by north side leaders—could make the money flow any faster. While many heaped blame on FEMA and other government agencies, Scott preferred to be thankful for what she had. At least she could live on her property, even if it was in a cramped FEMA trailer. The north side streets were hauntingly empty, but at least she could ride the bus to Walmart to meet up with friends and catch up on the latest gossip.

"It didn't all run smooth," she said of her own recovery. "But my daddy told me a long time ago things don't run smooth all the time anyway. So I have that attitude."

■ FRANCES DUNHAM AND her husband Herbert built their house on Coral Lane in 1959. It was close enough to the ferry landing that they could hear the boats running between the island and Bolivar Peninsula blow their horns every time they left the dock. But they never worried about flooding. Their end of the neighborhood was one of the highest points in the city, or so they were told when they bought the lot. The couple chose the neighborhood for its proximity to the port, where Herbert worked, and First Baptist Church, where they spent most of their time not devoted to work or sleep.

The Dunhams always evacuated for hurricanes, out of an abundance of caution rather than fear. But Ike was the first major storm Frances would have to prepare for without her husband. Herbert died in 2006, leaving his 81-year-old wife to figure out what to take with her and what to protect in place. Dunham's daughter, Donna, usually came to get her mother if she needed to leave the island. Although she could still drive, Dunham's license restricted her from going across the causeway or driving at night. But Donna was on vacation the week Ike churned into the Gulf of Mexico. Dunham's sister, who lived in Texas City, called on Thursday to tell her to pack up and leave as soon as she could. A friend from church offered to take her to the mainland, but Dunham didn't have much time to get ready. She tossed a few things in her suitcase but didn't bother with the more elaborate preparations she usually made—picking things up off the floor or putting her twenty photo albums in plastic trash bags. She did take the time to move her box of important papers to the top shelf of one of her bookcases, but only because her sister suggested it. Before she walked out the front door, Dunham poured out the milk in her refrigerator, hoping if she lost power it would come back on in time to keep everything else from spoiling.

During the evacuation, she hoped and prayed her house had survived. But when she heard the water rose as high as 14 feet downtown, she figured everyone was in trouble. Still she hoped and prayed. About a week later, Dunham's niece, a florist in Tennessee, got a call from a contractor working in Galveston who wanted to order flowers for his wife for their anniversary. Recognizing an opportunity to get some news of her aunt's house, Dunham's niece asked the man to drive down Coral Lane and see what he could see. He took a picture with his cell phone and e-mailed it to Donna. The water line, three feet high, was clearly visible across the white screen door.

Dunham didn't come back to the island until the day after the mayor allowed everyone home. The following Saturday her nieces and nephews came to help throw out what was ruined and clean up anything that could be saved. Like so many others, Dunham didn't have flood insurance. But unlike some, she had no complaints about FEMA or the Disaster Housing Assistance Program operated by the U.S. Department of Housing and Urban Development. FEMA sent her money right away, and she moved temporarily into an apartment on the island in early December.

A disaster recovery crew from Houston's Sagemont Church, which Dunham's daughter attended, hauled her ruined furniture and carpet to the curb. They cut down her mildewed drywall and sprayed a mold-reducing solution on the exposed studs. The crew's leader advised her to sell the house as it was because he knew the repairs would be expensive.

But she was determined to stay. With help from a deacon from her church, Dunham hired a local contractor to put the house back together. She finally moved home in May. Sitting in her newly remodeled living room, on furniture one of her nephews gave her, Dunham said she was blessed. But she wouldn't go as far as some and say Ike brought the island much-needed, positive change.

"It just made me do things I didn't want to do," she said. "My niece kept saying, 'But Aunt Frances, you got a new house.' And I said, 'But Diane, I was contented just the way it was.' "

■ **GALVESTON POLICE CHIEF** Charles Wiley returned home six months after the hurricane. He was one of the first people to move back into the townhouse complex, a testament to the progress that could be made when you didn't have to haggle with insurers or wait on FEMA.

Wiley had hazard insurance on the house, but no flood insurance. The island native, a strong believer in the seawall's power to beat back hurricanes, lived only a few blocks from the structure. He thought the house that close to the seawall could never flood. Hurricane Ike proved him wrong.

A contractor friend of Wiley's asked the police chief in the early weeks after the hurricane if Wiley wanted him to grab a crew of guys and just start gutting the place.

"I said, 'Yeah. Yeah. Just do that,'" Wiley recalled.

"Do you want to see it first?" the contractor asked.

"No, just do it."

"You have insurance?"

"No, I don't have any insurance," Wiley said. "Don't worry about the insurance, okay? The door's open. Go on in."

That afternoon Wiley swung by the townhouse to check on the contractors' progress. All of the stuff he'd spent a lifetime accumulating was piled on the curb. The appliances and cabinets mingled with bits of drywall in a mound that was as wide as the townhouse and as tall as a single-story building. Wiley drove by the pile, gave it a fleeting glance, and drove off. The next time he saw the place, the walls were gutted to the studs. (Wiley later found out that his wife sneaked into the house behind his back and salvaged the few possessions she could save. "She's more attached to stuff than I am," he said.)

Along with the house, Wiley lost both cars in the garage, a 2006 Yukon Denali and a Jeep Wrangler he used to shuttle back and forth to the Galveston Yacht Basin. At the basin, he kept his favorite mode of transportation: a brand new Godfrey Hurricane deck boat on which Wiley spent many weekends tooling around the bay, sipping cocktails, and smoking cigars with the Galveston bigwigs he had known for years.

Wiley's buddy, Eddie Barr, a former county commissioner, convinced him two days before Hurricane Ike struck to put the boat in dry storage at the marina. Wiley drove the boat around to the dry dock and made sure it was the last boat in. Last in, first out, he reasoned. Barr called him Friday morning to tell him that the Galveston Yacht Basin's dry storage area was on fire, and Wiley's boat, *Pier Pressure,* was at the top of the inferno.

After the hurricane, the Federal Emergency Management Agency doled out checks to people who didn't have insurance to cover the costs of temporary housing, or to pay for some repairs so people could get their lives back together. The Wileys applied for FEMA assistance and got squat. Wiley said one of the top FEMA officials stationed with him at The San Luis Resort asked him once if he'd had any luck with FEMA. Wiley told him no, he hadn't. The man urged him to go back to FEMA, to reapply, to appeal the decision. Wiley shook his head.

"I'm not doing that," he said. "I'm not going to go back and ask for something after the decision's made. That's it."

The FEMA official promised Wiley he'd have someone call him to straighten out the situation and give the Wileys the money they deserved. No one ever called.

"We got nothing from FEMA, not one nickel," he said later. "People all over this area got FEMA assistance and we got not a nickel. To hell with it. I've never asked for anything before and I'm not going to now."

The Wileys moved into an apartment complex for six and a half months. To piece the townhouse back together, they broke open their retirement accounts and the money they'd squirreled away for their grandchildren's college education.

"I called my daughter and said, 'We're going to have to figure out another way to pay for college. Dad ain't going to live in a shack.'"

By the time the Wileys moved back in April 2009, they'd spent $120,000 repairing the townhouse. That didn't include what they spent immediately after the storm, including buying new clothes and shoes. The Wileys returned home before anyone else in the area, even before the owner of a neighboring apartment complex gutted the hurricane-damaged building. For a while, the empty and wrecked Ashton Place apartments became a den for vagrants, squatters, crackheads, and truant children from the nearby schools. One night, Wiley saw a rat the size of a "kitty cat" scurrying up the side of the apartment complex's walls. He darted inside and grabbed his pistol, but the rat was gone by the time he ran back outside.

Still, despite the conditions around him, Wiley was happy to be back home and optimistic about Galveston's future.

"We are recovering at a pace much quicker than I expected," Wiley said. "It really is a testament to the resilience of Galvestonians. This is a strange place in more ways than one, but it's not a bad kind of strange. It's an eclectic, eccentric sort of strange. Maybe that's what draws a lot of us."

CHAPTER
FOURTEEN

OFFICIALS FROM ALABAMA and Mississippi visited Galveston not long after Ike's winds died down. They offered recovery advice to elected officials, city staff members, and business owners. One piece of hard-earned disaster wisdom really resonated: Hurricanes don't create trends, they just accelerate them.

The changes Galveston faced before the storm multiplied under Ike's wind and the waves. The island's middle class had already started streaming across the causeway before the storm. Galveston Independent School District lost so many students each year that it had already closed two elementary school campuses before Ike flooded the rest. The ten-year development boom that brought new condominium towers and beachfront subdivisions foretold the island's gradual transition to a resort community.

Ike pushed people off the fence, downtown business owner Laura Hurt said. People who had thought about leaving Galveston but needed a little incentive to take that step got it on September 13. They sold their houses and businesses and moved on. But Ike also galvanized the resolve of those who loved Galveston and couldn't imagine living or working anywhere else. While some popular island shops and restaurants didn't return after Ike, new ones took their places. More than 300 people volunteered to help write the island's recovery plan, an unprecedented amount of interest for any city committee. Island leaders, used to the bickering and infighting that often characterized community efforts, pointed to the recovery committee as a sign that Galvestonians had finally learned to put their differences behind them.

Hurricane Ike also revealed deep rifts in the community over public housing and the poor. The racial overtones of the rebuilding debate shocked many who had always considered the island a liberal and tolerant place. While many of Galveston's neighborhoods rebuilt after the storm, with aging houses getting the remodels they had needed for years, other neighborhoods still sat vacant more than 12 months later, their ravaged houses growing more decrepit every day. Every empty house represented a wounded family that might never recover financially from the blow of losing their home and all their belongings.

With the help of federal funding, the city's water, sewer, and drainage systems got the updates officials had talked about for decades but always lacked the money to start. Improvements to the power grid and emergency power supplies made it less likely that islanders would be kept from home after future storms due to a lack of basic services. But most of the city's houses wouldn't be any safer during the next big flood. And faced with the possibility of having to stay on the mainland while their houses rotted, many islanders swore they wouldn't leave next time.

Islanders feared Ike would set their city back half a century. Instead, the storm propelled Galveston into the future. In 48 hours, Ike forced people to answer the question they all would have had to face eventually: Is it worth it? Do the benefits of living on a fragile and vulnerable barrier island outweigh the risks? About 11,000 people decided the risk wasn't worth taking. They were the tentative ones, City Manager Steve LeBlanc said. The people who stayed knew Galveston would face another major storm sometime in the future, perhaps sooner than later. They would stay, no matter what. They were the determined ones. No storm could chase them from the city they loved.

Heartbreaking tales of loss peppered Galveston's history. But inspiring stories of regeneration always followed. Ike simply added another chapter to the story.

■ **BEFORE DAYA MYERS** and Laura Hurt made it back to Galveston in their aunt's tiny plane, they weren't sure whether they wanted to come back. But as soon as they landed at the island's crumpled airport, they knew they had come home. They were determined to reopen the Lunch-box Café, even though they didn't know how they would do it or how long it would take. Amid all the uncertainty over the island's future, Myers and Hurt wanted to be something their fellow Galvestonians could count on.

"We certainly couldn't be yet another thing they heard wasn't going to come back because a lot of people were making plans based on what other people were doing," Myers said. "Everyone just wanted reassurance."

Myers and Hurt wanted to reopen as quickly as possible, but their landlord didn't share their sense of urgency. When another building owner offered them a new, much larger space, they jumped at the chance. It was risky. With the island's population still about 20 percent less than its pre-storm level and with 3,000 fewer UTMB employees looking for a place to eat lunch, Myers and Hurt would have to sell many more sandwiches to break even in the larger space. They opened on January 15, four months and five days after they closed their last location. Hungry customers filled every table that first day and continued to keep the café full.

Unlike Myers and Hurt, many downtown business owners didn't have insurance. During the bleak winter months that followed the storm, several merchants announced they wouldn't reopen their stores or restaurants. Skip Martin, of Hava Cigar, was one. At first, Martin fully intended to reopen as quickly as possible. If he didn't reopen, the three years he spent building the business before the storm would be wasted. Plus he missed his customers, and they missed him. Every day, he got e-mails from islanders asking him when he thought he would start selling cigars again.

Martin thought he could get the store back to its pre-storm condition in about 18 months, as long as the rest of the city started to return to normal. But by November, the avalanche of storm casualties buried his plan to reopen. Layoffs at the University of Texas Medical Branch drastically cut into the store's customer base. Martin also started hearing from other regulars who had decided to abandon ship and move to the mainland. Rumors that American National Insurance Company might also move across the causeway, fears that eventually proved false, struck the final blow.

"When I heard all that, I knew our top line operating revenue would be less," Martin said. "It just wasn't economically feasible anymore."

Martin gave up on Galveston and opened a new store in Austin. The Hava Cigar space sat empty for almost a year until Martin's former partner, Charlie Head, decided to open another store in its place. When Myers and Hurt reopened the Lunchbox Café, most of the downtown district remained vacant. But by the time summer visitors started arriving in late May, about half the shops on The Strand had "open" signs hanging in their windows. New stores eventually replaced those, like Hava Cigar, that didn't return.

In most cases, the storm forced people to make decisions they had been toying with for years, Myers said. The damage and the monumental effort necessary to reopen either convinced store owners they loved their work or gave them the excuse they needed to walk away without feeling like they had given up. The determination to triumph over adversity rejuvenated the group that remained and encouraged others to join them.

■ As PART OF the city's recovery effort, officials with the Federal Emergency Management Agency strongly encouraged local officials to form a committee to draft a plan that would help guide post-storm policy and influence decisions about how to spend the federal disaster assistance money. The agency hardly needed to ask. Galveston officials loved forming committees, although its politicians had a reputation for ignoring its citizens' advice. But they promised for once to take this committee's recommendations seriously.

The recovery committee started with the 35 people already serving on the committee charged with updating the city's comprehensive plan, the document designed to guide long-term policy decisions. But so many others voiced interest in shaping the city's future that the city council agreed to open the group to anyone who wanted to join. The federal organizers tasked with forcing the committee to be productive watched in horror as its membership swelled to 330 people. They expected to deal with 15 people and host a few meetings. FEMA saw the bloated committee as unmanageable chaos. Committee Chairwoman Betty Massey saw it as hope for Galveston's future. Massey, executive director of the Mary Moody Northen Endowment, member of the Galveston Park Board of Trustees, and longtime community activist, knew everyone who usually served on city committees. But when the recovery committee met for the first time in January, she saw dozens of faces she didn't recognize.

"On the one hand, it looked overwhelming," she said. "On the other hand, I think you have to celebrate that so many people wanted to do this . . . These were people who had not been civically involved before, and I think that's terrific."

Massey divided the committee into 13 workgroups that addressed specific pieces of the recovery. They met weekly for almost three months to refine general visions for Galveston's future into specific projects. The final recovery plan, submitted to the city council in April, included 42 projects the committee asked the council to fund. Many projects, especially those dealing with street, sewer, and drainage improvements, had been on the city's wish list for years and didn't generate much controversy. Others, like the feasibility studies for a ring levee system for the island and a Dutch-style dike system for the entire Galveston Bay area, didn't get approved without a fight. Council members debated the environmental effects and scoffed at the cost to build such sophisticated storm protection systems.

But the group's commitment to unity won out. Committee members lobbied for each other's projects, even those they didn't believe in. The council gave way and approved the plan as presented. When it divvied up the first round of federal disaster recovery money, many of the projects got funded. More than a year later, several of the committee's subgroups continued to meet to champion their projects and assist in the recovery effort. Most notably, city officials credited the housing subgroup for helping to register homeowners for the federally funded repair program.

The committee succeeded because it spoke with a unified voice, an uncommon achievement in Galveston and a hopeful sign for the future, Massey said.

■ **CITY MANAGER STEVE** LeBlanc watched the island's population plummet after the storm. But a year later, the losses stabilized. Galveston had dropped below the 50,000 mark and probably would stay there. Although initially worried about the tax base, which determines the city's revenue, LeBlanc eventually declared himself satisfied with a smaller community. Smaller was fine, as long as the quality improved, he said. Based on the amount of federal money pouring in to fix public utilities, streets, and buildings, an improvement in quality seemed inevitable.

LeBlanc fully expected the island to become more of a resort community, a transformation already started before the storm struck. The island was an expensive place to live, and building and insurance costs would likely increase over time. Unless independently wealthy, people had to sacrifice to live on the island. With more than half his own staff living on the mainland, LeBlanc knew that even jobs wouldn't be enough to convince people to move back to the island.

But people who can afford to risk losing a second home to a hurricane will always be attracted to the coast, he said. People would continue to build new beach houses on the West End and buy condominiums with an ocean view. The memory of the storm would dampen enthusiasm for Galveston for a while, but people would forget. The ones who loved the island always did.

"The people that were tentative as far as remaining here have decided to move on," LeBlanc said. "The people who have decided to stay are here for the next one."

■ **WHILE LEBLANC SEEMED** willing to accept the changes Hurricane Ike brought to Galveston, Mayor Lyda Ann Thomas only wanted to see them reversed. Although term limits would force her from office 20 months after the storm, Thomas had a five-year plan for restoration. She estimated full recovery would take that long, based on what happened after hurricanes Carla and Alicia.

Thomas built her recovery plan around the assumption that full-time residents could be lured back, if the port continued to grow and conditions at the University of Texas Medical Branch remained stable. The middle class would return if the city partnered with the Galveston Housing Authority to build affordable, mixed-income housing. Young families would once again consider living in Galveston if the schools offered a good education. Executives from Houston would choose to live where they could walk on the beach after work if they could catch a high-speed commuter train into the city every morning. And no one would be afraid to live in Galveston if the island had a regional dike or levee system to protect it from future storms.

It was a good plan, she said. It was also an ambitious plan that many viewed as unrealistic. Thomas and other community leaders had worked toward the same goals for decades without making enough progress to stop the steady population loss multiplied by Ike. But with so much federal money pouring onto the island, the city had a real chance to make some headway, Thomas said. Look how far the city came in just a year, she said.

Although proud of the city's progress so far, Thomas said she never doubted her people would rise to Mother Nature's challenge. They always had.

"The city, as it has before, came together and made up its mind as a city, as citizens, to recover," she said.

■ **MIDDLE-SCHOOL SCIENCE TEACHER** Renee Brawner and her husband Brian decided not to rebuild their house in Bolivar Peninsula's Crystal Beach. The community they loved was gone and they couldn't stomach the risk of losing everything again. As she drove back and forth to school, Brawner watched new houses replace the ones Ike so easily obliterated. She couldn't understand it.

"I believe in that pioneer spirit and loving a place and all," Brawner said in her twangy East Texas drawl. "But good God, I can't do that again. It's just not worth that. There's a pioneer spirit, then there's just plain being stupid."

Crenshaw didn't reopen until February, when the school district decided enough students had returned to Bolivar Peninsula to justify calling its teachers back to work. But even then, each class had only about five students. Superintendent Lynne Cleveland told the school's small staff the campus would remain open until it became a financial burden on the district. Brawner felt sure Cleveland planned to lay off subject specialists and replace them with generalists who could teach all classes. And even then, she wasn't convinced the school would survive.

Feeling certain her job wouldn't last into the next school year, Brawner took a position with the East Chambers Independent School District in Winnie. She and Brian bought a house on the outskirts of Beaumont in December. Ending her commute in Winnie cut her daily drive time in half. It also ended the daily torture of driving past the blown out storefronts and cars still buried in the sand. Every day, as she sped past, she told herself not to look at the lone palm tree that stood next to her empty lot. But every day, her eyes went right to it. The desolation, the constant reminders of loss, started to play on her nerves.

"So many memories flooded back, to the point where they almost choked you sometimes, to where you just didn't know how to rationalize all your feelings," she said. "There were so many feelings. It wasn't just the home, it was my job there with the children that I just poured my heart into. It was Brian's work and our friends. Just our entire lives. I planned on being there forever."

But being away from Bolivar didn't stop the occasional onslaught of memories and a fresh sense of loss. While shopping for a new mattress in a Beaumont furniture store, a bright red fish statue caught Brawner's eye. Before the storm, she had one just like it, perched behind the glass door of her kitchen cabinet. Until she saw it, she'd forgotten she owned it. But once remembered, it had to be mourned, like everything else. She often wondered what happened to their home the night Ike came ashore. Did it slowly break to pieces, dropping her precious belongings into the churning surf? Or did it float off its pilings intact, only to smash apart on Goat Island? She wondered whether a beachcomber on South Padre Island might one day discover a broken piece of china from her kitchen.

Brawner committed to work in Winnie for a year. After that, she and Brian planned to reevaluate their options. Brian often told her he felt like a man without a country, and while she teased him about watching too many old Westerns, she knew what he meant. Sometimes they talked about moving somewhere else, even to another coast. But they never talked about going back to Bolivar.

"We don't really know what the future holds for us," she said. "Ike almost made us feel like we don't belong anywhere."

■ THREE WEEKS AFTER the storm, Bill and Kathy Moll moved back to their bayside home in Spanish Grant. Ike wiped out their downstairs garage and Bill's office, but the surge didn't get high enough to touch the rest of the elevated house. Not long after mail deliveries resumed in October, Bill discovered a bulky envelope in the mailbox. It contained his muddy and disheveled passport and a letter from the woman who found it in the pile of rubble at the end of the seawall. The Molls immediately drove to the spot, hoping to find some of the other items that washed out of their truck the day before the storm.

Their careful search unearthed a shredded red canvas bag full of Kathy's medication, all ruined. They also found an overnight kit with a comb and a hairbrush, but that was it. They could only hope that Kathy's jewelry and the $2,000 in cash fell into good hands, although Bill felt sure it had settled somewhere on the bottom of the Gulf of Mexico.

Although the couple slowly started to put their lives back together, repairing the beach house and the bottom floor of their home in Spanish Grant, Kathy had a hard time leaving Ike behind. She had nightmares. She didn't want to drive anywhere she might see destruction. And she refused to go by the spot on FM 3005 where they had to abandon their flooded truck and wade through the storm's early surge. Bill diagnosed his wife's condition as "post-Ike stress," something she didn't want to get help to overcome. Bill encouraged her to be thankful they were alive. Others weren't so lucky.

Bill's biggest post-Ike struggle had nothing to do with the storm. While the couple recovered in a Houston hotel room from their near drowning, the stock market crash wiped out their savings. Instead of enjoying a quiet retirement fishing and drinking fine wine, Bill had to resurrect his accounting business, without files, books, office equipment, or furniture. He struggled, but he didn't have a choice.

"You're talking about starting from zilch," he said. "But you just do it. The alternative is to sit there and feel sorry for yourself, or worse."

■ **LUPE RUSHING WENT** back to work when city hall reopened on September 28. With no boat and nothing else to occupy his time, Steven made quick progress on repairs to his family's home. He did most of the work himself, and even redesigned the kitchen to make it larger and more open to the dining room and back patio. The family moved home just in time for Tiffany to give birth to a healthy baby girl, Kaylie Paige, in February. Because he saved so much on contractor costs rebuilding the house, Rushing had enough insurance money left over to buy new furniture and a new shrimp boat, the *Tiffany Leann II*.

With so much of the shrimp fleet destroyed, the fishermen who could get boats harvested a bumper crop from Galveston Bay the year after Ike. Steven was so successful that he opened a bait camp in Sea Isle, on the island's West End. Sitting on her new couch in the room where she had tried to sleep as the floodwater slowly swallowed her home, Lupe acknowledged the storm turned into a blessing for her family. The terror they felt the night Ike came ashore and the emotional roller coaster they rode for months after now seemed like a bad dream, she said. But Steven proudly reminded her he predicted their survival.

"I kept telling her everything would be alright," Steven said, flashing his confident grin. "And see, I was right."

■ **THE MONTHS FOLLOWING** the storm blurred together for Karon and Willis Turner, the couple who braved the surge in a canal front home in Bolivar Peninsula's Crystal Beach so that they could save their beloved boat. The couple and the three people who rode out the storm with them lived in hotels around Southeast Texas for a while before a friend offered to sell them a trailer. All five of them—Karon, Willis, Mike Dunn, and the two companions—lived in the trailer for a few weeks before Karon and Willis purchased an RV. They parked it at a Baytown trailer park and spread the word to their Bolivar friends. Soon, the place was overrun with displaced peninsula residents, a virtual "Bolivar refugee camp," Karon joked.

The whole time they skipped from place to place, the phone never stopped ringing with calls from people wanting the Turners to repair their hurricane-damaged homes.

The Turners initially declined to reconstruct any houses, instead choosing only to do work that would help people get back in their homes: rebuilding missing staircases and shoring up sagging decks. Willis worked from daylight to dark, leaving Baytown as early as 5:30 AM and returning well past sunset. The commute got to be too much. Karon and Willis decided to open an RV park in the backyard of their damaged house on Crystal Beach Road. They set aside RVs for the construction workers they had to bring in to help tackle their overwhelming workload, and reserved a few others for the people whose homes they were rebuilding, a perk for customers who wanted to stay on the peninsula while the Turners worked on their houses. While Willis oversaw the reconstruction, Karon earned money inspecting septic tanks. All peninsula residents had to have their septic tanks inspected for damage before their water could be turned back on, and Karon was one of the few people on the peninsula qualified to do the work. For weeks, she did nothing but examine septic tanks for cracks and leaks. She'd make an appointment with someone and, by the time she arrived, the entire neighborhood would be lined up for inspections.

When the hurricane hit, Willis told Karon, "People will go bankrupt and people will be millionaires" from the destruction. He was right. Fourteen months after the hurricane, sitting on the deck of the newly repainted stock cruiser, Karon said Hurricane Ike had changed their lives for the better.

"To us, it was a blessing as far as work goes," Karon said. "We didn't lose that much stuff. We recovered [our] house. We lost stuff, but that's not as important as our lives. A lot more people who didn't fare as well as us are still trying to recover, still fighting with the insurance companies, still fighting with the bureaucrats, and that's what makes me sad, is to see the hoops that people have to jump through just to get their lives back."

■ BEACH PATROL CHIEF Peter Davis lived without running water or sewer service at his West End beach house for ten months. Recovery in neighborhoods west of the seawall lagged behind the recovery in other parts of the island, largely because many West End houses were second homes owned by people who lived elsewhere full time. The city also had trouble rebuilding the West End's roads and sewage and water pipes, which had been ripped from the ground by the pounding waves.

FEMA refused to pay to replace pipes and roads, such as Bermuda Beach Drive, which had been washed away by the hurricane. That infrastructure was just too vulnerable to future storms. Meanwhile, 68 West End homeowners joined a buyout program designed to remove hurricane-damaged structures from the public beach. Eighteen months after the storm, with the program tangled up in red tape, not one of those houses had been torn down. The once-beautiful, lavish beach houses sat decaying and falling apart, nothing more than outdoor bathrooms for people visiting the beach. The houses provided daily reminders to the few full-time West End residents, such as Davis, that Galveston was far from fully recovered.

In December, when things slowed down enough for Davis and his wife to take a break, they packed their "hippie" van—a pea-green Volkswagen painted with dark red fish scales—with their dogs and surfboards and headed to Veracruz, Mexico, where Davis sometimes teaches surfing classes. They stopped all along the Pacific Coast and spent some time in the mountains before heading back to Galveston. Overall, they were gone about a month.

"It was so nice getting away," Davis said. "It was so intense here. We're emotionally crippled now and we will be for a while more to go. You get in line at the grocery store and people are just beat down, or so irritable, or fighting over nothing. They just have this hopeless look."

Davis could relate. Two months after he took off to Mexico, his 70-year-old mother died suddenly. She wasn't even sick, Davis said. The spry woman, a lifelong resident of Galveston, was still teaching at the public school district when Hurricane Ike hit. Though her condo at the Galvestonian on the very East End of the island was spared damage, the management company had to make repairs before it could allow residents to come home. Davis' mother spent six weeks sleeping on a relative's couch, and worrying about whether or not she still had a job at the Galveston Independent School District. When Davis first brought her back to see her condo immediately after Hurricane Ike, his mother just stared in heart-wrenching silence at the damage.

In February, Davis got a phone call from the condominium staff. His mother had gotten in an argument with a contractor and collapsed. The University of Texas Medical Branch was still closed then, so Barbara Stephen Davis had to be flown to a Houston emergency room, where she died. The doctors said she died of a brain embolism; Davis knew it was a broken heart.

■ **Hurricane Ike was** not kind to the elderly, especially those like Davis, whose ties to the island went back four, five, and even six generations.

Fletcher Harris Jr., whose family had lived on the island for more than 100 years, died on Father's Day 2009. He was 85. At the visitation, an ex-mayor, a former district attorney, and current city and county officials lined up to pay their respects to the beloved curmudgeon. Photographs of Fletcher and framed war medals decorated the funeral home. Harris' "hurricane tool," the 10-inch crowbar with scuffed and chipped yellow paint, lay in the center of a table among framed photos of a smiling Fletcher. Dave initially planned to bury the crowbar with his father, but he couldn't bring himself to do it.

"I needed that as a remembrance," he said.

The Harris family buried Fletcher on a hot, sunny day at the Galveston Memorial Park in Hitchcock. They laid him to rest next to his parents, the last of the Harris family hurricane survivors.

■ **Emory Brockway started** making repairs to his house as soon as he received his building permit from the city. He settled his insurance claim not long after that. Determined to be independent from then on, Brockway used most of the money to pay off his mortgage. He spent the rest buying as much building material as he could afford. A friend helped him hang new drywall, install new windows, and replace the electrical wiring.

For three months, Brockway and his wife, Merlinda, lived in their gutted house without lights or heat. The fall was colder than most. Merlinda hung tarps from the ceiling to create a makeshift bedroom in the corner of their living room. The blue plastic helped break the wind coming through the front door but it did little to keep out the damp cold. Emory bundled up in sweaters, a puffy jacket, and a knit hat to stay warm. At night, Merlinda piled blankets on top of them as they huddled together on an air mattress and tried to stop shivering. Although loath to ask the government for anything, Emory did request a FEMA mobile home. It finally arrived in mid-December, but it took the agency and the city two more weeks to get the electrical connection hooked up.

Emory didn't go back to work at the convenience store until February. Merlinda didn't start working until June. Renovations at the house slowed when their insurance money ran out. After that, they made repairs as they could afford them. By the storm's first anniversary, the walls were up and painted and the windows were installed. Kitchen cabinets and appliances in boxes filled the living room. Emory waved his hand over them almost dismissively and pointed with pride at the new attic door leaning against the hallway wall, ready to be placed into the hole in the ceiling. Once in place, it would open like a trap door and release an 8-foot ladder. Emory smiled mischievously. Next time, they wouldn't have to scramble to safety, he said.

But Emory didn't really believe he would see another storm like Ike in his lifetime.

"It's a gamble, right here, right now. It's a gamble of sorts. But you know, considering this hasn't happened for 109 years, I'm going to gamble in the next 15 or 20 years it won't happen again.

"The odds are well over 100 to 1, right?"

AFTERWORD

L EIGH JONES AND Rhiannon Meyers rode out Hurricane Ike in Galveston, stationed by their editors at The San Luis Resort to report on the storm's aftermath and the city's response. They were among the first to get a look at the damage. For two weeks, they battled power shortages, spotty cell phone service, and unreliable Internet connections to transmit their storm coverage to readers desperate for news of their homes and their city. Jones and Meyers, both reporters for *The Galveston County Daily News*, continued to report on the storm's recovery for the next year.

■ **LEIGH JONES:** On Thursday, September 11, 2008, I glibly told National Public Radio's afternoon listeners that the storm preparations in Galveston were going well, all things considered. I spent Wednesday night putting my furniture up on blocks and watching my husband and a small group of friends armed with electric drills and hammers board up our windows. The whole production annoyed me, to be honest. I refused to buy in to the hurricane hysteria. I even told our friends, who weren't sure about evacuating, that they should stay put. The mayor hadn't called for a mandatory evacuation, and I was sure she would have, if the storm posed a real threat.

By the time I did my interview on NPR, Mayor Lyda Ann Thomas had changed her mind, and the evacuation was in full swing. At home, my husband frantically packed an overnight bag and gathered the few things he planned to take with him, including our three cats and two dogs. I would stay on the island, of course, and cover whatever Ike had in store. Up to that point, I scoffed at the possibility that the storm would actually hit Galveston and not turn away at the last minute. But watching my husband drive away, our pets peering forlornly through the doors of their cages, the magnitude of what we faced finally started to sink in.

As I left our house on Bayou Shore Drive, less than 100 yards from the edge of English Bayou, I fervently prayed that Ike would continue turning to the east. That night, Rhiannon and I stayed with Jennifer Reynolds, the photo editor for *The Daily News*, in her downtown loft. We stayed up late that night, watching the television news coverage. At 10 PM, forecasters grimly announced Ike would make a direct hit on Galveston. After that, I stopped thinking about our house and everything we owned. I knew I couldn't do my job if I continued to worry about what was happening there.

I found out Saturday evening that my house had flooded to the ceiling, although the water didn't drain enough for me to see it for myself until Monday. On Sunday, Rhiannon, Jennifer, and I interviewed a man who rode out the storm in his house near Offatts Bayou. He gave us a tour, pointing out his toppled furniture and mud-covered treasures. As we walked through the halls and peered into every dark room, tears started sliding down my face. I couldn't help it. That man's story was my story. His grief was my grief. Hurricane Ike bound us together in desolation.

I felt that connection with every sobbing, frustrated, angry, and determined Galvestonian I talked to or interviewed during the following twelve months. Every time I demanded answers from FEMA officials or city staffers, I was doing it for myself as much as for my readers. I agonized over every conversation I had with someone who couldn't get the help they needed and feared they wouldn't ever be able to recover. I knew exactly what they were going through. My husband and I lived with that kind of uncertainty for several months.

But we were much more fortunate than many people I interviewed for this book. We got a fair settlement from our insurance company, and about six months after the storm someone offered to buy what was left of our house. Although we could have rebuilt, we just didn't have the heart. We loved our life in Galveston, but it would never be what it was before the storm. I talked to so many people who refused to let Ike chase them from the place they loved. But we always felt that the storm propelled us forward. Ike gave us a new beginning. We just couldn't turn back.

We stayed in Galveston until just after Ike's one-year anniversary. Although we felt strongly that we needed to move on, it was not easy to leave the island. I will always be connected to Galveston and its residents by a shared experience of loss and rejuvenation. And I will be there in spirit every time another monster storm enters the Gulf of Mexico.

Leigh now lives in Atlanta, Georgia, with her husband James and their small menagerie. She works as an editor for the Daily Report, *a legal newspaper.*

■ **RHIANNON MEYERS:** "Get up!"

The room flooded with light, but it was the panic in photographer Jennifer Reynolds voice that made my eyes snap open.

"Downtown is flooding," she said as she darted around tossing things in bags. I bolted from the sleeping bag where I'd spent the night on the floor of Jennifer's downtown loft and rushed to the window to look. The streets were filled with water, which wasn't unusual in a heavy rainstorm. But it wasn't raining. A salty storm surge had already crept into town from Galveston Bay and Hurricane Ike was still more than 12 hours out.

Leigh and I followed Jennifer's lead, quickly wrapping up bedding and nonperishable food, as we hurried to get out of downtown before we got trapped there. When I walked outside to toss my sleeping bag in my car parked along the street, the water lapped halfway up the tires.

It was 5:30 AM when we made our way to The San Luis Resort, where we we'd reserved rooms alongside city staffers, cops, reporters, and firefighters to ride out the hurricane. Though it was still dark outside, I could easily see the foamy waves cresting over the seawall and splashing on the sidewalk. I was horrified. I willed myself to etch the image into my brain so I'd never forget what a hurricane looked like. Little did I know that image would haunt me for months in recurring nightmares about Hurricane Ike.

We spent the morning crisscrossing the island stuffed inside *The Galveston County Daily News'* tiny, white pickup. Jennifer drove and Leigh and I swapped turns sitting in the fold out seat in the cramped half cab, banging out details of the storm's early arrival on our laptops. Everyone we met that morning seemed just as surprised as we were at Hurricane Ike's early intensity and strength.

When it was no longer safe to drive the pickup across the rapidly flooding island, we hitched rides with cops who were still warning people to take shelter. When it wasn't safe for them to stay out in the storm, we retreated to The San Luis.

I wish I could say I was brave. The truth was, it was my first hurricane and I was terrified. When we hitched a ride with Galveston Police Lieutenant Joel Caldwell that Friday night in the final rescue attempts of the evening, I watched in horror from the backseat of Caldwell's pickup as lifeguards swam down the streets. As the wind rocked the truck side to side, I gripped my notebook so hard, my knuckles turned white. When the back half of the storm slapped The San Luis Resort, causing the hotel to shudder so violently that the pool lounger I was sleeping on inside the swanky ballroom shook me awake, I lost all the composure I'd been trying to maintain since 5 AM. I buried my face in my arm to muffle my sobbing until Jennifer caught me and talked me down.

I wish I could say I was so absorbed in my job that I never thought about what happened to my own house. But that's also not true. That Saturday afternoon, after the storm had passed and the winds died, I drove to my first floor apartment behind the seawall. When I walked in the door, the carpet squished under my feet. I can't remember if I cried. I do remember calling my husband to tell him what happened. "Don't worry about any of that," Mark said. "Just focus on your job." We lived at the newspaper for two weeks, sleeping on air mattresses on the floor and rinsing off in the grimy and cold pressroom shower, until my co-worker and friend Sara Foley offered us her miraculously unflooded house while we looked for a new place. We eventually moved into a downtown loft that we'd been eyeing before the hurricane hit. Its best selling point was that it was 30 feet off the ground.

I wish I could say I thought long and hard about whether I wanted to live in Galveston, that I weighed the benefits and risks of living on a hurricane-prone barrier island before deciding to stay. The reality is I never even thought about leaving. Galveston is the first place that has felt like home since I left my parent's house for college. I got married here in one of the few buildings that survived the 1900 Storm. I love the stately Victorian houses, the outline of the cruise ships on foggy nights, the color of the Gulf of Mexico at sunrise, and how, every night at dusk, the pelicans fly in jet fighter formation over the causeway on their way to roost for the night. Hurricane or no hurricane, Galveston is, and always will be, home.

Rhiannon Meyers lives in downtown Galveston with her husband Mark. She covers the city of Galveston for The Galveston County Daily News.

ACKNOWLEDGMENTS

THIS BOOK WOULD not have happened, or at least it would not have been as good, without Mark Collette, our first editor, writing coach, and biggest fan. Thank you for never softening your criticism or suppressing your enthusiasm.

We would not have had much of a book to write without the people who agreed to share their stories with us. Thank you for being vulnerable enough to tell us what it was really like to be battered by Hurricane Ike. We rejoice with those of you who have managed to put your lives back together. For those of you still waiting for help, we can only hope fervently that it comes soon.

We are especially grateful to the Rushings, the Brockways, and Dave Harris, on behalf of his father, Fletcher, for letting us make your stories such an integral part of this project.

To Jennifer Reynolds, our fellow Ike survivor, muse, driver, and personal sommelier, thank you for taking us seriously when we weren't sure how serious we really were.

To everyone who believed in this book and promised to buy a copy as soon as it came out, thank you for your encouragement. You helped us believe we could actually get this book to print.

We would also like to thank our bosses at *The Galveston County Daily News*–Dolph Tillotson, Heber Taylor, and Michael Smith–who didn't laugh when we told them we were writing a book and trusted us not to let our aspiration to be authors interfere with our work as reporters.

Leigh would like to thank her husband, James, for letting her take four months off work to finish writing. We would probably still be writing if you hadn't been willing to make that sacrifice.

Rhiannon would like to thank her parents, her sister Courtney, and her brother Justin for their steadfast support, and her husband Mark, whose incredible writing talent, sharp eye and unwavering optimism made this book possible.

NOTES

T HE MATERIAL IN this book came from fresh interviews conducted between March and November 2009. But all of the stories are woven around the knowledge we gained about the storm and the recovery while working as reporters for *The Galveston County Daily News*. We are indebted to the newspaper for making this project possible. In a few instances, we pulled stories and quotes directly from articles we wrote for *The Daily News*, which are documented here. We leaned heavily on our own work, and that of our colleagues, to refresh our memories about facts, dates, and details. All of those references also appear here. We obtained the e-mails cited in both the text and the notes through requests made under the Texas Public Information Act.

■ INTERVIEW LIST

LeeRoy Amador
Dr. Garland Anderson
John Augelli
Renee Brawner
Emory and Merlinda
    Brockway
Dakata Brodie
Dr. David Callender
Mike Christiansen
Lynne Cleveland
Casey and Sara Cutler
Peter Davis
Mike and Weez Doherty
Caroline Dorsett
Frances Dunham
Tx. Rep. Craig Eiland
Joe and Gloria Enriquez

John Giovannini
Gene Hafele
Dave Harris
Hud Hopkins
Laura Hurt
Charlie Kelly
Steve LeBlanc
David Marshall
Skip Martin
Betty Massey
Bill Moll
John Moran
Lou Muller
Daya Myers
Jennifer Nitschmann
Wendy O'Donohoe
Vic Pierson

Dr. Ben Raimer
Michael Rains
Dr. Joan Richardson
Lupe and Steven Rushing
Willie Ruth Scott
Mike Shriner
David Smith
Lyda Ann Thomas
Karon and Willis Turner
Mike Varela
Brandon Wade
Charles Wiley
Eric Wilson
Gene Williamson
Jim Yarbrough

■ **CHAPTER ONE**

p. 1   Hurricane Ike spun into life: Robbie Berg, "Tropical Cyclone Report: Hurricane Ike, 1–14 September 2008," National Hurricane Center, January 23, 2009 (www.nhc.noaa.gov/2008atlan.shtml).

p. 3   He stayed during Rita in 2005: T.J. Aulds and Sarah Viren, "Some county residents plan to stay put," *The Galveston County Daily News,* September 21, 2005.

p. 4   "Serious news programs . . .": Greta Van Susteren. "Fletcher Lives!" September 27, 2005 (www.foxnews.com/story/0,2933,170542,00.html).

p. 4   In a rare moment, before it became clear: T.J. Aulds and Sarah Viren, "Some county residents plan to stay put," *The Galveston County Daily News,* September 21, 2005.

p. 7   Those who panicked because: Ibid.

■ **CHAPTER TWO**

p. 11   did order the city's legal: E-mail message from Susie Green to Brandon Cook, September 10, 2008.

p. 11   Thomas coolly assured reporters: Leigh Jones, "Mandatory evacuation called for island's West End," *The Galveston County Daily News,* September 11, 2008.

p. 12   "Asking people to leave . . .": Ibid.

p. 12   In late July, Hurricane Dolly: Richard J. Pasch and Todd B. Kimberlain, "Tropical Cyclone Report: Hurricane Dolly, 20–25 July 2008," National Hurricane Center, January 22, 2009 (www.nhc.noaa.gov/2008atlan.shtml).

p. 13   The storm landed in Cuba: Robbie Berg, "Tropical Cyclone Report: Hurricane Ike, 1–14 September 2008," National Hurricane Center, January 23, 2009 (www.nhc.noaa.gov/2008atlan.shtml).

p. 13   Charlie Kelly . . . sent an e-mail: E-mail message from Charlie Kelly to city staff, September 8, 2008.

p. 13   the news had improved: E-mail message from Charlie Kelly to city staff, September 9, 2008.

p. 13   LeBlanc held a late afternoon: Staff reports, "No action required," *The Galveston County Daily News,* September 10, 2008.

p. 14   which killed 1,836: "Hurricane Katrina," Wikipedia (http://en.wikipedia.org/wiki/Hurricane_katrina).

p. 14   Millions of panicked Houston residents: Cindy Horswell, Edward Hegstrom, Allan Turner, Matt Stiles, Terri Langford, Cynthia Garza, Renee Lee, Todd

Ackeman, Mike Tolson, Lise Olsen, Dale Lezon, "Hurricane Rita: The Aftermath/Evacuation/Lessons come at high cost: 107 lives," *Houston Chronicle,* September 29, 2005.

p. 14 A bus evacuating nursing home: Ibid.

p. 15 As Hurricane Rita neared land: Richard D. Knabb, Daniel p. Brown, and Jamie R. Rhome, "Tropical Cyclone Report: Hurricane Rita, 18–26 September 2005," National Hurricane Center, March 17, 2006 (www.nhc.noaa.gov/2008atlan.shtml).

p. 16 Mayor Thomas decided: E-mail message between City Manager Steve LeBlanc and city council members, September 9, 2008.

p. 18 But all they got: Leigh Jones, "Mandatory evacuation called for island's West End," *The Galveston County Daily News*, September 11, 2008.

p. 18 Thomas told residents: Ibid.

p. 18 Both Thomas and LeBlanc bristled: Ibid.

p. 19 By 10 PM Wednesday, the National Weather Service: Robbie Berg, "Tropical Cyclone Report: Hurricane Ike, 1–14 September 2008," National Hurricane Center, January 23, 2009 (www.nhc.noaa.gov/2008atlan.shtml).

p. 19 trapped by rising water: Staff reports, "Tidal surge causes flooding on West End," *The Galveston County Daily News*, September 12, 2008.

p. 21 Hundreds made their way: Rhiannon Meyers, "Thousands board buses for Austin," *The Galveston County Daily News*, September 12, 2008.

p. 21 At least three people: Sara Foley "Hundreds wait for ride to safety" *The Galveston County Daily News,* September 12, 2008.

p. 21 Rumors that there wouldn't be enough buses: Ibid.

p. 23 About one-third of the island's 56,000 residents: Leigh Jones and Rhiannon Meyers, "Island begins rescue, recovery efforts," *The Galveston County Daily News,* September 14, 2008.

p. 23 Only 1,500 residents took the city: Leigh Jones, "About 1,500 take city's free bus ride to safety," *The Galveston County Daily News,* September 14, 2008.

■ CHAPTER THREE

p. 25 Donald Davis and Louis Gross: Rhiannon Meyers, "Rescuers already assisting those stranded by flood," *The Galveston County Daily News,* September 12, 2008.

p. 26 "I just came from our West End," E-mail message from Chris Gonzales to County Judge Jim Yarbrough, September 12, 2008.

p. 29   when Carla came ashore: "Hurricane Carla," Wikipedia (http://en.wikipedia.org /wiki/Hurricane_Carla).

p. 32   Thomas and Galveston Independent School District: E-mail message between City Manager Steve LeBlanc and Superintendent Lynne Cleveland, September 11, 2008.

p. 32   Cleveland agreed to throw in: Ibid.

p. 36   which drowned the older parts of the city: "Hurricane Carla Tides–Texas and Louisiana, September 7–13, 1961," provided by County Engineer Mike Fitzgerald.

p. 36   The Department of Homeland Security: E-mail message from the Department of Homeland Security to Judge Jim Yarbrough, September 12, 2008.

p. 37   Gene Hafele, chief of the local National Weather Service: Chris Paschenko, "Noon briefing bleak from emergency officials," *The Galveston County Daily News,* September, 12, 2008.

p. 37   "The state is working to get out . . .": Ibid.

p. 37   But 27 people holed up at Fort Travis: E-mail message from David Popoff to local officials, including Judge Jim Yarbrough, September 12, 2008.

p. 37   "The weather is allowing us . . .": Ibid.

p. 37   "Unbelievable!" E-mail message from County Commissioner Pat Doyle to Judge Jim Yarbrough, September 12, 2008.

p. 38   30,000 people had holed up in the Superdome: Jeff Duncan, "Superdome: Refuge of Last Resort," *The New Orleans Times-Picayune,* August 30, 2006.

p. 39   As they waited days: Ibid.

p. 39   Six people died: "Effects of Hurricane Katrina in New Orleans," Wikipedia (http:// en.wikipedia.org/wiki/Effects_of_Hurricane_Katrina_in_New_Orleans).

■ **CHAPTER FOUR**

p. 45   "It was a sort of infinite monster . . .": William Mercer Harris, "The Baptist Situation in Galveston and Vicinity," *The Home Mission Board.* Copy included in scrapbook at the Galveston and Texas History Center in the Rosenberg Library.

p. 45   By nightfall, the "enraged sea": Ibid.

p. 45   At 6:30 PM, a tornado: Toby Druin, "Hurricane! 1900 Storm Hit Baptists Hard," *Baptist Standard,* September 4, 2000 (www.baptiststandard.com/2000/9_4/pages /storm.html).

p. 45 "I saw our chapel blown . . .": William Mercer Harris, "The Baptist Situation in Galveston and Vicinity," *The Home Mission Board*. Copy included in scrapbook at the Galveston and Texas History Center in the Rosenberg Library.

p. 45 In a desperate attempt to get: Toby Druin, "Hurricane! 1900 Storm Hit Baptists Hard," *Baptist Standard,* September 4, 2000 (www.baptiststandard.com/2000/9_4/pages/storm.html).

p. 46 When dawn broke over the island: William Mercer Harris, "The Baptist Situation in Galveston and Vicinity," *The Home Mission Board*. Copy included in scrapbook at the Galveston and Texas History Center in the Rosenberg Library.

p. 46 historians estimate the storm: Michael A. Smith, "Post-storm rebuilding considered 'Galveston's finest hour,'" *The Galveston County Daily News*, published on www.1900storm.com in conjunction with the City of Galveston 1900 Storm Committee.

p. 46 Not only did it knock: Michael A. Smith, "Surprise Strike," *Ike: Stories of the Storm*, published by The Galveston County Daily News, p. 5.

p. 46 Houston television meteorologist: Laura Elder, "Defiant attitude, hubris form perfect storm," *The Galveston County Daily News*, May 28, 2003.

p. 47 In 1961, Hurricane Carla: "Hurricane Carla," Wikipedia (http://en.wikipedia.org/wiki/Hurricane_Carla).

p. 47 Huricane Alicia made a direct: "Hurricane Alicia," Wikipedia (http://en.wikipedia.org/wiki/Hurricane_Alicia).

p. 47 Frank warned in that 2003: Laura Elder, "Defiant attitude, hubris form perfect storm," *The Galveston County Daily News*, May 28, 2003.

p. 47 Like Ike, the 1900 Storm: "Two storms, similar paths" map, *Ike: Stories of the Storm*, published by The Galveston County Daily News, p. 6.

p. 47 In the years before 1900: Heidi Lutz, "One night of terror became a lasting part of Galveston's identity," *The Galveston County Daily News*, published on www.1900storm.com in conjunction with the City of Galveston 1900 Storm Committee.

p. 47 The city prospered from: Ibid.

p. 47 More than 70 percent: Ibid.

p. 47 Galveston was home to 37,000: Ibid.

p. 47 The country's rich: Ibid.

p. 48 Dr. Isaac Cline, a highly respected: Ibid.

p. 48 Anyone who suggested the island: Erik Larson, *Isaac's Storm: A Man, a Time, and the Deadliest Hurricane in History,* New York: Vintage Books, 1999, p. 84.

p. 48 The barometric pressure: Heidi Lutz, "One night of terror became a lasting part of Galveston's identity," *The Galveston County Daily News*, published on www.1900storm.com in conjunction with the City of Galveston 1900 Storm Committee.

p. 48 Cline hoisted the flag: John Edward Weems, *A Weekend in September,* New York: Henry Holt and Company, 1957, pp. 34, 35.

p. 48 He beseeched islanders: Heidi Lutz, "One night of terror became a lasting part of Galveston's identity," *The Galveston County Daily News*, published on www.1900storm.com in conjunction with the City of Galveston 1900 Storm Committee.

p. 48 He finally retreated to: Erik Larson, *Isaac's Storm: A Man, a Time, and the Deadliest Hurricane in History,* New York: Vintage Books, 1999, p. 191.

p. 48 A train trestle broke loose: John Edward Weems, *A Weekend in September,* New York: Henry Holt and Company, 1957, p. 111, 114–116.

p. 48 Pastor Harris watched: William Mercer Harris, "The Baptist Situation in Galveston and Vicinity," *The Home Mission Board.* Copy included in scrapbook at the Galveston and Texas History Center in the Rosenberg Library.

p. 49 "I saw the vacant stare . . .": Ibid.

p. 49 Galveston Mayor Walter C. Jones: Michael A. Smith, "Post-storm rebuilding considered 'Galveston's finest hour,'" *The Galveston County Daily News,* , published on www.1900storm.com in conjunction with the City of Galveston 1900 Storm Committee.

p. 49 After his father's death six years: I.H. Kempner, *Recalled Recollections,* Dallas: Egan Co., 1961, pp. 11–13.

p. 49 Kempner rode out the 1900: I.H. Kempner, *Recalled Recollections,* Dallas: Egan Co., 1961, p. 28.

p. 49 At one point, he tied: I.H. Kempner, *Recalled Recollections,* Dallas: Egan Co., 1961, p. 29.

p. 49 As Kempner returned to the house: I.H. Kempner, *Recalled Recollections,* Dallas: Egan Co., 1961, p. 29.

p. 50 Kempner and Wheeler were welcomed: I.H. Kempner, *Recalled Recollections,* Dallas: Egan Co., 1961, p. 29.

p. 50 "We tried to gain access . . .": I.H. Kempner, *Recalled Recollections,* Dallas: Egan Co., 1961, p. 29.

p. 50 the mayor charged Kempner: I.H. Kempner, *Recalled Recollections,* Dallas: Egan Co., 1961, pp. 30–31.

p. 50 After the hurricane destroyed the city's tax: I.H. Kempner, *Recalled Recollections,* Dallas: Egan Co., 1961, p. 33.

p. 50 The city used that money to secure: Michael A. Smith, "Post-storm rebuilding considered 'Galveston's finest hour,'" *The Galveston County Daily News,* published on www.1900storm.com in conjunction with the City of Galveston 1900 Storm Committee.

p. 50 In 1901, the city hired: Ibid.

p. 50 The city would literally: Ibid.

p. 51 All island buildings had to be elevated: Ibid.

p. 51 Construction on the seawall: Ibid.

p. 51 "The public defenses against . . .": Ibid.

p. 51 five hurricanes struck the island: "Hurricane Strikes vs Population for Galveston, Texas," National Oceanic and Atmospheric Administration (http://csc-s-maps-q .csc.noaa.gov/hurricanes/pop2_action.jsp?county=galveston&state=tx).

■ CHAPTER FIVE

p. 65 "Can you imagine me . . .": Rhiannon Meyers, "'God taught me a lesson' about taking Ike lightly," *The Galveston County Daily News,* September 14, 2008.

■ CHAPTER SIX

p. 75 At least 10 people died: Chris Paschenko, "Remains are from Crystal Beach man," *The Galveston County Daily News,* January 2, 2010.

p. 75 Three people remained missing: Laura Recovery Center (www.lrcf.net/Ike/index .html).

p. 81 The flight mechanic hauled up: Coast Guard News' video of Bolivar Peninsula rescue (www.coastguardnews.com).

p. 83 left in a tank that holds: Lt. Dan Leary and Sarah Foster-Snell, "A 'Stunning' Mountain Rescue: Air Crew Takes HH-65C to New Heights," U.S. Coast Guard September newsletter, March 27, 2008 (www.uscg.mil/Acquisition/deepwater /newsletters/sept06/newsletter_sept06-03.asp).

p. 85 Gail Ettenger, a 58-year-old chemist: Associated Press, "Islanders insisted on staying, died in Ike," *USA Today,* October 4, 2008.

p. 86 Ettenger, her voice shaking with fear: Ibid.

p. 86 Marian Violet Arrambide: Ibid.

p. 86   Searchers found Williams' body: Chris Paschenko, "Ike remains are from Crystal Beach man," *The Galveston County Daily News,* January 2, 2010.

■ CHAPTER SEVEN

p. 94   Further east, in Gilchrist: Rhiannon Meyers, "Volunteer fire crews in shambles after Ike," *The Galveston County Daily News,* September 29, 2008.

p. 96   The storm surge had peeled: Leigh Jones and Rhiannon Meyers, "Island begins rescue, recovery efforts," *The Galveston County Daily News,* September 13, 2008.

p. 97   Amador stopped the truck: Rhiannon Meyers, "Isle residents swap horrific survival stories," *The Galveston County Daily News,* September, 13, 2008.

p. 98   Segura had decided to ride: Ibid.

p. 98   "This was a real close call . . .": Ibid.

p. 108   They bummed cigarettes: Ibid.

p. 109   Seventeen buildings had collapsed: Leigh Jones and Rhiannon Meyers, "Island begins rescue, recovery efforts," *The Galveston County Daily News,* September 13, 2008.

p. 111   "We will do everything . . .": Leigh Jones and Rhiannon Meyers, "Island begins rescue, recovery efforts," *The Galveston County Daily News,* September 13, 2008.

■ CHAPTER EIGHT

p. 113   Meanwhile, city crews struggled: Rhiannon Meyers, "Filthy, unhealthy conditions rampant on island," *The Galveston County Daily News,* September 16, 2008.

p. 118   The line backed up: Leigh Jones, "Galveston suspends 'look and leave,'" *The Galveston County Daily News,* September 16, 2008.

p. 123   Outraged residents sent fiery e-mails: Dolph Tillotson, "Who's in charge?," *The Galveston County Daily News,* September 17, 2008.

p. 127   The street-by-street search: Leigh Jones, "Five now confirmed dead," *The Galveston County Daily News,* September 14, 2008.

p. 128   The death count in Galveston: Chris Paschenko, "Remains are from Crystal Beach man," *The Galveston County Daily News,* January 2, 2010.

p. 129   Within two days of the hurricane: Rhiannon Meyers, "Mobile kitchens set up on island," *The Galveston County Daily News,* September 15, 2008.

p. 129   By mid-September, the Salvation Army: Salvation Army press release, "Warns Residents That Storm's Path Threatens Major Population Center and Heightens Danger," September 12, 2008.

p. 130 The evangelical charity also: Salvation Army press release, "Hurricane Ike makes Landfall, The Salvation Assesses Damage and Prepares to Assist Those Impacted by the Storm."

p. 130 By Monday, September 15: Salvation Army press release, "Fast Facts: Hurricane Ike," September 15, 2008

p. 130 what would later become: Adapted with permission from a September 21, 2008 article in *The Galveston County Daily News*. Rhiannon Meyers, "Islanders turn to old-fashioned picnics to survive," *The Galveston County Daily News*, September 21, 2008.

p. 133 Carriage horse owner: John Nova Lomax, "Hurricane Ike's Wake," *Houston Press*, January 8, 2009.

p. 135 Deborah Snyder intended: Leigh Jones, "Shelter helps reunite pets, owners," *The Galveston County Daily News*, September 26, 2008.

p. 135 the biologists at: Adapted with permission from an October 1, 2008 article in *The Galveston County Daily News*. Rhiannon Meyers, "Many Moody Gardens animals live despite conditions," *The Galveston County Daily News*, October 1, 2008.

p. 140 *USS Nassau*: Mass Communication Specialist 3rd Class David Wyscaver, "Galveston Mayor, USS Nassau Coordinating Hurricane Ike Relief Efforts," U.S. Navy press release, September 18, 2008, (http://www.navy.mil/search/display .asp?story_id=39851).

p. 141 weighed anchor: "USS Nassau Concludes Hurricane Ike Disaster Response Efforts," U.S. Navy press release, September 24, 2008 (http://www.navy.mil /Search/display.asp?story_id=39964).

p. 143 They did an interview: Associated Press, "Riding out Ike on an island, with a lion," MSNBC, September 14, 2008 (http://www.msnbc.msn.com/id/26746849 /ns/weather-hurricane_ike//).

p. 144 county officials announced that all: Chris Paschenko, "Judge calls for removal of Bolivar residents," *The Galveston County Daily News*, September 15, 2008.

■ CHAPTER NINE

p. 148 Only 16,000: Laura Elder and Leigh Jones, "Few people on island had flood insurance," *The Galveston County Daily News*, September, 19, 2008.

p. 148 Susan Parker: Leigh Jones, "Two households look toward recovery," *The Galveston County Daily News*, September 24, 2008.

p. 149 "Darlin', I love you": Ibid.

p. 149   federal government spent $190 million: Federal Emergency Management Agency statistics.

p. 149   The public housing projects echoed: Adapted with permission from: Rhiannon Meyers, "Public housing residents angry, confused," *The Galveston County Daily News,* September 24, 2008.

p. 155   Two days after Hurricane Ike: Adapted with permission from: Rhiannon Meyers, "Many displaced islanders not coming back," *The Galveston County Daily News,* September 27, 2009.

p. 157   Sea-Arama: Laura Elder, "A city rises in the debris of another," *The Galveston County Daily News,* September 26, 2008.

p. 157   "toxic" sludge: Leigh Jones, "Study: Ike did not leave toxic sludge," *The Galveston County Daily News,* January 24, 2009.

p. 157   Port officials raced: Laura Elder, "Port vows to keep business, recover quickly," *The Galveston County Daily News,* September, 20, 2008.

p. 158   Submerged meters: Rhiannon Meyers, "Electrician, plumber OK needed to turn on meters," *The Galveston County Daily News,* September 23, 2008.

p. 158   17,000 houses: Ibid.

p. 158   daycare centers: Rhiannon Meyers, "Only three private day cares open on island," *The Galveston County Daily News,*" October 13, 2008.

p. 158   Mail delivery: Leigh Jones, "Some mail delivery begins on island," *The Galveston County Daily News,* September 29, 2008.

p. 159   watering the trees: Rhiannon Meyers, "Broadway oak trees bouncing back," *The Galveston County Daily News,* October 18, 2008.

p. 159   Forest service arborists: Ibid.

p. 159   40 percent of the trees: Leigh Jones, "Lack of leaves is not good for island's trees," *The Galveston County Daily News,* April 15, 2009.

p. 159   11,000 on public property: Leigh Jones, "Officials ready to start cutting down dead trees," *The Galveston County Daily News,* June 8, 2009.

p. 160   5,000 trees: Leigh Jones, "Wood from Broadway trees now available," *The Galveston County Daily News,* September 29, 2009.

p. 160   Woodworkers, furniture makers: Leigh Jones, "Isle's downed trees will become ship parts, art," *The Galveston County Daily News,* July 14, 2009.

p. 161   Ashton Villa: Chris Paschenko, "Ashton Villa reopens despite ongoing repairs," *The Galveston County Daily News,* July 4, 2009.

p. 161   cost almost $1 million: Ibid.

p. 161   Other historic landmarks: Laura Elder, "Historic properties escape major damage," *The Galveston County Daily News*, September 15, 2008.

p. 161   started a window restoration project: "Window Restoration," Willet Hauser Architectural Glass, Inc., February 11, 2009.

p. 162   Galveston school district reopened: Rhiannon Meyers, "GISD takes huge leap toward normalcy," *The Galveston County Daily News,* October 8, 2008.

p. 163   Pickens had the students fold: Ibid.

p. 164   destroyed nearly 3,000 peninsula homes: Chris Paschenko, "County could potentially permit 2,000 homes," *The Galveston County Daily News*, October 25, 2008.

p. 164   in class for just a few weeks: "A&M-Galveston moving to college station," *Associated Press*, September 17, 2008.

p. 165   1,500 Sea Aggies: Staff reports, "Alumni give TAMUG $200,000 for recovery," *The Galveston County Daily News*, October 17, 2008.

p. 165   48,000 students: Jeannie Kever, "A&M Galveston must relocate," *Houston Chronicle*, September 23, 2008.

p. 165 $12 million: R.G. Ratcliffe, "Auditor puts Hurricane Ike damage at A&M Galveston at $12.4 million," *Houston Chronicle* Texas Politics blog, March 31, 2009.

p. 165   temporary repairs: Laura Elder, "Pelican Island Bridge repairs may take millions," *The Galveston County Daily News*, September 30, 2008.

p. 165   Sea Aggies returned to Galveston: Chris Paschenko, "TAMUG students come home to graduate," *The Galveston County Daily News*, December 15, 2008.

■ **CHAPTER TEN**

p. 171   Months after the catastrophic 1900 Storm: Pastor William Mercer Harris' speech at 1901 Baptist congregation. Copy included in scrapbook at the Galveston and Texas History Center in the Rosenberg Library.

p. 172   President George W. Bush flew to the island: Staff reports, "President takes tour of storm-devastated island," *The Galveston County Daily News*, September 16, 2008.

p. 173   the presidents joined forces: Leigh Jones, "Former presidents visit island," *The Galveston County Daily News*, October 15, 2008.

p. 174   "I don't think . . .": Ibid.

p. 174   raised only $2.2 million: Leigh Jones, "Presidential recovery fund makes donations," *The Galveston County Daily News,* July 26, 2009.

p. 174 Everyone was disappointed: Ibid.

p. 175 $267 million: Leigh Jones, "Island's share of federal relief funds increased," *The Galveston County Daily News*, February 18, 2009.

■ CHAPTER ELEVEN

p. 177 William L. Prather: Heber Taylor, "A clear picture in eight words," *The Galveston County Daily News,* October 20, 2008.

p. 178 regents had authorized: Laura Elder, "UTMB to cut 3,800 jobs," *The Galveston County Daily News*, November 13, 2008.

p. 178 Tom Craddick: Rhiannon Meyers, "Legislators tour UTMB damage," *The Galveston County Daily News*, September 25, 2008.

p. 180 annual losses: Laura Elder, "Callender has seen issues like UTMB's before," *The Galveston County Daily News*, May 9, 2007.

p. 180 learn new ways to operate: Leigh Jones, "Shine to UTMB faculty: Change is coming," *The Galveston County Daily News*, January 9, 2007.

p. 181 Regents tapped Callender: Laura Elder, "Callender has seen issues like UTMB's before," *The Galveston County Daily News*, May 9, 2007.

p. 181 $18 million annual operating loss: Ibid.

p. 181 Callender unveiled his plan: Laura Elder, "Medical branch seeks path out of $35 million hole," *The Galveston County Daily News*, August 3, 2008.

p. 183 Ogden, a conservative: Laura Elder, "'Tightfisted Aggie' steps up to help UTMB," *The Galveston County Daily News*, October 9, 2008.

p. 183 $5 billion surplus: Ibid.

p. 183 Dewhurst and Ogden persuaded: Ibid.

p. 183 Callender announced: Leigh Jones, "Callender briefs employees on UTMB's future," *The Galveston County Daily News*, October 29, 2008.

p. 183 Dewhurst and Ogden insisted: Leigh Jones, "State leaders: UTMB layoffs not imminent," *The Galveston County Daily News*, October 29, 2008.

p. 183 It came on November 12: Laura Elder, "UTMB to cut 3,800 jobs," *The Galveston County Daily News*, November 13, 2008.

p. 183 met behind closed doors: Laura Elder and Rhiannon Meyers, "UT regents to discuss UTMB personnel matters," *The Galveston County Daily News*, November 12, 2008.

p. 185 Straus reached across: T.J. Aulds, "Eiland named Citizen of the Year," *The Galveston County Daily News*, April 26, 2009.

p. 185   Callender hired: Laura Elder, "UTMB hires Atlanta firm to assist in downsizing," *The Galveston County Daily News*, November 16, 2008.

p. 185   Kurt Salmon Associates recommended: Laura Elder, "Consultant's report: Move most of UTMB operations," *The Galveston County Daily News*, February 12, 2009.

p. 186   In 1881: Historical account provided by the Sealy & Smith Foundation.

p. 188   For three hours: Laura Elder, "Dozens plead to keep UTMB in Galveston," *The Galveston County Daily News*, February 21, 2009.

p. 188   H. Scott Caven Jr.: Staff reports, "Perry taps Houstonian for UT Board of Regents," *Houston Chronicle*, February 15, 2009.

p. 188   Robert Rowling: R.G. Ratcliffe, "UT regents quit over bonus flap," *Houston Chronicle*, February 6, 2009.

p. 188   they agreed to fund: Laura Elder, "Regents resolve to rebuild UTMB on the island," *The Galveston County Daily News*, March 11, 2009.

p. 188   the regents wanted local: Ibid.

p. 190   120 students: Bronwyn Turner, "UTMB students win support from legislators," *The Galveston County Daily News*, March 18, 2009.

p. 191   Eiland struck a deal: Leigh Jones, "UTMB funding bill survives committee vote," *The Galveston County Daily News*, March 24, 2009.

p. 191   More than 200: T.J. Aulds, "UTMB funding passes state house," *The Galveston County Daily News*, April 17, 2009.

p. 191   only five lights: Ibid.

p. 191   The budget bill passed: Laura Elder, "UTMB secures recovery funding," *The Galveston County Daily News*, June 2, 2009.

p. 194   state's only community medical college: Leigh Jones, "County judge begins push for hospital district," *The Galveston County Daily News*, July 30, 2009.

p. 194   Yarbrough decided he couldn't risk it: T.J. Aulds, "Commissioners OK tax hike for health care," *The Galveston County Daily News*, September 3, 2009.

■ CHAPTER TWELVE

p. 197   Genell Simmons sat sobbing: *Ike: Stories of the Storm,* published by The Galveston County Daily News, p. 94.

p. 199   35 hotels: Leigh Jones, "Housing in short supply around county," *The Galveston County Daily News*, September 22, 2008.

p. 199   LeBlanc told reporters: Leigh Jones, "City sets up small, temporary shelter," *The Galveston County Daily News*, September 24, 2008.

p. 200   The shelter opened: Leigh Jones, "Tent shelter set up for displaced residents," *The Galveston County Daily News*, September 25, 2008.

p. 200   42 people: Ibid.

p. 200   team of teachers: Rhiannon Meyers, "Time in shelters doesn't turn back learning curve," *The Galveston County Daily News*, October 3, 2008.

p. 201   The Red Cross Shelter quickly filled: Sara Foley, "Red Cross shelter gives some comfort," *The Galveston County Daily News,* September 29, 2008.

p. 201   They spent the first few chaotic: Sara Foley, "Evacuees in Austin desperate to return," *The Galveston County Daily News,* September 20, 2008.

p. 201   Housing authority officials condemned: Rhiannon Meyers, "Housing projects condemned," *The Galveston County Daily News,* September 24, 2008.

p. 202   a homeowner shot a shelter resident: Rhiannon Meyers, Sara Foley, and Leigh Jones, "Neighbors: Shooting shows tensions with shelter," *The Galveston County Daily News,* October 7, 2008.

p. 202   LeBlanc appealed: Rhiannon Meyers and Leigh Jones, "Frustration mounts as shelter closing looms," *The Galveston County Daily News,* October 22, 2008.

p. 202   helped all 300 people: T.J. Aulds, "New shelter opens on island near airport," *The Galveston County Daily News,* October 27, 2008.

p. 202   Franjetta Jones: Rhiannon Meyers, "Future unclear for GHA residents," *The Galveston County Daily News,* October 26, 2008.

p. 202   1,474 displaced: Leigh Jones, "Not everyone qualifies for hotel voucher extension," *The Galveston County Daily News,* October 28, 2008.

p. 202   Latina Vallery: Leigh Jones, "Hundreds may be homeless with FEMA vouchers ending," *The Galveston County Daily News,* November 12, 2008.

p. 203   finally got word: Leigh Jones, "Eviction notices turn out to be a mistake," *The Galveston County Daily News,* November 13, 2008.

p. 203   flood-damaged floors: Rhiannon Meyers, "Housing all locked up on isle," *The Galveston County Daily News,* November 8, 2008.

p. 203   stopped mandating interior inspections: Ibid.

p. 204   FEMA officials at first: Leigh Jones, "Many roadblocks delay FEMA mobile homes," *The Galveston County Daily News,* November 20, 2008.

p. 204   140 trailers: Chris Paschenko and Leigh Jones, "Officials eyeing spots for FEMA mobile homes," *The Galveston County Daily News,* November 14, 2008.

p. 204   commissioners nixed the plan: T.J. Aulds, "County defers Justice Center trailer plan," *The Galveston County Daily News,* November 20, 2008.

p. 204   positive image: Ibid.

p. 205   Larry Crow: Ibid.

p. 205   Lee Sander: Ibid.

p. 205   The agency finally got permission: Rhiannon Meyers, "GISD offers city land for mobile homes," *The Galveston County Daily News*, November 17, 2008.

p. 205   961 families: Leigh Jones, "FEMA trailer park opens in Galveston," *The Galveston County Daily News*, March 13, 2009.

p. 205   Galveston Housing Authority condemned all four: Rhiannon Meyers, "Housing projects condemned," *The Galveston County Daily News*, September 24, 2008.

p. 206   Two weeks later: Rhiannon Meyers, "Future of public housing depends on repair cost," *The Galveston County Daily News*, November 16, 2008.

p. 206   According to housing authority statistics: Rhiannon Meyers, "Island's poor, homeless wonder where they'll live," *The Galveston County Daily News*, November 2, 2008.

p. 206   intended to emulate Biloxi: Rhiannon Meyers, "Galveston Housing Authority to emulate Biloxi," *The Galveston County Daily News*, November 30, 2008.

p. 206   Sheila Jackson Lee: Leigh Jones, "Congresswoman makes case for public housing," *The Galveston County Daily News*, December 4, 2008.

p. 207   Jackson Lee announced: Ibid.

p. 207   Housing authority board members agreed: Rhiannon Meyers, "Two public housing complexes to be demolished," *The Galveston County Daily News*, January 29, 2009.

p. 207   Lone Star Legal: Rhiannon Meyers, "Complaint halts planned public housing demolition," *The Galveston County Daily News*, March 5, 2009.

p. 207   he agreed to include: Rhiannon Meyers, "GHA to move forward with demolition," *The Galveston County Daily News*, March 16, 2009.

p. 207   more than 100 families: Rhiannon Meyers, "117 families on Cedar Terrace waiting list," *The Galveston County Daily News*, March 19, 2009.

p. 207 $60 million: Leigh Jones, "Housing authority wants $60 million," *The Galveston County Daily News*, March 25, 2009.

p. 207   An online petition started: Leigh Jones, "Petition opposes public housing rebuilding plans," *The Galveston County Daily News*, March 29, 2009.

p. 208   returned to the city council: Leigh Jones, "Possible holdup in GHA project," *The Galveston County Daily News*, April 12, 2009.

p. 208   the housing authority board abandoned plans: Leigh Jones, "GHA abandons plans for 1,500 new homes," *The Galveston County Daily News*, May 2. 2009.

p. 208   "I just want . . .": Ibid.

p. 208   backpedal again: Leigh Jones, "Public housing to be torn down," *The Galveston County Daily News*, May 15, 2009.

p. 209   accused the agency: Leigh Jones, "Housing authority facing renewed opposition," *The Galveston County Daily News*, September 30, 2009.

p. 209 $25 million: Leigh Jones, "Council Oks housing repair funding plan," *The Galveston County Daily News*, May 29, 2009.

p. 209   hired Civic Design: Leigh Jones, "GHA hires design firm," *The Galveston County Daily News*, June 17, 2008.

p. 209   hosted three public meetings: Leigh Jones, "Designers unveil new public housing layouts," *The Galveston County Daily News*, August 6, 2009.

p. 209   largest neighborhood association: Leigh Jones, "Housing authority facing renewed opposition," *The Galveston County Daily News*, September 30, 2009.

p. 210   postponed his presentation: Leigh Jones, "GHA delays plans to rebuild," *The Galveston County Daily News*, October 14, 2009.

p. 210   unveiled new designs: Leigh Jones, "GHA unveils new public housing plan," *The Galveston County Daily News*, October 20, 2009.

p. 210   shouting match: Leigh Jones, "Meeting on housing plan ends in shouting match," October 20, 2009.

p. 210   penned a letter: Rhiannon Meyers, "Housing focus of Ike spending complaint," *The Galveston County Daily News*, November 1, 2009.

p. 211   commissioners in December approved: Rhiannon Meyers, "GHA approves public housing rebuilding plan," *The Galveston County Daily News*, December 15, 2009.

p. 211   They lobbied the planning: Rhiannon Meyers, "Planning commission OKs GHA rebuilding plan," *The Galveston County Daily News*, February 17, 2010.

p. 211   city council members met: Rhiannon Meyers, "City releases $25 million for GHA rebuilding," *The Galveston County Daily News*, February 26, 2010.

p. 212   After nine hours: Ibid.

■ CHAPTER THIRTEEN

p. 213   More than 800,000: Laura Elder, "Coverage is not a premium for some," *The Galveston County Daily News*, September 14, 2009.

p. 214   About 1,500 houses: Leigh Jones, "City wants grant tweaked," *The Galveston County Daily News*, January 8, 2009.

p. 225   rebuilt 154 homes: T.J. Aulds, "15 families home for the first time since Ike," *The Galveston County Daily News*, December 23, 2009.

p. 225 $160 million: Leigh Jones, "Council OKs housing repair funding plan," *The Galveston County Daily News*, May 29, 2009.

■ CHAPTER FOURTEEN

p. 235   included 42 projects: Leigh Jones, "City approves list of recovery projects," *The Galveston County Daily News*, April 10, 2009.

INDEX

Varela, Mike, 41–42
vehicles
    abandoned, 126, 127
    city, safeguarding, 22
    as debris, 158
    emergency, 107
    in floodwaters, 31, 55–56, 61,
        68–69, 79–83, 158, 229
    rescues from, 79–83
"vertical evacuation," 47
volunteers, 110, 129, 130, 133, 134, 135,
    225

W

Wade, Belinda, 27, 28
Wade, Brandon, 15, 18, 27, 28, 40, 41,
    98, 100, 101, 127, 169, 171
Walker, Latrice, 151
"Wall Street of the South," 186
wastewater treatment plant, 90, 103,
    139–140
water, drinking, 21, 129
water pumping station, 90, 98, 102–103,
    139–140, 141
Webber, Danny, 216
West, Royce, 190
West End, 106, 169
    buyout program, 242
    damage to, compared to downtown,
        101
    evacuations, last minute, 28
    flooding, 19, 26
    routes off of, 27
"We will survive," 159
Wheeler, Safford, 50
White, Bill, 225

Whittaker, Greg, 135, 136, 137
Wiley, Charles, 58, 70, 109, 110, 119,
    121, 228–230
Williams, John, 151
Williams, Shane, 86
Williamson, Gene, 57, 58, 175
Wilson, Eric, 40, 41, 98, 102, 103, 139,
    140, 141
Womack, Deandre, 150–151
Woods, Jasmine, 150
Woods, Tarris, 226

Y

Yarbrough, Jim, 19, 20
    emergency management, 15, 16, 17
    evacuation, mandatory, Bacliff, 17
    evacuation, mandatory, Bolivar
        Peninsula, 17, 77
    evacuation, mandatory, Galveston
        Island, 20
    evacuation, mandatory, San Leon,
        17
    hospital district, 184, 193, 194
    Hurricane Carla, 29–30
    press conferences, 17, 20
    storm preparations, personal, 30
    Thomas, defense of, 23
Young, Delores, 152

Z

Zaffirini, Judith, 192
Zajack, Dennis, 103
Zendt, John, 136